M000019438

Coins:
Questions
& Answers

5th Edition

by Clifford Mishler

Whitman
Publishing, LLC
PUBLISHING SINCE 1934

Coins:
Questions
& Answers

© 2008 Whitman Publishing, LLC
3101 Clairmont Road · Suite C · Atlanta GA 30329

Correspondence concerning this book may be directed to the publisher, at the address above.

ISBN: 0794822738
Printed in Canada

Disclaimer: This book is presented as a collecting guide only. Expert opinion should be sought in any significant numismatic purchase.

Advertisements within this book: Whitman Publishing, LLC, does not endorse, warrant, or guarantee any of the products or services of its advertisers. All warranties and guarantees are the sole responsibility of the advertiser.

About the images in this book: In general, coin denominations of 50 cents and higher are pictured at actual size; denominations below 50 cents and coins that are unusually small (e.g., gold dollars) are generally pictured at 150 percent of their actual size. Paper money is typically pictured at page width. Other items, such as medals, encased postage, and so on, may be enlarged for visibility. Appendix B lists the actual sizes of U.S. coins and currency.

For a complete catalog of antiques/collectibles reference books, supplies, and storage products, visit Whitman Publishing online at
www.whitman**books**.com

TABLE OF CONTENTS

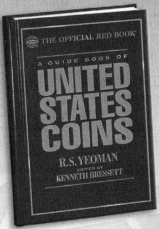

INTRODUCTION

The genesis of the book you are holding in your hands dates to nearly 45 years ago, shortly after I joined the *Numismatic News* staff in Iola, Wisconsin, back in the late winter of 1963. Among my early tasks and responsibilities was that of responding to the never-ending flow of informational inquiries from collectors arriving in the daily mail. The questions poured forth ceaselessly, perhaps upwards of a couple hundred monthly, a couple thousand or so annually, I expect, each and every one seriously tendered and deserving of informed responses. Back in those pre-computer days, responding with personal letters was a laborious task. The more popular or interesting questions were answered in print as well.

It quickly became apparent to me that many of the topics embraced were puzzling, not only to beginning and novice collectors, but frequently to casual collectors as well, not to mention the topics that sometimes prove challenging even to advanced collectors whose focused interests rested outside a given interest realms. Not infrequently, it was found necessary to do some research, digging deeper into the subject that the knowledge I possessed to provide answers that would fully "fit" the specifics of the inquiry.

Expanded and enhanced, this latest edition of *Coins: Questions & Answers* provides a quick tour of the historic and fascinating byways traveled by those who enjoy exploring the basic disciplines of the North American coin-collecting community. It is intended to be enlightening and enticing to the beginner, providing scholarly guidance along some of the more popular coin-collecting trails, and at the same time being refreshing to even the most advanced collectors.

An ultimate problem solver, this book is, of course, certainly not; no question-and-answer book of manageable size could claim to provide the reader with more than an introduction to the diverse facets of the hobby which its sweep encompasses. That would require an encyclopedia; perhaps a thousand compilations equal in volume to that presented here would even fall far short of achieving such a challenging objective.

Rather, it is my hope that this latest of a number of editions of this book, presented today by Whitman Publishing, will provide each reader with a point of beginning . . . the beginner with the motivation to proceed . . . the novice with the desire to progress . . . the casual collector with the determination to advance . . . and the advanced collector with a greater appreciation for the diversity encompassed within the realm.

So, read on, join the hunt in learning more of *what you should know . . . regardless of your present interest level . . . but perhaps never would have asked!*

I.
THE WORLD OF
NUMISMATICS

About the images in this book: In general, coin denominations of 50 cents and higher are pictured at actual size; denominations below 50 cents and coins that are unusually small (e.g., gold dollars) are generally pictured at 150 percent of their actual size. Paper money is typically pictured at page width. Other items, such as medals, encased postage, and so on, may be enlarged for visibility. Appendix B lists the actual sizes of U.S. coins and currency.

CHAPTER ONE

General Information

Q. *What is meant by the terms numismatics and numismatist?*

A. Numismatics is the study and/or collection of coins, paper money, tokens, medals, orders, and decorations, and similar monetarily related or styled objects. A numismatist is one who has a comprehensive knowledge of numismatics. A collector isn't necessarily (indeed, seldom is) a numismatist in a technical sense; a numismatist needn't be a collector. He can be an archaeology associate, the curator of a national or institutional collector, a dealer, a scholar, or simply a serious student of numismatics.

Q. *I have often heard people refer to the grade of a coin. What do they mean?*

A. They are referring to the relative condition, or state of preservation of the coin in question. Grading a coin is basically a subjective exercise, but there are three grading "standards" that have been stated in textbook form and are widely referenced by dealers and collectors when they are judging the relative merits of a coin to determine its grade.

Each of these standard grading references possesses unique distinctions. The first published (1958), and least referenced today, is Brown and Dunn's *A Guide to the Grading Standards of United States Coins;* it is based on textual descriptions accompanied by line drawing illustrations of the various coinage types which are individually highlighted by grade to emphasize the degree of wear allowable for each condition level. Another title, James F. Ruddy's *Photograde,* was first published a decade later (1970); it offers textual descriptions representing similar characteristics of quality for each grade, accompanied by illustrative art in the form of reproductions of actual coin photos.

In 1977 the American Numismatic Association published *The Official ANA Grading Standards for United States Coins.* Where the previous titles presented grading descriptions which represented the opinions of the individual authors, the new title was a committee effort that represented the consensus of many individuals. It also introduced to general use in the grading of U.S. coins a numerical system intended to enhance and provide uniformity in the application of grading standards, the adjectival standards having been subjected to many variations of description and interpretation over the years. The latest of this study—the sixth edition (2006), which embodies the latest consensus of individual experts and the current realities of the commercial marketplace—is published and distributed by Whitman Publishing.

Liberty Seated silver dollars in two grades. Left, VG-8; right, MS-65.

Q. *When a coin is described as being of MS-65 quality, what does that designation mean?*

A. It is a numerical description of a quality which would be adjectivally described as being a step above "brilliant" uncirculated, but not quite "gem," or "choice" in adjectival terminology. It is one of a number of numeric designations on a scale from 1 to 70 used to designate coin grades, the former representing the lowest identifiable quality, the latter, the highest. Numeric designators below 60 are accompanied by abbreviations of their adjectival counterparts; those from 60 through 70 by the letters MS, for "Mint State." In declining order of quality, the officially described designators and their generally accepted adjectival counterparts are:

MS-70	Perfect Uncirculated
MS-69	Near Perfect Uncirculated
MS-68	Gem (Exceptional) Uncirculated
MS-67	Gem Uncirculated
MS-66	Choice Uncirculated

MS-65	Select Uncirculated
MS-64	Brilliant Uncirculated
MS-63	Uncirculated (Attractive Eye Appeal)
MS-62	Uncirculated (Good Eye Appeal)
MS-61	Uncirculated (Unattractive)
MS-60	Uncirculated (Poor Eye Appeal)
AU-55	Choice About Uncirculated
AU-50	About Uncirculated
AU-40	Extremely Fine
VF-30	Choice Very Fine
VF-20	Very Fine
F-12	Fine
VG-8	Very Good
G-4	Good
AG-3	About Good
Fair-2	Most Details Smooth
Poor-1	Identifiable by Type

Individuals frequently describe coins by applying unofficial variations of these designators, like "Gem MS-65," "MS-65+," or similar. Such indications are generally intended to enhance the reception of a coin which is clearly superior in quality to that represented by the next lower designator, although it will not meet the requirements of the next higher designator.

Q. *What is the meaning of abbreviations like ANA, ANS, and PNG that I see some people list following their names, and dealers in conjunction with their business names?*

A. Such letter combinations would generally represent abbreviations for national, regional, state, and major specialized organizations, the major collector and dealer organizations of North America being:

American Numismatic Association (ANA)—Membership Department, American Numismatic Association, 818 N. Cascade Ave., Colorado Springs, CO 80903-3279. Annual dues: regular $36, senior (65 and older) $31, junior (under 23 years old) $20, associate $13. Publications: *The Numismatist*, a monthly magazine. Objectives and services: The largest nonprofit educational organization dedicated to advancing the knowledge of numismatics and facilitating better cooperation and closer relations within the hobby community. Maintains the Dwight N.

Manley Numismatic Library, the world's largest circulating numismatic lending library, and the Edward C. Rochette Money Museum featuring fantastic numismatic displays; sponsors national conventions semi-annually—National Money Show and World's Fair of Money; sponsors young numismatist and educational programs through Numismatic Theatre and Workshop convention programming and correspondence courses; offers an annual Summer Seminar campus learning experience; sponsors the annual National Coin Week public awareness initiative; and provides direct access to grading and conservation services for numismatic items.

American Numismatic Society (ANS)—Membership Department, American Numismatic Society, 96 Fulton St., New York, NY 10038. Annual membership: $50 (associates). Publications: *American Numismatic Society Magazine*, three issues published annually; also publishes other scholarly works on a selective basis that are offered to members at special prices, including two annual volumes, *American Journal of Numismatics* and *Numismatic Literature*. Objectives and services: The oldest nonprofit educational organization, founded in 1858, dedicated to the advancement of numismatic knowledge in the United States and internationally. Presents Coinage of the Americas Conference every fall and college level Graduate Seminar in numismatics every summer, and several other specialized educational lecture series. Maintains voluminous research collections and library resources for the use of its members and scholars. Loans specimens from its collections to museums and historical organizations throughout the country, in addition to maintaining an outstanding numismatic exhibition at the Federal Reserve Bank of New York.

Canadian Numismatic Association (CNA)—Executive Secretary, Canadian Numismatic Association, 5694 Highway #7 East, Suite 432, Markham, ON L3P 1B4, Canada. Annual dues: regular $35 (Canadian funds), junior $16.50. Publications: *The CN Journal*, a journal published 10 months of the year with two issues combining two months. Objectives and services: The encouragement and promotion of the science of numismatics with special emphasis on materials pertaining to Canada. Founded in 1950, the CNA annually sponsors Canada's oldest ongoing numismatic convention, which is hosted at different sites across the country, and the services of a comprehensive Numismatic Book Lending Library, including audiovisual programs. Members also have access to a sponsored coin collecting insurance program, an educational Numismatic Correspondence Course, and one-day educational seminars held in major centers across the country from time to time. The organization supports the involvement of local coin clubs and specialized organizations, many of the latter meeting annually in conjunction with the CNA convention.

Professional Numismatists Guild (PNG)—Robert Bruggeman, Executive Director, Professional Numismatists Guild, 3950 Concordia Lane, Fallbrook, CA 92028. An organization comprised of upwards of 250 leading coin-dealing professionals, who are required to meet high financial and professional standards, including adherence to a strict *Code of Ethics* in support of its proclaimed *Collector's Bill of Rights* which provides for binding arbitration in the event of an disagreement between a member dealer, his dealership or company, and a customer.

1785 copper, Bust Facing Right. Although it's more than 200 years old, a post-colonial copper of this type can be purchased for a few hundred dollars in nice condition.

Q. *Which United States coins are most valuable?*

A. There is no general answer to this question. Some very old U.S. coins command modest values, while some relatively recent issues are worth thousands of dollars. Supply and demand govern what a coin is worth. Any coin that is very popular among collectors will have a strong demand and a relatively high value. Another factor is condition or state of preservation. Coins in perfect, new condition are always in demand and are the most valuable. Those that have suffered the ravages of use and time are usually of little interest or value to collectors, unless they are an issue of relative high rarity.

1793 large cent with Chain reverse.

Q. *Which was the first coin ever made by the U.S. Mint?*

A. The large-size cent of 1793 was the first coin produced by the mint at Philadelphia. For a while it was a toss-up as to whether the cent or the half cent would be first, but production problems and available materials gave the edge to the cent. Both coins were issued in 1793 but the half cent production didn't get underway until a few months after cents were placed in production.

Q. *Is it true that the first U.S. cents were rejected by the public?*

A. This is partially true. Cents—for that matter, all small change—were in such short supply that all coins were welcome and needed in the economy. The first issue of cents had a chain of 15 links on the reverse, however, to symbolize the union at that time, which had grown to 15 states, with the addition of Vermont (1791) and Kentucky (1792) to the original 13. Some people said the chains reminded them of a mark of bondage, however, and refused to use them. Because of this public outcry, the design was changed mid-year, with the chain being replaced by a wreath.

Q. *Why are old cents so popular with collectors?*

A. There are two very basic reasons. The first is that cents have been made nearly every year since the beginning of the U.S. Mint in 1793. The only exception was in 1815, when the mint was closed because of the combined circumstances of an epidemic and the lack of copper. The long run of dates makes cent collecting interesting and meaningful, because they cover every phase of coinage artistry and the history of our country. The second reason is that the low denomination can be collected without generally spending a great deal of money, because the issues were generally produced in larger quantities than other denominations. Unlike silver or gold coins, cents—with but a few exceptions—can be purchased at prices to fit most budgets.

Q. *Aren't many old large cent varieties needed for a collection?*

A. The more serious collectors pursue assembling sets of early cents and half cents not only for each date, but also with examples of each recognizable die variety or minor die variation in the positioning of letters or the treatment of design elements. Because of the specialized interest in these coins by die variety collectors, that kind of collecting appeals more to serious collectors than to beginners or investors. There are no rules about collecting, but most collectors do try to locate one coin of each date, mint, and major variety in design, or those listed in general catalogs of a series.

Q. *Are Indian Head cents still popular with collectors? They are no longer in circulation.*

A. The copper-nickel alloy coins that were made starting in 1857 with the Flying Eagle cents and the bronze Indian Head cents that followed were issued in great numbers and have long been a favorite collecting area for beginners, probably second only to Lincoln cents. Most old-time collectors remember starting their hobby by putting together sets of Indian Head or Lincoln cents taken from circulation. It is no longer possible to find the old Indian cents in change, nor the wreath back Lincoln cents minted from 1909 through 1958, and while assembling sets is not as popular as it once was, these coins remain among the most broadly sought items in American numismatics.

Q. *Can all of the old Lincoln cents still be found in change?*

A. Yes and no. All of the dates and mintmarks likely still exist to be found in circulation with enough searching, but it is about as likely as winning the lottery. Most dates prior to 1959 are seldom encountered, with a few being certifiably unlikely to be encountered in change, such as the 1914-D, 1909-S, or 1931-S. Still, such coins are still tucked away in household stashes of coins deposited in boxes, jars, or dresser drawers as souvenirs or curiosities. Until around 1970, the challenge of assembling a set of Lincoln cents from circulation was still the first collecting activity for most beginners. Interest in this changed somewhat when most of the early date coins were finally drained from circulation and collectors could only complete their sets by purchasing the scarcer "key" dates from dealers or other collectors.

1856 Flying Eagle cent. Typically, copper coins are not popular as investments, but are collected for historical or other reasons—but one might make an exception for the 1856 small cent, which in AU-50 condition could fetch about $13,000. Most other Flying Eagle cents in similar condition are worth about $200.

Q. *Are old cents considered a good investment?*

A. Copper coins have never been considered prime investment material, although in recent years, top grade specimens of some issues have reached well into the five-figure range, with a few even reaching into the six-figure bracket. For one thing, very few early date cents are still available in the choice quality range. Copper coins are difficult to store and preserve in high grade, because their delicate surface is affected by moisture and atmospheric conditions much more readily than silver coins. Most investors prefer large silver and gold coins, because they are available in high-grade condition, are generally more attractive, and are easier to preserve. As a consequence, the values of copper coins and low denomination silver coins are very much a factor of collector demand rather than investor pressure, and in many cases they have not gone up in value at the same rates as so-called "investor coins."

Q. *Doesn't the scarcity of high-grade coppers make them really valuable?*

A. The demand by collectors for uncirculated large cents is seemingly endless. If the investor community ever takes to buying these coins in near perfect condition, they will find that there are very few available.

A relatively miniscule quantity have retained their original color or are unblemished by dark spots or other problems that are so easily caused by careless handling, storage or environmental exposure. It is likely that early date coppers would go up in value tremendously if there was a demand for them outside the mainline numismatic community. Pieces dated from 1793 through 1814 are usually found in grades no higher than Extremely Fine, and later dates up to 1878 are hard to find in grades above low-range Uncirculated. Any early copper coin with the original red color and no brown or black spots is always in high demand and worth a substantial premium.

Q. *Does anyone collect recent date cents? Are any of them worth saving?*

A. Most cents made since 1954 have little or no premium value unless they grade in the uncirculated range. Most individuals collecting from circulation do not save them for their value, but because of the challenge of finding and putting together a set of each date and mintmark. There are some interesting varieties of recent vintage that are worth looking for because of their exceptional value. These would include the doubled-die cents of 1955, 1972, 1983, and 1995, the 1960 and 1970-S (high 7) small date, and letter spacing varieties for the AM in "America" on the 1992-D, 1998, 1999, and 2000 issues, which are variously worth a few dollars to a few hundred.

Q. *What are "odd denomination" coins?*

A. Very few people know that the United States once issued two-cent and three-cent coins as part of our regular monetary system. These were intended as a convenience in making change or, in the case of the three-cent pieces, also for the purchase of postage stamps. Two-cent coins were made from 1864 through 1873, and three-cent pieces were made first as silver coins and later as nickel issues from 1851 through 1889. Other odd denomination coins include the copper half cent, a twenty-cent piece (only from 1875 through 1878), and the $2.50 and $3 (from 1854 to 1889) gold coins. There was also a $4 "Stella," a gold coin for which there was a great push in 1879 and which is listed in most catalogs along with other "regular issue" U.S. coins, but which was never authorized for circulation production, although 425 examples of one variety of this pattern were produced and distributed to political figures, dignitaries, and otherwise made widely available at the time. These odd denomination coins hold great interest for collectors and noncollectors alike because in today's monetary environment they seem so strange. (See chapter 9, "Discontinued Denominations," for more.)

Q. *Are "odd denomination" coins collected by date, like regular issues?*

A. Yes, they are, in the instances of six of the seven dominations, the $4 "Stella" being the exception. These coins are an essential part of any U.S. type set. A complete date set of two-cent pieces numbers 12 coins, of which 10 were minted for circulation. A complete date and mint set— the New Orleans Mint produced the issue in 1851—of silver three-cent pieces numbers 24 coins, of which 23 were minted for circulation, not including several over-date issues. A complete date set of nickel three-cent pieces numbers 26 coins, of which 23 were minted for circulation. A complete set of twenty-cent pieces numbers seven coins minted over four years, with the Carson City Mint producing the issue in 1875 and the San Francisco Mint in 1875 and 1876 (of which only four were produced and released for circulation). While the $2.50 gold piece was produced in a number of types and at six mints over 134 years from 1796 through 1929, three-dollar gold pieces were produced principally at the Philadelphia Mint, with four issues from San Francisco and one each from Dahlonega and New Orleans—a complete collection numbers 44 coins, of which five were not produced for circulation, including the unique 1870-S. These issues are always a topic of heightened interest, conversation, and amazement by those not acquainted with the numismatic history of our country. Investors and collectors are attracted to these series because of their unique character.

Q. *Why did the United States make three-cent coins?*

A. The primary reason was to accommodate the purchase of stamps. But, in addition, a three-cent coin could be used in many combinations that should have made it very convenient. The only problem with it is that few people are accustomed to computing in threes, and that ultimately spelled the death knell of the denomination.

Q. *If the three-cent coins were not very popular, why were there two different kinds made in two different metals?*

A. Silver three-cent coins were made from 1851 through 1873. They were originally made of 75 percent silver to inhibit the populace from melting them down to recover their silver content. In 1854 the composition was changed to 90 percent silver, but the weight was lowered and the coins continued to be shunned because they were not considered to be worth their weight in silver. The small size and unusual denomination made them inconvenient for daily use. From 1865 to 1889 a larger version of the three-cent coin was made in nickel. It was identical in size to the dime, but of a different design. Unlike the tiny silver piece, it was readily accepted in circulation.

Q. *What are my chances of finding Uncirculated two-cent or three-cent coins for my collection?*

A. You are unlikely to discover any of these coins lying in a dresser drawer, where they might have been deposited as curiosities, but you can buy them from coin dealers and other collectors. Don't expect to find perfect pieces, because these coins did not hold up well to long-term storage. Both of these coins are made of metals that react to environmental exposure, and they are frequently encountered with tiny black spots on the surface. The copper two-cent pieces, in particular, have a tendency to turn dull and lose their original red color with age. Any of these coins that are still in their original pristine condition are worth substantial premiums.

Q. *Is there a safe way to store copper and nickel coins to prevent environmental damage?*

A. Moisture is the greatest threat to storing any copper-, nickel-, or silver-based coins. Collectors who live near the ocean face the greatest problems in protecting their coins from high humidity and salt air. Coins sealed in tight containers have the best chance of escaping the ravages of moisture in the air. Remember that cardboard and paper can act like a sponge by trapping and holding moisture near coins. Solid plastic holders are usually best.

Q. *Is it true that most collectors prefer silver coins over the copper and nickel pieces? Which are the most popular coins?*

A. Silver coins are by far the most avidly collected. In the past, one-cent pieces might have been the most popular, but today prices for silver coins—compare, for instance, Lincoln cents and Mercury dimes of the era between World War I and World War II—are in many instances lower, and their relative rarity based on mintages much greater, so collectors feel they are a better value. The popularity of silver coins seems to be tied to the size, ranging from dimes up to silver dollars. "Morgan" silver dollars minted from 1878 through 1921 are probably the most popularly collected coins of the mid-1800s to mid-1900s era.

Q. *Are all Morgan dollars valuable? What should I look for when selecting some for my collection?*

A. All U.S. silver dollars contain approximately three-quarters of an ounce of pure silver and are worth that much in melt value. As a rule most silver dollars of this type are available in substantial qualities in near-mint Uncirculated condition and are worth a slight premium over their bullion value. Just about any dollar in new mint condition will be valued by collectors. Silver dollars are valued on the basis of the rarity and desirability of each date and mintmark and according to how near perfectly preserved they are. The highest grade coins are worth the most money. Even relatively common date coins may be worth thousands of dollars if they are judged to possess high Mint State quality.

Q. *Is it illegal to own gold coins?*

A. Not anymore. You can own all the gold you can afford. Controlling legal restrictions on private ownership of gold were changed effective December 31, 1974, making it legal to buy, sell, and hold all U.S. and foreign gold coins. Most gold coins and bullion were illegal to own from 1934 to late 1974 because of a government regulation intended to prevent the demand for (and price of) gold from going too high. This was a sad time in our American numismatic history.

Q. *How does one go about collecting gold coins? Are they readily available from coin dealers?*

A. Gold coins are collected just like silver and copper pieces, but they are usually a bit scarcer and substantially more costly. Many people collect only gold coins because of their beauty and rarity. Gold coins are usually collected as type coins—that is to say, one of each different design, rather than by date and mint—because both their intrinsic and numismatic values are much higher than other coins. Gold pieces can be purchase from coin dealers, but are only infrequently found in household accumulations. Most dealers carry a selection of different types in inventory, but one has to embark on a search-and-find mission to obtain specific dates and mints.

Q. *Is it true that the U.S. Mint once made $2.50 and $3 gold coins?*

A. These odd denominations were made to accommodate commerce. The $3 coin, like the three-cent piece, was made as a convenience for purchasing stamps. The $2.50 gold piece, called a quarter eagle, was one of the first coins ever made at the U.S. Mint and continued to be popular until near the end of the gold coinage era.

Q. *What is a "double eagle"?*

A. The United States $10 gold coin was originally called an eagle. That makes the $20 coin a double eagle, the $5 a half eagle, and the $2.50 coin a quarter eagle. The gold dollar never had a nickname.

Q. *Does the United States still mint gold coins?*

A. Technically, yes; but in a practical sense, no. Gold coins have been minted every year since 1984 as premium-priced commemoratives, generally as $5 denominated coins, with the exceptions of 1985, 1990, 1998, 2004, and 2005. Gold bullion coins, denominated as $5, $10, $25, and $50 coins in weights of 1/10, 1/4, 1/2, and 1 ounce, have also been minted annually since 1986. Marketed as American Eagle bullion coins, those struck in 1986 through 1991 are dated in roman numerals and later with Arabic numerals. The cost of these coins is based on the spot value of gold and has no relation to the face value indicated on them. They are marketed in both uncirculated and proof editions, with the uncirculated editions being priced about 3 percent above the spot price of gold bullion at the time of sale. The proof versions are sold at an additional premium. Uncirculated mintages do not carry mintmarks, while the proof mintages are mintmarked with a "P" for Philadelphia or a "W" for West Point. The 1986 $25 pieces were minted only in Uncirculated, while the $5 and $10 pieces of both 1986 and 1987 were not minted as Proofs.

Source of the gold bullion design. Comparison of the original design of the double eagle (top) with the design of the modern $50 gold-eagle bullion coin.

Q. *Do bullion coins look like the regular U.S. gold coins?*

A. The design on the obverse of the gold bullion American Eagles is a modern copy of the old Saint-Gaudens image of a Standing Liberty taken from the $20 gold coin that was minted from 1907 to 1933. The same obverse design is used on all of the $5, $10, $25, and $50 bullion, while the reverses present a representation of a family of eagles, as created by Miley Busiek.

Q. *Did the U.S. Mint make a mistake in calling the quarter-ounce bullion gold eagle a $10 coin?*

A. It looks that way, but it is really not the case; it's just an example of the marketing folks prevailing with a sequence of denomination-content relationships that do not make sense. The $50 coin contains one ounce of gold. The $25 coin contains a half ounce of gold. Most people believe the quarter-ounce should be denominated $12.50 instead of $10, to make it consistent with the 1/10-ounce $5 piece and the upper two coins in the series.

Q. *Are there other bullion coins besides the gold eagles?*

A. The U.S. Mint has produced bullion silver dollars since 1986 and began marketing platinum bullion coins in 1997. None of those coins will ever be found in circulation because their bullion value far exceeds the face values indicated on them. Like their gold counterparts, platinum bullion coins are known as American Eagles, but they are logically denominated: $100, one ounce; $50, one-half ounce; $25, one-quarter ounce; and $10, one-tenth ounce. Bullion coins made of gold, silver, or platinum can be purchased only through coin and bullion dealers. The value of these of the Uncirculated editions of these pieces fluctuates frequently on the basis of the "spot" price quoted for raw bullion each day.

1877 Indian Head cent; 1860 half dime.

Q. *A friend of mine has an 1877 Indian Head cent for which he had been offered several hundred dollars. I have an older 1860 half dime for which I have been offered only a few dollars. As my coin is somewhat older, shouldn't it be worth more?*

A. The age of a coin is not of itself significant in determining a coin's value. Coins of the ancient Greeks and Romans, or Medieval kings and Crusaders, can also be purchased for relatively nominal amounts. The value of a coin, as with any commodity, is determined by the interaction of supply and demand. Demand, as it applies to a specific coin, is determined by the popularity of the series and the availability and condition of the coin.

Your friend's 1877 Indian Head cent is one of the "key coins" of a series widely collected by date and mintmark. In that year only 852,500 cents were produced, the lowest mintage in the series by far, with annual mintages generally falling in the 10 to 50 million range. Given the survival factor of this issue within the series, specimens in just "good" condition command values in the mid-three figure range, while those in the select "uncirculated" range go for mid-four figure values. On the other hand, in the instance of the 1871 half dime, there were 1,873,000 examples struck—more than twice as many as in the case of the 1877 Indian Head cent—that being the 11th highest mintage in the entire Liberty Seated half dime series (1837 to 1873). Specimens of this piece go for under $20 in "good" and in the low-three figure range for select "uncirculated" examples. There's a very adequate supply in contrast to the demand.

Q. *What benefits does a collector derive from joining a local coin club or national organization?*

A. Three principal benefits can be derived from active membership in a local coin club; the mental stimulation of associating with people of like interests, the opportunity to increase knowledge through the club's program of guest speakers and by conversation with advanced collectors (most clubs also maintain libraries of a selection of basic numismatic references of value to their memberships), and the opportunity to upgrade and add to your collection by trading or selling your duplicates and by making purchases, often below market levels, from fellow members. Membership in a national organization affords an expanded opportunity for learning through advanced articles in the organization's publications and by access to larger lending libraries.

Q. *What useful purpose is served by attending a national or major convention?*

A. Obviously, a national convention enlarges the opportunity for fellowship and the buying and selling of numismatic items. However, the average collector also appreciates the opportunity to browse among the exhibits, to study displays in every field of the numismatic endeavor, and to see the fabulous rarities—the aristocrats of Coindom—he could see nowhere else and will likely never own personally.

Q. *What is meant when a reference is made to the bourse area and bourse tables?*

A. "Bourse" is a French noun meaning purse, bag; stock exchange; scholarship, fellowship. In practice, it indicates a meeting of the purse and produce, or the marketplace. In numismatics, the bourse is that area of a show or convention facility set aside for the purpose of dealers in numismatic items and supplies offering their wares to attendees. The table space a dealer rents is called his bourse table.

Q. *What categories of "collectibles" are covered by the Hobby Protection Act?*

A. The Hobby Protection Act of November 29, 1973, requires that reproductions and imitations of numismatic and political items be permanently marked as copies. Numismatic items include coins, tokens, paper money, and commemorative medals. Political items include political buttons, posters, literature, stickers, and advertisements. The Act applies only to items manufactured after enactment of the law, and does not apply to any "official" reissue or restrike of any original numismatic item by the United States or any foreign government.

Q. *The motto IN GOD WE TRUST first appeared on a coin of the United States in 1864, during the Civil War. Is that the year it became the national motto?*

A. Although the presence or absence of the motto on our coins has been a highly emotional issue since 1864, and despite the fact that the inclusion of the motto in coin design was made mandatory by the Act of July 11, 1965, IN GOD WE TRUST did not become the national motto of the United States until July 30, 1956, when it was so decreed by a resolution of the 84th Congress and was approved by President Eisenhower.

Q. *When did the motto E PLURIBUS UNUM first appear on our coins? Is use of the motto required by law?*

A. The first use of the motto E PLURIBUS UNUM ("one composed of many") on the coinage of the United States was on the 1795 Liberty Cap and Heraldic Eagle type gold half eagle. Its use was not directed by law until the Act of February 12, 1873, required that the motto be inscribed on all coins bearing a representation of an eagle. Nevertheless, the motto did not appear on the 20-cent piece minted from 1875 through 1878, which bore an eagle on the reverse.

Q. *I have often wondered what the Secret Service expects me to do if I am handed a piece of paper currency I recognize to be a counterfeit.*

A. There are certain things you can do if it doesn't expose you to personal danger. Do not return the note to the individual who handed it to you. Telephone the nearest police station and give the answering officer all of the pertinent information available to you. Write your name or initials and the date on the note in ink before surrendering it to the police or Secret Service.

CHAPTER TWO

❦

Common Terms and Abbreviations

Q. *In various publications having to do with coin collecting I have noted a number of abbreviations which are very confusing to me. Could you explain the meaning of the ones most frequently encountered?*

A.

Ae	Bronze
Ag or Au	Gold
Al	Aluminum
ANA	American Numismatic Association
ANACS	A grading service; originally the ANA Certification Service
ANS	American Numismatic Society
Ar	Silver
Ars.	Arrows (at date)
Avg.	Average
Bil.	Billon (silver alloy of less than 50 percent)
Br.	Brass
ca.	About (era in time)
Cmkd.	Countermarked
C-N, CN, or Cop-Nic	Copper-Nickel alloy
CAN	Canadian Numismatic Association
Comm.	Commemorative coin
Cu	Copper
D.G.	Dei Gratia (By the Grace of God)
Diad.	Diademed
Drap.	Drapery
1864-L	An Indian Head cent with "L" on the headdress ribbon

F-numeral	A catalog number from one of several books created under the authorship of Robert Friedberg
Ind. Hd.	Indian Head
IND:IMP	Emperor of India
KL-numeral	A catalog number from the book *Standard Catalog of United States Paper Money*
KM-numeral	A catalog number from the book *Standard Catalog of World Coins*
Laur.	Laureate
LD	Large Date
3-Leg.	3-legged: A major error 1937-D nickel variety
Let. Ed	Lettered Edge
Lg.	Large
Lib.	Liberty
LL	Large Letters
Micro	Smaller than usual mintmark
mm	Millimeters (coin diameter)
MM or mmk.	Mintmark
N.C. or NC	No Cents
N.D. or ND	No Date
NGC	Numismatic Guarantee Corp.: A coin grading service
Ni	Nickel
NM	None Minted
Obv.	Obverse
P-numeral	A catalog number from the book *Standard Catalog of World Paper Money*, originally authored by Albert Pick.
Pb	Lead
PCGS	Professional Coin Grading Service: A coin grading service
Pl.	Plain Edge
PNG	Professional Numismatists Guild: A dealer organization
Pt	Platinum
R-numeral (as R-1)	Indicates degree of rarity on one of various scales
Rev.	Reverse

SD	Small Date
SL	Small Letters
Sm.	Small
Sn	Tin
Std.	Seated
Stg.	Standing
T or Ty.	Type
Var.	Variety
V.D.B.	Victor David Brenner
W.C. or WC	With Cents
w/o	Without
Wtd.	Wanted
Y-numeral	A catalog number from the book *Modern World Coins* or *Current Coins of the World*
Z	Zinc
42/41	Example of an overdate
*	An asterisk in a catalog indicating that the described coin is illustrated

Buffalo nickels. Left to right, from top: Unc. (Uncirculated), EF (Extremely Fine), VF (Very Fine), and F (Fine).

Q. *The abbreviations I see associated with conditions of coins have me confused. Could you clarify?*

A.

P	Poor; less desirable than FAIR, yet identifying features can usually be distinguished.
FR	Fair; quite badly worn and highly undesirable, except for the rarest issues.
AG	About Good; most lettering and designs discernible.
G	Good; worn, but lettering and design all clear.
VG	Very Good; heavy signs of wear, but not altogether unattractive.
AF	About Fine; moderate signs of wear overall.
F	Fine; perceptible signs of wear, but still a very desirable piece.
VF	Very Fine; showing inconsequential signs of wear.
EF, EXF, or XF	Extremely Fine; no definite signs of wear, but having a less than desirable surface than an uncirculated coin.
AU	Almost or About Uncirculated; only the most minor distractions.
Poor-1 to AU-58	Degrees of wear on a circulated coin loosely tied to the above adjectival descriptions.
MS	Mint State; followed by numeric designations from 60 through 70, representing varying degrees of quality from basic uncirculated to perfect quality as originally minted.
Unc.	Uncirculated; no signs of wear other than possible bag marks, but not necessarily brilliant. Interchangeably applied term for MS-60.
BU	Brilliant Uncirculated; sharply struck with full mint luster. May exhibit toning. Used interchangeably with MS-64.
Gem	Gem Quality; interchangeable with MS-67/68.
PR or PF	Proof; a piece produced by a technique involving specially prepared dies and planchets and usually struck multiple times. Proof-60 to Proof-70 quality designations applied; impaired or damaged Proofs may be assigned Proof-40 to Proof-58 designations.
Cr. Unc. or CU	Crisp Uncirculated; paper money which has not been in circulation or mishandled.

Descriptive Identification of a Coin

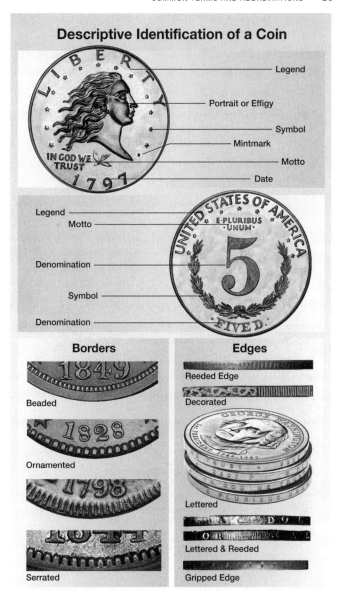

Legend

Portrait or Effigy

Symbol

Mintmark

Motto

Date

Legend

Motto

Denomination

Symbol

Denomination

Borders

Beaded

Ornamented

Serrated

Edges

Reeded Edge

Decorated

Lettered

Lettered & Reeded

Gripped Edge

Q. *I am a novice collector and would like for you to define for me some of the common numismatic terms in the collector's vocabulary?*

A. **altered.** Deliberately changed, usually with a view to increasing the face value or numismatic value of a coin or note.

ancient coin. Generally any coin issued before circa AD 500.

billon. A low grade precious metal alloy used for some minor coin issues, consisting usually of a mixture of less than 50 percent silver alloyed with copper and sometimes coated with a silver wash.

bullion. Uncoined precious metal in the form of bars, plates, ingots, etc.; also a reference used to designate the precious metal content of a coin.

bust. The head represented as a coin device, including at least a portion of the collar bone.

Civil War tokens. Private issue pieces usually made to the approximate size of the current U.S. cents which circulated during the Civil War because of a scarcity of U.S. Mint–produced small change.

coin. Usually a piece of metal marked with a device, issued by a governing authority and intended to be used as money.

commemorative. A coin issued to mark, honor, or observe an event, place, or person, or to preserve its memory.

copper coin. A coin containing over 96 percent pure copper. Lower grade alloys are usually termed bronze or brass.

copy. A reproduction or imitation of an original.

crown. A general term historically embracing most silver coins from about 20 to 30 grams in weight and from about 33 to 50 millimeters in size. The term now applies to nickel-alloy coins of similar weight and size.

current. Coins and paper money still in circulation.

device. The principal element, such as a portrait, shield, or heraldic emblem, of the design on the obverse or reverse of a coin, token, or medal.

die. A hardened metal punch, the face of which carries an intaglio or incuse mirror-image of the device to be impressed on one side of a planchet.

duplicate. A piece identical to another, except that it need not be in an identical state of preservation.

edge. That portion of a coin, generally plain or reeded, which displays the thickness between its obverse and reverse.

error. A coin, token, medal, or paper money item evidencing a mistake made in its manufacture.

exergue. The lower field of a coin, usually on the reverse below a wreath.

exonumist. A collector whose interests encompass numismatic items outside those issued for official government monetary purposes.

facsimile. An exact copy or reproduction.

field. The blank space on a coin not occupied by the design.

forgery. An unauthorized copy made with intent to deceive.

fractional coin. A coin, the face value of which is a fractional unit of the denominated currency; historically, generally minted of silver, but today of a base metal.

fractional currency. A paper money note with a face value of less than $1.

Hard Times token. An unofficial large-cent size copper struck in a wide variety of types from 1833 to 1844, serving as de-facto currency and bearing either a politically inspired legend or advertising, as a store card.

hub or hob. A hardened metal positive impression of a design to be reproduced in reverse on a die, to be used in striking coins.

incuse. Design or lettering elements that are recessed into the surrounding surface of a coin.

intrinsic. As applied to value, the net bullion value as distinguished from face value.

legal tender. Currency explicitly determined by a government to be acceptable in the discharge of debts.

legend. The inscription on a numismatic item.

lettered edge. A design characteristic of coins, whereby a piece—when viewed by the edge—will reveal a statement of the coin's denomination or a patriotic legend. On U.S. coins, lettered edges appeared only on half cents and large cents minted from 1792 to 1805, halves and silver dollars minted prior to 1836, and on the Saint-Gaudens eagle and double eagle issues, until resurrected with the introduction of the Presidential dollars series in 2007. The lettering appears incuse on the early issues and the modern Presidential dollars series, but is raised on the eagles and double eagles.

medal. Usually a piece of metal, marked with a design or inscription, made to honor a person, place, or event.

medieval coin. A coin struck from circa AD 500 to 1500.

milled coin. In contrast with a hammered coin, a piece produced by pressure indirectly rather than being directly applied, on which the edge has been rolled or upset.

minor coin. A silver coin of less than crown weight or any coin struck in base metal.

mint luster. The sheen or "bloom" on the surface of an Uncirculated numismatic item. Once removed, mint luster can never be restored.

mintmark. A letter or other symbol, sometimes of a private nature, indicating the mint of origin.

mint set. One coin of each denomination produced by a given mint in a given year without regard to condition. Mint sets purchased directly from a mint contain uncirculated coins.

misprint. A printing error on a piece of paper money.

modern coin. A coin struck after circa AD 1500.

money. A medium of exchange.

mule. A coin made by combining the dies of two different coin types.

NCLT. An acronym designating official government issue "Non-Circulating Legal Tender" coins, generally struck of silver or gold in denominations not intended to circulate commercially.

obverse. The side of a numismatic item which bears the principal device. With a few exceptions, the obverse is the date side of regular-issue U.S. coinage.

overdate. Date made by superimposing one or more numerals on a previously dated die.

patina. A natural surface coloring, induced by oxidation, acquired by all unprotected coins with the passage of time. Usually applied to the green film formed on copper and bronze. Patina can also be produced artificially, as by introducing certain chemical elements.

pattern. Coins struck to test a design being considered for adoption as a regular issue, usually dated in a year prior to the introduction of the coin into production.

plain edge. A design characteristics of all U.S. small cents and nickels, half cents and large cents minted after 1795, all two-cent and three-cent pieces, the 20-cent coin, and the Sacagawea dollar series.

planchet. The disc of metal or other material on which the dies of a coin, token, or medal are impressed.

Proof. A coin or bank note prepared as an example of a given issue.

Proof set. A set of one Proof coin of each current denomination for a specific year, or a series of issues, produced by or in the name of a recognized government.

reeded edge. The design characteristic present on most U.S. silver and gold coin issues, and their successor clad metal coinages, consisting of a continuous encirclement of raised vertical lines.

reissue. A numismatic item issued again after an extended lapse of time.

restrike. A numismatic item produced from original dies at a later date.

reverse. The side of a numismatic item opposite to that on which the principal device is impressed.

right and left. To the viewer's right and left.

scrip. Paper currency, usually of denominations less than one dollar, issued as a design being considered for adoption as a regular issue, usually dated in a year prior to the introduction of the note into production. Also substitutes for currency by private persons or organizations to fill a demand for circulation not being met by government currencies.

script. Words represented on a numismatic item, usually in a form resembling handwriting.

silver coin. A coin usually consisting of 50 percent or greater silver content.

specimen. A coin or bank note prepared as a example of a given issue.

spurious. A false piece made to deceive, often an original creation rather than a copy of a known item.

store card. A token bearing a business name and/or address and often intended as a local or ad-hoc medium of exchange.

token. Usually a piece of durable material unofficially issued for monetary, adverting, service, or other purposes.

token coinage. Coinage, the intrinsic value of which is less than its face or precious metal content; e.g., a clad metal quarter vs. the old .900 fine silver quarter.

type set. A collection composed of one coin of each basic design within a given range of issues.

uniface. A struck coin, token, or medal bearing a design on one side only.

unique. Existing in only one known specimen.

vectures. Transportation tokens.

CHAPTER THREE

Educating the Budding Collector

Q. *I just want to collect coins. What's the point of reading a bunch of books?*

A. Anyone can save unusual coins from their pocket change, or acquire random, interesting items from coin shops. The result is an accumulation more than it is a collection, which is a group of coins that are acquired deliberately and with knowledge, and that often have a common factor (e.g., a collection of colonial coins; a collection of Buffalo nickels; a collection of coins designed by Christian Gobrecht; a collection of coins minted in Carson City).

 To turn a jar full of wheat pennies into a collection, you need knowledge, most of which must, of necessity, be gained through reading. Even seasoned collectors who have forgotten more than most people will ever learn continue to read voraciously; many of them even go on to write other books. (One noted numismatist, David M. Bullowa, said that the beginning collector would be wise to spend 20 to 25 percent of his or her coin budget on a numismatic library.)

Q. *There are hundreds and hundreds of books and articles about coins. Where should I start?*

A. It depends on what you want to collect. The following are the absolute minimum a collector should own and read, based on your specialty:

U.S. coins (all)	Breen, Walter. *Walter Breen's Complete Encyclopedia of U.S. and Colonial Coins.* New York (1988).
	Yeoman, R.S. *A Guide Book of United States Coins,* current edition (as of 2008, the 62nd). Atlanta.

Tokens	Rulau, Russell. *Standard Catalog of United States Tokens 1700–1900*. Iola, Wisconsin (1997).
Federal paper money	Friedberg, Arthur L., and Ira S. Friedberg. *Paper Money of the United States*, current edition (as of 2008, the 18th). Clifton, New Jersey (2006). *A Guide Book of United States Paper Money*, current edition (as of 2008, the 2nd). Atlanta (2008).
	Bowers, Q. David. *Whitman Encyclopedia of U.S. Paper Money*. Atlanta (2008).

Q. *The books above include guides to retail or wholesale values. Why not just subscribe to a magazine or an Internet service, whose values are updated weekly or even daily, rather than buy a book that won't be updated for at least a year?*

A. Smart collectors *do* keep up with rapid market changes, using periodicals and the Internet. But short-term price fluctuations are only part of a much larger picture. To begin with, few of the coins in the market see a huge change in value over the course of a week, a month, or even a year, so most of the suggested values in a book will be reasonably accurate for about 12 months after publication. Examples of exceptions are as follows:

Gold—Gold-coin values can fluctuate rapidly with the market price for the metal, but this mostly affects worn coins whose numismatic value is less than their bullion value. The numismatic value is likely to change much more slowly.

Rarities—A coin might get a huge boost in value when another of its kind achieves a record-high auction price. This only applies to very high-priced rarities, however, not to the vast majority of coins.

Trendy issues—A "hot" coin (say, a certain year and mintmark of Morgan silver dollar) might drop sharply in value if the discovery of a hoard of identical coins makes them almost commonplace. This is quite rare.

The biggest limitation of price lists, though, is that they're meaningless if you don't know how to use them. For example, assume that a magazine values an 1892 Liberty Head quarter at $325 when graded at MS-63. But suppose you're looking at a coin that hasn't been graded by a professional service, and the handwritten description on the cardboard holder just says "Unc." Is "Unc." worth more or less than MS-63? Or say you're at a coin show, and in front of you are three professionally graded

1892 quarters, all certified at MS-63. One has nice luster and few marks, but it does have a noticeable scratch right on Liberty's cheek. The other looks duller, but it doesn't have any major marks—just a few small nicks and dings. The third one has rainbow-colored toning on the reverse. How do you compare these?

It's important to keep up with pricing trends, but if you don't understand the basic principles of collecting, a price list won't do you any good.

Q. *I saw a crate-load of old auction catalogs on eBay. Are those worth having?*

A. An auction catalog written for a high-quality sale by a knowledgeable and talented cataloger can be as informative and enjoyable to read as a book. In fact, many auction catalogs are written by premier numismatic authors, who not only collect and write but also work for or are principals in numismatic firms.

Q. *There are scores of these catalogs out there. Is there a guide book of some kind to help me choose?*

A. Numismatist John W. Adams wrote an excellent, two-volume survey of numismatic auction catalogs called *United States Numismatic Literature*, covering those published through 1975. Adams assigned a "quality rating" to each catalog, based on his opinion of the contents. The best were given the highest rating, A+, while those that deserved no more than passing notice were assigned a "C–." In general, look for those that Adams rated B or finer, adding any others that are of interest to you. (E.g., if you are interested in pattern coins, a B catalog with a lot of patterns is a better buy than an A+ catalog filled with rare early U.S. gold, but not a single pattern in sight.)

Q. *If I can't get a copy of the Adams book, what are some general rules of thumb in choosing auction catalogs for my library?*

A. In general, catalogs of the past 50 years will have better numismatic, historical, and other content than those of the previous century (although there are excellent catalogs from back in the 1800s). Most such catalogs are quite inexpensive, and a useful and extensive library of them can be formed for very little. A thumbnail sketch of famous collections that produced outstanding catalogs when auctioned includes the Garrett, Eliasberg, Norweb, Childs, Harry W. Bass Jr., and John J. Ford Jr. collections, along with the sale of the treasure from the S.S. *Central America*.

Pay attention, too, when the auction was held by a noteworthy firm. Several worth looking for are, in alphabetical order, American Numismatic Rarities, Bowers and Merena, Bowers and Ruddy, Bullowa, Christie's, David W. Akers, DLRC, Heritage, Larry and Ira Goldberg, Lyn F. Knight, Mid-American, New England Rare Coin Galleries, Pacific Coast Auction Galleries, Paramount, R.M. Smythe & Co., RARCOA, Sotheby's, Spectrum, Stack's, Steve Ivy, and Superior.

Q. *What about periodicals?*

A. As of this printing, some of the major journals and magazines were these:
American Journal of Numismatics—Second Series
The Asylum
Banknote Reporter
Canadian Coins News
The Celator (ancient coins)
COINage Magazine
Coin Dealer Newsletter (a.k.a. "the Greysheet")
Coin Prices Magazine
Coins Magazine
Coin World
Colonial Newsletter
The Currency Dealer Newsletter
Error Trends Coin Magazine
Numismatic News
The Numismatist
Paper Money
World Coin News
Worldwide Coins Magazine

Q. *Where can I go for more information on numismatic publications?*

A. The Numismatic Bibliomania Society (http://www.coinbooks.org/), through its journal, *The Asylum*, and its E-Sylum on the Internet (https://my.binhost.com/lists/listinfo/esylum), connects hundreds of enthusiasts. Other resources include the libraries of the American Numismatic Association (http://www.money.org), the American Numismatic Society (http://www.numismatics.org), and the Harry W. Bass Foundation (http://harrybassfoundation.org).

Q. *In addition to the basic titles mentioned early in this chapter, what books are recommended for specific topics and specialties?*

A. Although the following is not an exhaustive list, it should get any collector started down the path of his or her area of interest:

History of the U.S. Mint

Evans, George. *Illustrated History of the U.S. Mint With a Complete Description of American Coinage* (Philadelphia, various eds., 1885–1901).

Lange, David W. *History of the United States Mint and Its Coinage* (Atlanta, 2005).

Colonial Coins

American Numismatic Society. *Studies on Money in Early America* (New York, 1976).

Bowers, Q. David. *Whitman Encyclopedia of Colonial and Early American Coins* (Atlanta, 2008).

Carlotto, Tony. *The Copper Coins of Vermont* (Chelsea, Michigan, 1998).

The Colonial Newsletter (publication of the American Numismatic Society, 1960 to date).

Crosby, S.S. *The Early Coins of America* (Boston, 1875; reprinted 1945, 1965, 1974, 1983).

Kessler, Alan. *The Fugio Cents* (Newtonville, Massachusetts, 1976).

Maris, Edward. *A Historic Sketch of the Coins of New Jersey* (Philadelphia, 1881; reprinted 1965, 1974, 1987).

Martin, Syd. *The Hibernia Coinage of William Wood (1722–1724)* (n.p., 2007).

Miller, Henry C., and Ryder Hillyer. *The State Coinages of New England* (New York, 1920).

Mossman, Philip L. *Money of the American Colonies and Confederation* (New York, 1993).

Nelson, Philip. *The Coinage of William Wood 1722–1733* (London, 1903; reprinted 1959).

Newman, Eric P. *Coinage for Colonial Virginia* (New York, 1956). *The 1776 Continental Currency Coinage; Varieties of the Fugio Cent* (New

York, 1952). *The United States Fugio Copper Coinage of 1787* (Ypsilanti, Michigan, 2007).

Newman, Eric P., and Richard G. Doty. *Studies on Money in Early America* (New York, 1976).

Noe, Sydney P. *The New England and Willow Tree Coinage of Massachusetts*
(New York, 1943). *The Oak Tree Coinage of Massachusetts* (New York,
1947). *The Pine Tree Coinage of Massachusetts* (New York, 1952). (All
reprinted 1973).

Rulau, Russell, and George Fuld. *Medallic Portraits of Washington* (Iola,
Wisconsin, 1999).

Vlack, Robert. *An Illustrated Catalogue of the French Billon Coinage in the
Americas* (Boston, 2004).

Wurtzbach, Carl. *Massachusetts Colonial Silver Money* (n.p., 1937).

Half Cents

Breen, Walter. *Walter Breen's Encyclopedia of United States Half Cents
1793–1857* (South Gate, California, 1983).

Cohen, Roger S., Jr. *American Half Cents—The "Little Half Sisters"* (2nd
ed.; Bethesda, Maryland, 1982).

Leone, Frank. *Longacre's Two Cent Piece Die Varieties and Errors* (College
Point, New York, 1991).

Manley, Ronald P. *The Half Cent Die State Book, 1793–1857* (n.p., 1998).

Large Cents

Breen, Walter. *Walter Breen's Encyclopedia of Early United States Cents
1793–1814* (Wolfeboro, New Hampshire, 2001).

Grellman, J.R. *Attribution Guide for United States Large Cents 1840–1857*
(3rd ed.; Bloomington, Minnesota, 2002).

Newcomb, H.R. *United States Copper Cents 1816–1857* (New York, 1944;
reprinted 1983).

Noyes, William C. *United States Large Cents 1793–1794* (Ypsilanti,
Michigan, 2006). *United States Large Cents 1793–1814* (Bloomington, Minnesota, 1991). *United States Large Cents 1795–1797* (Ypsilanti, 2007). *United States Large Cents 1816–1839* (Bloomington,
1991).

Penny-Wise (official publication of Early American Coppers, Inc.).

Sheldon, William H. *Penny Whimsy: A Revision of Early American Cents,
1793–1814* (New York, 1958; reprinted 1965, 1976).

Wright, John D. *The Cent Book 1816–1839* (Bloomington, Minnesota,
1992).

Small Cents

Bowers, Q. David. *A Guide Book of Lincoln Cents* (Atlanta, 2008).

Lange, David W. *The Complete Guide to Lincoln Cents* (Wolfeboro, New Hampshire, 1996).

Snow, Richard. *A Guide Book of Flying Eagle and Indian Head Cents* (Atlanta, 2006).

Steve, Larry, and Kevin Flynn. *Flying Eagle and Indian Cent Die Varieties* (Jarretteville, Maryland, 1995).

Taylor, Sol. *The Standard Guide to the Lincoln Cent* (Anaheim, California, 1999).

Wexler, John, and Kevin Flynn. *The Authoritative Reference on Lincoln Cents* (Rancocas, New Jersey, 1996).

Two-Cent Pieces

Flynn, Kevin. *Getting Your Two Cents Worth* (Rancocas, New Jersey, 1994).

Kliman, Myron M. *The Two Cent Piece and Varieties* (South Laguna, California, 1977).

Leone, Frank. *Longacre's Two Cent Piece Die Varieties and Errors* (College Point, New York, 1991).

Nickel Five-Cent Pieces

Bowers, Q. David. *A Guide Book of Buffalo and Jefferson Nickels* (Atlanta, 2007). *A Guide Book of Shield and Liberty Head Nickels* (Atlanta, 2006).

Fletcher, Edward L., Jr. *The Shield Five Cent Series* (Ormond Beach, Florida, 1994).

Lange, David W. *The Complete Guide to Buffalo Nickels* (Virginia Beach, Virginia, 2006).

Nagengast, Bernard. *The Jefferson Nickel Analyst* (2nd ed.; Sidney, Ohio, 1979).

Peters, Gloria, and Cynthia Mahon. *The Complete Guide to Shield and Liberty Head Nickels* (Virginia Beach, Virginia, 1995).

Wescott, Michael. *The United States Nickel Five-Cent Piece* (Wolfeboro, New Hampshire, 1991).

Half Dimes

Blythe, Al. *The Complete Guide to Liberty Seated Half Dimes* (Virginia Beach, Virginia, 1992).

Breen, Walter. *United States Half Dimes: A Supplement* (New York, 1958).

Logan, Russell, and John McClosky. *Federal Half Dimes 1792–1837* (Manchester, Michigan, 1998).

Newlin, H.P. *The Early Half-Dimes of the United States* (Philadelphia, 1883; reprinted 1933).

Valentine, D.W. *The United States Half Dimes* (New York, 1931; reprinted 1975).

Dimes

Ahwash, Kamal M. *Encyclopedia of United States Liberty Seated Dimes 1837–1891* (n.p., 1977).

Davis, David, Russell Logan, Allen Lovejoy, John McCloskey, and William Subjack. *Early United States Dimes 1796–1837* (Ypsilanti, Michigan, 1984).

Flynn, Kevin. *The 1894-S Dime: A Mystery Unraveled* (Rancocas, New Jersey, 2005). *The Authoritative Reference on Roosevelt Dimes* (Brooklyn, New York, 2001).

Greer, Brian. *The Complete Guide to Liberty Seated Dimes* (Virginia Beach, Virginia, 2005).

Kosoff, A. *United States Dimes From 1796* (New York, 1945).

Lange, David W. *The Complete Guide to Mercury Dimes* (2nd ed.; Virginia Beach, Virginia, 2005).

Lawrence, David. *The Complete Guide to Barber Dimes* (Virginia Beach, Virginia, 1991).

Quarter Dollars

Bowers, Q. David. *A Guide Book of Washington and State Quarters* (Atlanta, 2006).

Bressett, Kenneth. *The Official Whitman Statehood Quarters Collector's Handbook* (New York, 2000).

Briggs, Larry. *The Comprehensive Encyclopedia of United States Seated Quarters* (Lima, Ohio, 1991).

Browning, A.W. *The Early Quarter Dollars of the United States 1796–1838* (New York, 1925; reprinted 1992).

Cline, J.H. *Standing Liberty Quarters* (3rd ed.; Dayton, Ohio, 1996).

Duphorne, R. *The Early Quarter Dollars of the United States* (n.p., 1975).

Fivaz, Bill, and J.T. Stanton. *The Cherrypickers' Guide to Rare Die Varieties* (Atlanta, 2006).

Haseltine, J.W. *Type Table of United States Dollars, Half Dollars, and Quarter Dollars* (Philadelphia, 1881; reprinted 1927, 1968).

Kelman, Keith N. *Standing Liberty Quarters* (Nashua, New Hampshire, 1976).

Lawrence, David. *The Complete Guide to Barber Quarters* (Virginia Beach, Virginia, 1989).

Half Dollars

Flynn, Kevin. *The Authoritative Reference on Barber Half Dollars* (Brooklyn, New York, 2005).

Fox, Bruce. *The Complete Guide to Walking Liberty Half Dollars* (Virginia Beach, Virginia, 1993).

Haseltine, J.W. *Type Table of United States Dollars, Half Dollars, and Quarter Dollars* (Philadelphia, 1881; reprinted 1927, 1968).

Lawrence, David. *The Complete Guide to Barber Halves* (Virginia Beach, Virginia, 1991).

Overton, Al C. *Early Half Dollar Die Varieties 1794–1836* (3rd ed.; Colorado Springs, Colorado, 1990).

Peterson, Glenn R. *The Ultimate Guide to Attributing Bust Half Dollars* (Rocky River, Ohio, 2000).

Wiley, Randy, and Bill Bugert. *The Complete Guide to Liberty Seated Half Dollars* (Virginia Beach, Virginia, 1993).

Silver Dollars

Bolender, M.H. *The United States Early Silver Dollars From 1794 to 1803* (5th ed.; Iola, Wisconsin, 1987).

Bowers, Q. David. *A Guide Book of Morgan Silver Dollars: A Complete History and Price Guide* (3rd ed.; Atlanta, 2007). *The Rare Silver Dollars Dated 1804* (Wolfeboro, New Hampshire, 1999). *Silver Dollars and Trade Dollars of the United States: A Complete Encyclopedia* (Wolfeboro, 1993).

Fey, Michael S., and Jeff Oxman. *The Top 100 Morgan Dollar Varieties* (Morris Planes, New Jersey, 1997).

Haseltine, J.W. *Type Table of United States Dollars, Half Dollars, and Quarter Dollars* (Philadelphia, 1881; reprinted 1927, 1968).

Logies, Martin A. *The Flowing Hair Silver Dollars of 1794* (n.p., 2004).

Newman, Eric P., and Kenneth E. Bressett. *The Fantastic 1804 Dollar* (Racine, Wisconsin, 1962).

Van Allen, Leroy C., and A. George Mallis. *Comprehensive Catalogue and Encyclopedia of U.S. Morgan and Peace Silver Dollars* (New York, 1997).

Willem, John M. *The United States Trade Dollar* (2nd ed.; Racine, Wisconsin, 1965).

Gold Pieces ($1–$20)

Akers, David W. *Gold Dollars* (and other gold denominations; Englewood, Ohio, 1975–1982).

Bowers, Q. David. *A Guide Book of Double Eagle Gold Coins* (Atlanta, 2004). *The Harry W. Bass Jr. Museum Sylloge* (Dallas, Texas, 2001). *United States Gold Coins: An Illustrated History* (Wolfeboro, New Hampshire, 1982).

Breen, Walter. *Major Varieties of U.S. Gold Dollars* (and other gold denominations; Chicago, 1964). *New Varieties of $1, $2.50, and $5.00 United States Gold* (Chicago, 1968).

Dannreuther, John W., and Harry W. Bass Jr. *Early U.S. Gold Coin Varieties* (Atlanta, 2006).

Fivaz, Bill. *United States Gold Counterfeit Detection Guide* (Atlanta, 2005).

Garrett, Jeff, and Ron Guth. *Encyclopedia of U. S. Gold Coins, 1795–1933* (2nd ed.; Atlanta, 2007).

Gillilland, Cory. *Sylloge of the United States Holdings in the National Numismatic Collection of the Smithsonian Institution. Volume 1: Gold Coins, 1785–1834* (Washington, D.C., 1992).

Goe, Rusty. *The Mint on Carson Street* (Reno, Nevada, 2003).

Taglione, Paul F. *A Reference to United States Federal Gold Coinage. Volume 4: An Investment Philosophy for the Prudent Consumer* (Boston, 1986).

Winter, Douglas. *Charlotte Mint Gold Coins: 1838–1861* (Wolfeboro, New Hampshire, 1987). *Gold Coins of the Dahlonega Mint 1838–1861* (Dallas, Texas, 1997). *New Orleans Mint Gold Coins, 1838–1909* (Wolfeboro, 1992).

Winter, Douglas, and Lawrence E. Cutler. *Gold Coins of the Old West: The Carson City Mint 1870–1893* (Wolfeboro, New Hampshire, 1994).

Commemoratives

Bowers, Q. David. *Commemorative Coins of the United States: A Complete Encyclopedia* (Wolfeboro, New Hampshire, 1991). *A Guide Book of United States Commemorative Coins* (Atlanta, 2008).

Bullowa, David M. *The Commemorative Coinage of the United States 1892–1938* (New York, 1938).

Mosher, Stuart. *The Commemorative Coinage of the United States 1892–1938* (New York, 1940).

Slabaugh, Arlie. *United States Commemorative Coinage* (Racine, Wisconsin, 1975).

Swiatek, Anthony, and Walter Breen. *The Encyclopedia of United States Silver and Gold Commemorative Coins 1892–1954* (New York, 1981).

Taxay, Don. *An Illustrated History of U.S. Commemorative Coinage* (New York, 1967).

Tokens and Medals

Betts, C. Wyllys. *American Colonial History Illustrated by Contemporary Medals* (New York, 1894).

Brunk, Gregory G. *American and Canadian Countermarked Coins* (Rockford, Illinois, 1987).

Coffee, John M., Jr., and Harold V. Ford. 1996. *The Atwood-Coffee Catalogue of United States and Canadian Transportation Tokens* (5th ed.; Boston, 1996).

Doty, Richard G. (editor). *The Token: America's Other Money.* American Numismatic Society, Coinage of the Americas Conference (New York, 1994).

DeWitt, J. Doyle. *A Century of Campaign Buttons 1789–1889* (Hartford, Connecticut, 1859).

Fuld, George, and Melvin Fuld. *U.S. Civil War Store Cards* (Lawrence, Massachusetts, 1975).

Fuld, Melvin, and George Fuld. *Patriotic Civil War Tokens* (Iola, Wisconsin, 1982).

Hibler, Harold E., and Charles V. Kappen. *So-Called Dollars: An Illustrated Standard Catalog With Valuations* (New York, 1963).

Jaeger, Katherine, and Q. David Bowers. *100 Greatest American Medals and Tokens* (Atlanta, 2007).

Jaeger, Katherine. *A Guide Book of United States Tokens and Medals* (Atlanta, 2008).

Julian, R.W. 1977. *Medals of the United States Mint: The First Century, 1792–1892* (El Cajon, California, 1977).

Loubat, J.F. *The Medallic History of the United States of America, 1776–1876* (2 vols.; New York, 1878).

Low, Lyman Haynes. *Hard Times Tokens* (New York, 1899).

Miller, Donald M. *A Catalogue of U.S. Store Cards or Merchants' Tokens* (Indiana, Pennsylvania, 1962).

Rulau, Russell. *Standard Catalog of United States Tokens 1700–1900* (Iola, Wisconsin, 1997).

Rulau, Russell, and George Fuld. *Medallic Portraits of Washington* (Iola, Wisconsin, 1999).

Schenkman, David E. *Civil War Sutler Tokens and Cardboard Scrip* (Bryans Road, Maryland, 1983).

Patterns

Akers, David W. *United States Gold Patterns* (Racine, Wisconsin, 1975).

Judd, J. Hewitt. *United States Pattern Coins* (10th ed., edited by Q. David Bowers; Atlanta, 2008).

Pollock, Andrew W., III. *United States Patterns and Related Issues* (Wolfeboro, New Hampshire, 1994).

Private and Territorial Gold

Adams, Edgar H. *Official Premium Lists of Private and Territorial Gold Coins* (Brooklyn, New York, 1909). *Private Gold Coinage of California 1849–1855* (Brooklyn, 1913).

Bowers, Q. David. *A California Gold Rush History Featuring Treasure from the S.S. Central America* (Wolfeboro, New Hampshire, 2001). *The History of United States Coinage as Illustrated by the Garrett Collection* (Los Angeles, 1979).

Breen, Walter. *California Pioneer Fractional Gold* (2nd ed., revised and expanded by Robert D. Leonard et al.; Wolfeboro, New Hampshire, 2003).

Clifford, Henry H. "Pioneer Gold Coinage in the West—1848–1861." Reprint from *The Westerners Brand Book, Book Nine* (Los Angeles, 1961).

Doering, David. *California Fractional Gold* (Seal Beach, California, 1982).

Griffin, Clarence. *The Bechtlers and Bechtler Coinage and Gold Mining in North Carolina 1814–1830* Spindale, North Carolina, 1929).

Kagin, Donald H. *Private Gold Coins and Patterns of the United States* (New York, 1981).

Lee, Kenneth W. *California Gold: Dollars, Half Dollars, Quarter Dollars* (Santa Ana, California, 1979).

Owens, Dan. *California Coiners and Assayers* (Wolfeboro, New Hampshire, 2000).

Seymour, Dexter C. *The 1830 Coinage of Templeton Reid.* American Numismatic Society Museum Notes No. 22. (New York, 1977).

Philippine and Hawaiian Issues

Allen, Lyman L. *U.S. Philippine Coins* (Oakland Park, Florida, 1998).

Medcalf, Donald, and Ronald Russell. *Hawaiian Money Standard Catalog* (2nd ed.; Mill Creek, Washington, 1991).

Shafer, Neil. *United States Territorial Coinage for the Philippine Islands* (Racine, Wisconsin, 1961).

Proof Coins and Proof Sets

Lange, David W. *A Guide Book of Modern United States Proof Coin Sets* (Atlanta, 2005). *A Guide Book of United States Proof Sets 1936–2004* (Atlanta, 2005).

Tomaska, Rick Jerry. *Cameo and Brilliant Proof Coinage of the 1950 to 1970 Era* (Encinitas, California, 1991).

Type Coins

Bowers, Q. David. *A Guide Book of United States Type Coins* (2nd ed.; Atlanta, 2008).

Garrett, Jeff, and Ron Guth. *100 Greatest U.S. Coins* (2nd ed.; Atlanta, 2005).

Guth, Ron, and Jeff Garrett. *United States Coinage: A Study by Type* (Atlanta, 2005).

Colonial and Continental Paper Money

Newman, Eric P. *The Early Paper Money of America* (4th ed.; Iola, Wisconsin, 1997).

Prince Society, Inc. *Colonial Currency Reprints* (Boston, 1910).

Obsolete Bank Notes

Bowers, Q. David. *Obsolete Paper Money Issued by Banks in the United States 1782–1866* (Atlanta, 2006).

Haxby, James A. *Standard Catalog of United States Obsolete Bank Notes 1782–1866* (4 vols.; Iola, Wisconsin, 1988).

Confederate Paper Money

Criswell, Grover C. *Comprehensive Catalog of Confederate Paper Money* (Port Clinton, Ohio, 1996).

Allen, H.D. "The Paper Money of the Confederate States With Historical Data." *The Numismatist* (June 1917–February 1919).

Bradbeer, William W. *Confederate and Southern States Currency* (Mount Vernon, New York, 1915).

Chase, Philip H. *Confederate Treasury Notes* (Philadelphia, 1947).

Fuller, Claud E. *Confederate Currency and Stamps* (Nashville, Tennessee, 1949).

Haseltine, John W. *Descriptive Catalog of Confederate Notes and Bonds* (Philadelphia, 1876).

Lee, William. *The Currency of the Confederate States of America* (Washington, D.C., 1875).

Massamore, George W. *Descriptive and Chronological Catalog of Confederate Currency* (Baltimore, 1889).

Shull, Hught. *A Guide Book of Southern States Currency* (Atlanta, 2007). *A Guide Book of Confederate Currency* (Atlanta, 2009).

Slabaugh, Arlie R. *Confederate States Paper Money* (10th ed.; Iola, Wisconsin, 2000).

Thian, Raphael P. *Register of the Confederate Debt* (Boston, 1880; reprinted 1972)

Tremmel, George B. *A Guide Book of Counterfeit Confederate Currency* (Atlanta, 2007).

Federal Bank Notes, 1861 to Date

Friedberg, Arthur L., and Ira S. Friedberg. *Paper Money of the United States* (18th ed.; Clifton, New Jersey, 2006). *A Guide Book of United States Paper Money* (2nd ed.; Atlanta, 2008).

Hessler, Gene. *The Comprehensive Catalog of U.S. Paper Money* (6th ed.; Port Clinton, Ohio, 1997). *The Engraver's Line* (Port Clinton, 1993). *U.S. Essay, Proof, and Specimen Notes* (2nd ed.; Port Clinton, 2004).

Huntoon, Peter. *U.S. Large Size National Bank Notes* (Laramie, Wyoming, 1995).

Kelly, Don C. *National Bank Notes* (4th ed.; Oxford, Ohio, 2004).

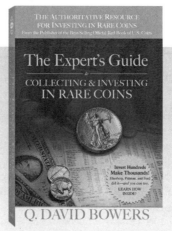

For more information: See the *Expert's Guide to Collecting and Investing in Rare Coins* for advice on getting started in the hobby.

II.
U.S. COINAGE

About the images in this book: In general, coin denominations of 50 cents and higher are pictured at actual size; denominations below 50 cents and coins that are unusually small (e.g., gold dollars) are generally pictured at 150 percent of their actual size. Paper money is typically pictured at page width. Other items, such as medals, encased postage, and so on, may be enlarged for visibility. Appendix B lists the actual sizes of U.S. coins and currency.

Chapter Four

Basics of
U.S. Coinage

Q. *What coins have been officially issued by the United States, and are they all still legal tender?*

A. With a single exception (the 1873 to 1885 trade dollar), all coins ever officially issued for circulation or as commemoratives remain legal tender to this day, as do all issues of paper money. Here is a list of the U.S. coinage standards and their years of actual and official issue:

Circulating Coinage, Copper and Silver

Half cents	copper	1793–1857
1¢ (large)	copper	1793–1857
1¢ (small)	copper-nickel	1857–1864[1]
	bronze	1864–1942, 1944–1982[2]
	zinc coated steel	1943
	copper-plated zinc	1982–date
2¢	bronze	1864–1873
3¢	.900 fine silver	1851–1873
	nickel	1865–1889
5¢ (nickels)	copper-nickel alloy	1866–1942, 1946–date
	copper-silver-manganese alloy	1942–1945
5¢ (half dimes)	.8924 fine silver	1794–1837
	.900 fine silver	1837–1873
10¢	.8924 fine silver	1796–1837
	.900 fine silver	1837–1964
	clad/cupronickel on copper	1965–date[6]

20¢	.900 fine silver	1875–1878
25¢	.8924 fine silver	1796–1838
	.900 fine silver	1838–1964
	.800 fine silver clad to .209 fine silver	1976[3]
	clad/cupronickel on copper	1965–date[6]
50¢	.8924 fine silver	1794–1836
	.900 fine silver	1836–1964
	.800 fine silver clad to .209 fine silver	1965–1970, 1976[3]
	clad/cupronickel on copper	1965–date[6]
$1 (regular circulating)	.8924 fine silver	1794–1803
	.900 fine silver	1840–1873, 1878–1935
	.800 fine silver clad to .209 fine silver	1971–1976[3]
	clad/cupronickel on copper (38.1 mm diameter)	1971–1978
	clad/cupronickel on copper (26.5 mm diameter)	1979–1999
	clad/manganese brass on copper	2000–date
$1 (trade)	.900 fine silver	1873–1885[4]

Circulating Coinage, Gold

$1	.900 fine gold	1849–1889
$2.50	.9167 fine gold	1796–1834
	.8992 fine gold	1834–1839
	.900 fine gold	1840–1929
$3	.900 fine gold	1854–1889
$5	.9167 fine gold	1795–1834
	.8992 fine gold	1834–1838
	.900 fine gold	1839–1929
$10	.9167 fine gold	1795–1804
	.900 fine gold	1838–1933
$20	.900 fine gold	1849–1933[5]

Commemorative Coinage

25¢	.900 fine silver	1892 Isabella; 1999–2008 statehood quarters
	clad/cupronickel on copper	1999–2008
50¢	.900 fine silver	1892–1954 Classic issues; 1982 Washington; 1993 Bill of Rights
	clad/cupronickel on copper	1986–date
$1	.900 fine silver	1900 Lafayette
	.900 fine gold	1903–1922 Classic issues
	.900 fine silver	1983–date
$2.50	.900 fine gold	1915–1926 Classic issues
$5	.900 fine gold	1986–date
$10	.900 fine gold	1984 Los Angeles XXIII Olympiad; 2003 First Flight Centennial
	platinum and gold bimetallic	2000 Library of Congress
$50	.900 fine gold	1915 Panama-Pacific Exposition[7]

Bullion Coinage, American Eagles[8]

$1	.9993 fine (1 oz.) silver	1986–date
$5	.9167 fine (1/2 oz.) gold	1986–date
$10	.9167 fine (1/4 oz.) gold	1986–date
	.9995 fine (1/10 oz.) platinum	1997–date
$25	.9167 fine (1/2 oz.) gold	1986–date
	.9995 fine (1/4 oz.) platinum	1997–date
$50	.9167 fine (1 oz.) gold	1986–date
	.9995 fine (1/2 oz.) platinum	1997–date
$100	.9995 fine (1 oz.) platinum	1997–date

Bullion Coinage, American Buffalos[8, 9]

$50	.9999 fine gold (1 oz.)	2006–date

1 Flying Eagle cents dated 1856 are frequently included in date sets, but these were not authorized issues and are regarded as patterns; with a mintage of only 2,000, this issue is exceedingly rare.

2 Various slight metallic-composition variations were employed in the manufacture of bronze cents from 1864 to 1982, ranging from a composition of 95 percent copper and 5 percent tin and zinc, to 95 percent copper and 5 percent zinc from 1962 to 1982.

3 Struck exclusively for sale to collectors, but still legal tender.

4 This dollar was intended for circulation outside the United States, primarily in the Far East, but was legal tender to the extent of $5 during the period of 1873–1876.

5 While nearly a half-million examples of the 1933 double eagle were minted, and 11 examples are known to have escaped the melting pot, only one specimen is legal to own, it having been sold at a public auction with the approval of the Treasury Department for $7.59 million in July of 2002.

6 Commencing in 1992, silver dimes, quarters, and halves—including the issues in the 50 State Quarters® series of 1999–2008, of the pre-1965 standard were struck as Proofs for inclusion in special premium-quality Proof sets.

7 During the period of Classic commemorative issues (1892–1954), 60 major issue types were produced, this being the only one that was not produced in a standard denomination and metal, and also the only $50 gold piece officially produced by the U.S. Mint.

8 These bullion coins are legal tender for the monetary value indicated thereon, but are not minted for circulation purposes, the value of their respective bullion contents being significantly in excess of the indicated monetary value at the time of issue. At the time of issue the uncirculated versions are sold to authorized buyers, based on the spot price of the respective metals; the buyers in turn distribute them to secondary distributors and other retailers at appropriate premium increments, while the Proof versions are sold directly to the public by the United States Mint.

9 In 2008 the Mint announced plans to offer fractional pieces as well.

Q. *What mints have operated at one time or another to strike U.S. coins?*

A. The U.S. Mint has carried out coin production at facilities in eight cities. At the present time, all coins minted for circulation are struck at facilities situated in Philadelphia and Denver, while Proof, commemorative, and bullion issues are produced at facilities located in San Francisco and in West Point, New York.

The mintmarks, locations, and years of operation of the eight historical U.S. minting facilities are as follows:

CC	Carson City, Nevada	1870–1893
C	Charlotte, North Carolina (gold coins only)	1838–1861
D	Dahlonega, Georgia (gold coins only)	1838–1861
D	Denver, Colorado	1906–date
O	New Orleans, Louisiana	1838–1861 and 1879–1909
P	Philadelphia, Pennsylvania	1792–date*
S	San Francisco, California	1854–1955 and 1968–date
W	West Point, New York	1984–date

* Coins minted at the Philadelphia Mint did not carry mintmarks from 1792 through 1979, with the exception of the wartime five-cent pieces of 1942 through 1945 and the 1979 Anthony dollars. Commencing in 1980 all coins struck there have carried the "P" mintmark, with the exception of the cent.

Q. *Are there any specific reasons why the United States does not change the design of its coins as frequently as do foreign countries?*

A. A law enacted by Congress on September 26, 1890, specified that changes in the design of regular-issue U.S. coins cannot be made more frequently than once every 25 years, unless Congress enacts legislation mandating a specific change.

Treasury officials have historically maintained that the counterfeiting of our coins and currency is made more difficult by infrequent design change, reasoning that familiarity intimately acquaints the public with the designs and enables them to more readily detect counterfeits. (If you believe this reasoning to be valid, ask a non-collector to describe the reverse designs of the coins in his pocket change.)

The validity of this historic reasoning has been invalidated by the experience with recent special issues of circulating coins, specifically the Bicentennial-coin issues of 1976, the 50 State Quarters® Program of 1999–2008, and the innovative Westward Journey Nickel Series™ of 2004–2006. The nickel experiment, in particular, may lead to a more enlightened approach in the future, although the likelihood of the retention of Lincoln, Jefferson, Roosevelt, Washington, and Kennedy portraiture on the obverses of the cent, nickel, dime, quarter, and half dollar, respectively, is highly probable given historical and political considerations.

Proof and uncirculated coins. Comparison of Proof (left) and uncirculated coin surfaces shows such qualities as great detail and sharper lines on edges of letters and numbers.

Q. *What are Proof coins and sets?*

A. The term "Proof" refers to the method of manufacturing a coin, not to its condition. Originally, Proof coins were struck for presentation, souvenir, exhibition, and display purposes. They are now, commencing in 1936 and continuously since then with the exception of the years 1965 to 1967, produced principally for sale to collectors who desire the finest possible specimens of the nation's current coinage.

Ideally, the Proof coin is minted with a maximum of preparation and care, using highly polished dies and planchets free of imperfections. Each coin is multiple-struck at slow speed with extra pressure to bring up sharp, high-relief details. Proofs are distinguished by their brilliant mirror finish, sometimes with frosted highlights, and high-relief rims; since 1968 they bear "S" or "W" mintmarks as appropriate.

Proof sets of current U.S. circulating coinage are produced annually at the San Francisco Mint. Each set issued commencing in 2000 has consisted of one example of each current circulation denomination (presently 1¢, 5¢, 10¢, 25¢, 50¢, and $1; Proof 1999 Anthony dollars were struck, but not included in 1999 Proof sets; the dollar has been included beginning in 2000 with the introduction of the Sacagawea issue), all bearing the "S" mintmark. Each annual five-coin 50 State Quarters® Program series has also been offered as a separate Proof set.

Sets of various descriptions have been produced in recent years, commencing in 1983. Since the introduction of the statehood-quarter series in 1999, the variations have ranged from 10- or 11-coin sets representing all of the coins released to circulation, to similar sets bearing the dime, half dollar, and five quarters in silver. Issue prices have ranged from $13.95 (five-piece quarter set, face value $1.25) to $37.95 (11-piece silver sets of 2004 and 2005, each including the five statehood quarters and two nickels of that year; face value $2.96). The five-coin sets available from 1950 through 1964 were priced at $2.10 each (91¢ face value); the price of annual sets did not reach the $10 level until 1980. Current-year ordering information may be obtained by calling 1-800-USA-MINT or accessing the Web site (www.usmint.gov).

Q. *What does the term "prooflike" imply?*

A. Prooflike coins possess the basic visual characteristics of true Proof coins, but are generally produced as single-strike impressions from any new production die. They are not true Proof coins, as they are not double struck, and as a consequence some of the highlight features and the rims may not be sharply defined; but they do generally command a premium. The term "prooflike" applies to the condition of a coin, not to its method of manufacture.

Proof sets. Proof set packaging has changed frequently through the years; this is a rigid plastic mounted 1982 set containing five coins, plus a special medal.

Q. *What is the difference between a Proof set and a Mint set?*

A. A Proof set consists of specially manufactured specimen coins of brilliant finish, high relief, and exquisite detail. A Mint set consists of Uncirculated coins issued annually by the U.S. Mint, assembled from select early strikes. Presently these sets consist of one coin of each denomination struck for circulation at the Philadelphia and Denver mints: two each of the 1¢, 5¢, 10¢, 50¢, and $1 coins, along with ten 25¢ coins (except in 2004 and 2005, when there were four 5¢ coins). Current-year ordering information may be obtained by calling 1-800-USA-MINT or accessing the Web site (www.usmint.gov).

Proof sets. From 1955 through 1964 U.S. Mint Proof Sets were "Mint Sealed" in six pocket polyethylene-coated cellophane "flat packs," which in turn were shipped in sealed envelopes.

Q. *What does the term "Mint-sealed Proof set" mean?*

A. During the early 1960s, a "Mint-sealed Proof set" was, in practice, considered to be one still sealed in the original brown craft envelope in which it came from the U.S. Mint. These sets were bought and sold by an incomparable act of faith, with no one actually knowing the contents of the envelope, or its condition. Later this practice was modified to the more logical insistence that the Proof set still be sealed within the polyethylene-coated cellophane package ("flat pack") enclosed in the envelope, as employed starting in 1955 and continuing through 1964. Today the sets are sonically sealed in a rigid plastic case that can also serve as a display package. Prior to mid-1955, Proof coins were individually packaged in cellophane or polyethylene coin envelopes, and these were packaged in a small, postal-tape-sealed box ("box pack") for shipment, the boxes being a uniform 2-3/8 inches square beginning in 1950.

Q. *Is it true that the first real person to appear on an authorized U.S. coin was a foreigner?*

A. Actually, three of the first four were foreigners. The first identifiable person to appear on a regular-issue or commemorative U.S. coin was the Italian navigator Christopher Columbus, who is generally credited with discovering America. The second person was a woman, Queen Isabella of Spain, who with King Ferdinand sponsored Columbus's voyage of discovery. Her portrait appears on the Columbian Exposition commemorative quarter dollar of 1893. Overlapping portraits of Washington and Lafayette, the French hero of the American Revolution, appeared on the 1900 Lafayette commemorative silver dollar. This was the first U.S. coin to bear the portrait of an American, and the first to bear the portrait of a president of the United States.

The next coins to carry the portraits of identifiable persons were special commemorative gold-dollar issues: the Louisiana Purchase Exposition pair of 1903, one bearing a likeness of Jefferson and the other that of McKinley; and the Lewis and Clark Exposition issue of 1904–1905, with a portrait of Lewis on one side and Clark on the other. The first U.S. coin issued for circulation to bear the likeness of an identifiable person was the Lincoln cent, introduced in 1909.

Q. *What is a "Frosted" Proof coin or set?*

A. In the generally accepted application of the term, Frosted Proofs have a brilliant, mirror-like field (often referred to as "cameo" in today's marketplace) with contrasting dull or "frosted" surfaces on the raised design and lettering elements. When the dies for manufacturing these coins were created, only the raised surfaces (which would become the recessed fields of the coins) were polished, resulting in the frosted appearance of the raised design elements.

From 1936 to 1977/78, Proof set production was executed to the "brilliant" standard; that is, all surfaces were brilliant and mirror-like both in the field and on the raised surfaces. Early strikes from die sets created for this production had a frosted appearance on the raised design and lettering, but the die surfaces were soon polished by the striking process. Coins evidencing the frosted cameo features generally command a premium. Commencing in 1977/78, Proof set production was performed to the frosted standard, with the raised surfaces and lettering on dies being chromium plate–treated to maintain the frosted appearance for extended production runs.

Proofs can also be produced with the frosted surfaces reversed, meaning that the fields appear frosted while the design and lettering elements are brilliant. Similarly, they can also be made with all surfaces frosted.

Q. *Can you define for me the word "specie?"*

A. The definition of specie is "coin or coined money" or, colloquially, "hard" money. Payment "in specie" was a condition of contracts in the days when the bullion value of a coin equaled or nearly approximated its face value, giving it a real worth independent of the fiscal integrity of the issuing agency.

Today, the wealth of a nation is computed in terms of resources, productivity, and trade balances; much of the world's coinage has an insignificant intrinsic value; and paper currencies are no longer backed by pledges to redeem their value in silver or gold. Thus the stipulation "payment in specie" has become meaningless.

Q. *Is there a federal law against altering dates and mintmarks on coins?*

A. Federal law prohibits the possession or passing of any coin that has been altered for the purpose of increasing its monetary or numismatic value. The sale of such altered coins in a transaction involving U.S. mail violates the prohibition against using the mails to defraud.

Q. *What is a "Matte" Proof? How does it differ from a "sandblast" Proof?*

A. Both Matte and sandblast Proofs have a softly lustrous, granular appearance in sharp contrast with the brilliant mirror finish associated with modern Proofs. The finish of a Matte Proof was created prior to striking, by blasting the die surfaces with fine sand propelled by a jet of compressed air. Matte Proof Lincoln cents were produced from 1909 to 1916, and Buffalo nickels from 1913 to 1916, along with some 1921 and 1922 Peace dollars. Gold Proof coins produced from 1908 to 1915 were of the sandblast or "Satin" (dull) finish style; this effect was achieved by striking the coins on a medal press with regular dies, then blasting the coin surfaces with fine sand particles. Neither of these Proof types was popular with collectors of the day, and they are quite difficult to discern from high-quality circulation strikes.

Q. *What is a "Special Mint Set?"*

A. Special Mint Sets of U.S. coins were issued by the Treasury Department for the years 1965, 1966, and 1967 in lieu of Proof sets and regular Mint sets (the offerings of which were discontinued due to the coin shortage of 1964). These sets included one coin of each denomination, cent through half dollar, and carried no mintmark. They were struck one at a time from specially selected but unpolished blanks, on high-tonnage presses using polished dies, and handled individually after striking. They have better detail in the relief than regular coins, and a better appearance than the uncirculated coins contained in regular Mint sets of 1964 and earlier and of 1968 and later, with some specimens displaying "frosted" or "cameo" design features. The 1965 sets were housed in vinyl packets similar to those employed for Proof sets from 1955 to 1964; those of 1966 and 1967 were contained in special plastic holders. They sold for $4 per set.

Q. *What constitutes a United States "Mint set?"*

A. A Mint set is, by concise definition, a set of coins incorporating the denominations struck at a given mint in a given year. In the case of "official" Mint sets, containing coins of uncirculated quality, as assembled and sold by the U.S. Mint annually since 1947 (except for 1950, 1965–1967, and 1982–1983) include examples of each coin placed in regular production at each mint during a given year. From 1947 to 1958 these sets included two examples of each coin from each mint; thereafter the sets have included only a single example of each coin from each mint. The sets from 1947 to 1958 were packaged in cardboard holders, causing the coins to quickly and detractively tarnish; commencing in 1959 the packaging was changed to polyethylene-coated cellophane packaging ("flat packs") enclosed in envelopes.

No Mint sets were produced for 1965–1967, when Special Mint Sets were offered. Proof-set production resumed in 1968; then, in 1982 and 1983, special, individual, uncirculated "Souvenir" sets were sold at the Philadelphia and Denver Mint gift shops. Each Souvenir Set contained only the coins produced at those respective mints. From 1947 to 2004, coins in these sets were selected from those produced for circulation, with little special consideration for quality; commencing in 2005 they were selected from special production runs that resulted in coins with a satin finish.

Q. *Why was it thought necessary to find a substitute for silver in U.S. coins above the five-cent denomination?*

A. By 1964 a world shortage of newly mined silver for industrial and coinage applications had developed; this, coupled with the fact that the mushrooming use of coin-operated machines had resulted in massive quantities of coinage stagnating in circulation due to the frequency of collections, constituted the primary reason. The increasing artistic and industrial demands for silver—to say nothing of the vast requirement of silver to meet coinage demands—vastly exceeded the amount being mined.

Q. *Was the United States the first country to issue a clad coinage of the "sandwich" variety?*

A. Silver was successfully fused to copper sheets and employed for "sandwich" coinage purposes as early as the eighth century by the Greeks.

Q. *Why was a clad composition, instead of pure nickel, chosen for the new, silver-less coinage?*

A. The clad coinage material was engineered to exactly duplicate the electrical properties of the silver coins that had been minted to the same standard since the mid- to late 1830s. This was to ensure that they would function in all existing coin-operated vending machines, including the more sophisticated ones that accepted only those coins having the electrical properties of .900 fine silver. Converting all of the nation's vending machines to accept a pure nickel coinage would have been a lengthy and very expensive undertaking.

Q. *What is the metallic composition of the components of the clad planchet?*

A. All of the regular-issue clad coins being struck at this time (dimes, quarters, and half dollars) have a solid copper core clad with a 75 percent copper and 25 percent nickel alloy, as did the Eisenhower dollars struck from 1971 to 1978 and the Anthony dollars struck from 1979 to 1999. Uncirculated and Proof Eisenhower dollars (1971–1976) struck for souvenir and collector purposes, and the Kennedy half dollars of 1965 through 1970, have a core of 79.1 percent copper and 20.9 percent silver clad with an 80 percent silver and 20 percent copper alloy, giving them a resulting overall fine silver content of 40 percent. Sacagawea and Presidential dollars, introduced in 2000 and 2008, respectively, consist of a pure copper core layered with a manganese-brass composition that is 77 percent copper, 12 percent zinc, 7 percent manganese, and 4 percent nickel.

Q. *How are the copper-nickel sheets bonded to the copper core to make planchets for the clad or sandwich coins?*

A. While it may sound like a contradiction of terms, the three layers are literally exploded together. Sheets of the copper-nickel alloy are placed against the top and bottom surfaces of a pure copper strip, and are then fused to it by detonation of an explosive material on the outer faces of the sandwich.

Q. *In what year did mintmarks first appear on U.S. coins?*

A. The mintmark first appeared on U.S. coinage in 1838 with the establishment of branch mints at New Orleans (O), Dahlonega (D), and Charlotte (C). Subsequently, with the exception of coins minted in 1965–1967, mintmarks have always appeared to denote the manufacturing origin of all U.S. coins, with the exception of those minted at Philadelphia. Since 1980 even the coins struck at Philadelphia, with the exception of one-cent pieces, have carried the Philadelphia (P) mintmark.

Q. *I have a coin folder that has a hole for a 1965-D Lincoln cent, yet the coin is not listed in any catalog I have encountered. Why?*

A. Coin-folder and album manufacturers have in the past occasionally found the need to anticipate coin issues, drawing upon precedent, in order to maintain production and delivery schedules. Thus, when the production of your album was ordered in mid-1964, it was assumed that the Denver Mint would be minting coins bearing the traditional "D" mintmark in 1965. Such coins were never created, however, because U.S. Mint director Eva Adams in 1964 announced by decree that mintmarks would not appear on 1965-dated clad metal coins, nor the issues of future years. (Mintmarks were restored to the nation's coinage, by the way, in 1968 in response to congressional action, at which time the placement on all denominations was moved to the obverse.)

The action taken in eliminating mintmarks was intended to alleviate a national coin shortage (which was officially attributed in large part and unjustly to coin collectors) by reducing the demand for the number of specimens of a date to be collected or set aside in rolls by speculators. Thus, the coins struck at Denver during that three-year period cannot be distinguished from those struck at Philadelphia.

Q. *What is a U.S. Bicentennial Coin Set?*

A. Proof and uncirculated three-coin sets of Bicentennial commemoratives (each consisting of a 40 percent silver Washington quarter, Kennedy half, and Eisenhower dollar) were made available to the public on November 15, 1975. The Proof set was priced at $15, and the set of uncirculated specimens at $9. These three coins were also offered in cupronickel-clad coin Proof sets along with 1975- or 1976-dated cents, nickels, and dimes at $7 per set, and as uncirculated Mint sets for $6 per set.

Q. *What do the 1905-S Coronet gold quarter eagles and the 1915-O Liberty Head or Barber silver half dollars have in common?*

A. Both exist as excellent counterfeits of coins that never existed. The San Francisco Mint did not strike quarter eagles in 1905, and the New Orleans Mint ceased operating as a coining facility in 1909. In fact, while the San Francisco Mint struck half eagles, eagles, and double eagles up through 1916, it did not strike any quarter eagles after 1879.

Q. *Jefferson and Hamilton favored the copper half cent as a coin useful to the poor. Who argued for the inclusion of a silver half dime among the early coinage denominations, and what was his argument?*

A. On September 28, 1790, Thomas Paine, political theorist and propagandist for the American Revolution, proposed to Jefferson that a silver five-cent piece be included in the nation's coinage system, then in its preliminary planning stages. In Paine's view, copper coins were but tokens required by convenience, having no real value. He argued that copper should be "excluded as much as possible" from the nation's coins, and that a small silver coin should be available to those who wished to minimize their possession of copper.

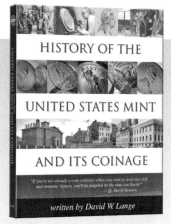

For more information: *History of the United States Mint and Its Coinage* (Lange) is an excellent study of U.S. coins.

CHAPTER FIVE

Early American Coins

Q. *Is the Pine Tree Shilling a rare coin?*

A. No, but it *is* a scarce and desirable coin, commanding premiums determined by variety and condition ranging from a few hundred dollars well into the five-figure range.

The Pine Tree coinage—shillings, sixpence, and threepence—was issued under the authority of the General Court of Massachusetts from 1667 to 1682, but all were dated 1652. The British Crown forbade the issuing of coinage by the colonies to prolong their dependence on Mother England. The Crown's displeasure was made known in 1652 upon the appearance of the Massachusetts NE or New England shilling. All subsequent related issues—including the Willow Tree issues of 1653–1660 and the Oak Tree issues of 1660 through 1667, which included a twopence value—carried that date as the colony continued to defy the crown.

Q. *What were the "Elephant Tokens"?*

A. They originated in the late 17th century and are generally regarded as half-penny tokens, of which there are three basic types. The most plentiful type is undated and bears a shield and legend—GOD PRESERVE LONDON—on one side, presumed by some to be a reference to the city's 1665 outbreak of plague or the great fire of 1666, but is more likely a general entreaty for divine intervention. The other two types—GOD PRESERVE CAROLINA AND THE LORDS PROPRIETERS and GOD PRESERVE NEW ENGLAND—are both dated 1694, and are believed to have been struck in England as promotional pieces to increase interest in the American colonies, rather than to be circulated there.

Q. *If "Hibernia" was the English name for Ireland, how do you account for the listing of such a coin in the category of American Colonial coins?*

A. The Hibernia farthing and halfpenny pieces of 1722 through 1724 were coined, under Royal patent granted by King George I, by William Wood for use in Ireland. However, their preparation became so involved in political scandal and graft that the Irish people refused to accept them. Shipped to the colonies (where they were eagerly received), they entered circulation alongside Wood's related Rosa Americana (American Rose) coinage.

Q. *Did any of the original 13 states issue their own coins after the Declaration of Independence was proclaimed?*

A. During the period when the loosely federated colonies were governed as independent states (1776–1787), under the Articles of Confederation and before our present Constitution was adopted, all of them considered their own coinage. Many authorized and carried out production.

States that authorized and issued coinages were as follows: New Hampshire was the first in 1776, followed by Connecticut and New Jersey in 1785, and Massachusetts in 1786. Vermont, which was an independent republic until 1791, also authorized coins in 1785. A New York coinage was issued by a consortium calling themselves a "Manufactory of Hardware," but there is no record that the operation was state authorized.

Q. *I have been told that shortly after the American Revolution, a number of coins honoring George Washington were issued in England. Is this true?*

A. It should be remembered that the American Revolution was not without considerable sympathy in England, even among members of Parliament.

A significant variety of Washington pieces were struck during the period from 1783 to 1795, among which were several halfpenny-value tokens of English origin, in addition to those denominated in cents. Many of these issues incorporated patriotic slogans and such design elements as eagles, shields, and stars, features that ultimately would be incorporated on coins produced by the U.S. Mint.

Q. *Are all of the Washington pieces complimentary to our first president?*

A. One is tempted to suppose that Washington found all of the pieces to be distasteful, as he opposed having his portrait on coins. In particular, he undoubtedly found those depicting a laureate bust most objectionable, that being a style traditionally reserved for royalty. An extremely rare 1784-dated piece, presumed to be of American origin, bears a distorted portrait and is referenced as the "Ugly Head" copper, and it cannot be considered complimentary.

Spanish milled dollar.

Q. *Has a foreign coin ever been legal tender in the United States?*

A. The Spanish eight reales, or milled dollar (popularly referred to as the "Pillar Dollar" or "piece of eight"), and its fractional units were legal tender in the United States until 1857. This renowned coin, the favorite trade coin of international commerce over a three-century time-frame (from the 17th well into the 19th), was the principal coin of the American colonies. While U.S. dollars were first minted in 1794, production was relatively sporadic and in small quantities prior to the introduction of the Morgan dollar in 1878.

Common use of the fractional parts (or "bits") of the Spanish milled dollar still influences American slang. The one-real coin, being one-eighth of the Spanish dollar, had a value of 12-1/2¢ U.S.; two reales were valued at 25¢ and so on. Thus originated the commonly heard reference of a quarter being "two bits."

Q. *Reading Old West history, I have seen where authors casually reference the terms "dobe dollar" and "short bit." What were these references to?*

A. The Texas drovers who pushed slab-sided longhorns up the Great Western and Chisholm trails to Dodge City and Abilene in those violent years following the Civil War were acutely suspicious of paper currency, their resistance having built up from experience with Confederate money. When they couldn't get U.S. cartwheels or California gold pieces, they preferred to take their pay in Mexican silver pesos, which they called 'dobe dollars. The 'dobe dollar circulated freely between the Mississippi and the Rockies long after the legal tender status of all foreign coins was terminated by law in 1857.

Mining camps and cow-towns in the Old West had many businesses that used the Spanish real or "bit" (valued at 12-1/2¢ U.S.) as a pricing unit. The "bit" could be a round one-real coin, or it could be a pie-shaped piece created by cutting a piece of eight into quarters, then cutting the quarters in half to create two normal or 12-1/2¢ bits. If the quarter was divided on a 60-40 basis, the larger piece, known as a "long bit," was valued at 15¢, and the smaller piece or "short bit" at 10¢. At that time and in those areas, a U.S. dime also was frequently called a "short bit."

Hogge Money shilling.

Q. *What was the first coinage to be specifically struck for the English-American colonies, and when was it issued?*

A. The first coinage for the English-American colonies was the "Hogge Money" of Bermuda, coined in London and introduced into the colony between 1612 and 1616 (that self-governing crown dependency's founding being dated to 1609, when Sir George Sommers shipwrecked there on his way to the Virginia plantations). Known for many years thereafter as the Sommer Islands, Bermuda takes its present name from Spanish adventurer Juan Bermudez, who is believed to have shipwrecked in the archipelago in 1515 on his way to the West Indies. Among his cargo were a few hogs that were left behind. "Hogge Money" was made of lightly silvered brass or copper; issued in twopence, threepence, sixpence, and shilling denominations, it circulated for only a few years.

Q. *What was the first coinage struck in America for the English-American colonies?*

A. While the Spaniards established a mint at Mexico City in 1535, and Spanish-real-denominated coins eventually became the de facto currency of the English colonies in the New World, the first coins actually struck in English North America were the silver threepence, sixpence, and shilling "New England" coinage. These coins were struck between June 11 and October 19, 1652, at a mint just outside Boston established by the order of the General Court with John Hall as mintmaster. This "NE" coinage was discontinued due to its crude workmanship and simple design, which encouraged clipping and counterfeiting, and was succeeded by the "Willow Tree" coinage struck from 1653 to 1660.

1787 Fugio cent.

Q. *What was the first coin to be issued by authority of the United States and when was it issued?*

A. Commerce was plagued by a flow of underweight state coppers and forgeries of English coppers in the years immediately following the American Revolution. The "Fugio" cent was authorized by Congress on April 21, 1787, in an effort to remedy this frustrating economic situation. Congress directed that the coins bear a representation of a sundial, the date 1787, FUGIO ("time flies"), and the motto MIND YOUR BUSINESS on the obverse, with 13 linked circles and the motto WE ARE ONE on the reverse. Since the incorporation of these mottos often is attributed to Benjamin Franklin's suggestion, the coins are sometimes referred to as Franklin Cents.

As the United States did not have a mint in 1787, a contract for the striking of 300 tons of Fugio coppers was awarded to New Haven's James Jarvis, part owner of a company that had coined coppers for the state of Connecticut. Most of the 400,000 Fugio coppers struck were produced in early 1788—with the copper being salvaged from bands that had held together the powder kegs sent to America by the French—after which Jarvis defaulted on his contract.

1787 Massachusetts cent.

Q. *The Law of April 2, 1792, committed the United States to a decimal-standard coinage; therefore isn't it true that the first official coins of the country to bear values expressed in terms of the decimal standard were the half dimes and dimes struck at the U.S. Mint in 1792?*

A. Congress, in assembly under the Articles of Confederation (1781–1789), resolved as early as July 6, 1787, that the U.S. monetary unit "shall be one dollar," and that "the several pieces shall increase in a decimal ratio" from a base of one cent. Thus, up to the time the Constitution took effect with New Hampshire's ratification of the document on June 21, 1788, states were permitted to coin money, with the Congress serving as a regulating authority. Under that authority in 1787 and 1788, Massachusetts struck the first official coins bearing the one-cent denomination as established by Congress. The half dimes and dime coins, and cents as well, dated 1792 and struck in Philadelphia under the authority of Congress subsequent to the enactment of the law of April 2, 1792 (establishing the U.S. Mint), are considered patterns, with at least the half dimes being produced on private premises.

Brasher doubloon.

Q. *I have been told that the famous Brasher doubloon wasn't really a coin at all. Is this true?*

A. Although the celebrated, historically significant, and rare (value $2.5 million to $3 million) Brasher doubloons are generally considered to be the first "gold coins" minted in the United States, there are two conflicting theories for their existence. Inasmuch as the doubloons were struck to the approximate diameter of cents then being issued under the authority of individual states, it has been proposed that the dies were actually intended for cents, as Brasher had petitioned the New York State Assembly for the right to coin coppers. It is doubtful that Brasher would have placed his name so prominently on a die intended for an official copper coinage, or that he would have prepared patterns in gold rather than copper. The other theory suggests that, with his petition being rejected by the assembly, Ephraim Brasher added his name to the die and struck a number of specimens of doubloon weight and standard as an extension of his goldsmithing endeavors.

There is no doubt that Brasher's doubloons could have served as a medium of exchange at the time. They weighed about 408 grains, giving them an intrinsic value roughly equal to that of the Spanish gold doubloon ($16) or 16 Spanish milled dollars. They were valued at $15 in New York currency. The "EB" (Ephraim Brasher) hallmark that appears on all of the doubloons was also counterstamped on various foreign coins of the time under his commission to test and verify other gold coins then in circulation.

1783 Nova Constellatio 5-unit pattern.

1783 Nova Constellatio 500 quint.

Q. *Is it true that a coinage expressed in "mark," "quint," and "bit" denominations was once considered for adoption in the United States?*

A. On January 15, 1782, Robert Morris proposed a system of coinage devised by Gouverneur Morris, who had been assistant financier of the Confederation, designed to carry out the idea of a decimal-coinage system for the United States. The accounting "unit" of the system was to be one-quarter grain of fine silver (480 grains = 1 ounce troy), which equated to 1/1440th Spanish dollar, with the lowest coined unit to be a "bit" or "cent" of 100 units (25 grains silver, plus 2 grains copper); the 500-unit designation was the "quint" (125 grains silver, plus 10 grains copper), and the 1,000-unit designation the "mark" (250 grains silver,

20 grains copper). Patterns of the three denominations were designed and struck in silver, but the coinage never advanced beyond that stage. They are all dated 1783, with all but one variety being unique; two examples of one of two "bit" varieties are known; in 1977 a five-unit coin with the legend ". . . 5" and struck in copper surfaced.

These silver Nova Constellatio patterns shouldn't be confused with the Nova Constellatio *coppers.* The latter were struck in England in large quantities dated 1783 and 1785 as a private coinage venture by Governour Morris and partners, who imported them into New York, where they circulated. Uncirculated examples of these issues may be acquired for four-figure premiums, while examples in Very Good to Fine condition are priced in the $100 to $200 range.

Q. *I recently picked up a copy of a colonial coin that depicts a deer on one side along with the legend VALUE ME AS YOU PLEASE. Can something so arbitrarily valued have served as money?*

A. What you have is one of the Higley or Granby coppers of Connecticut, which come in several varieties. These tokens were first struck by Dr. Samuel Higley in 1737. He owned a copper mine at Granby, where he mined and smelted his own ore, engraved his own dies, and struck and released the pieces for circulation. Higley died in 1737 and was succeeded by his brother, John. The original issue carried the value as three pence. When the circulation of these coppers soon exceeded local demand, their value in trade was sometimes challenged. With commendable ingenuity, a new design was created featuring the VALUE ME AS YOU PLEASE legend along with a roman numeral III as a suggestion of value.

Q. *Which of the states was the first to consider issuing its own coinage after the colonies proclaimed the Declaration of Independence?*

A. In 1776, the House of Representatives of New Hampshire authorized William Moulton to produce an issue of copper coins. Cast patterns were prepared, but there is no evidence that they actually circulated or were even approved.

1776 Continental dollar.

Q. *What was the first silver dollar–size coin ever proposed for the United States?*

A. That distinction belongs to the 1776-dated Continental Currency dollars, struck in silver, pewter, and brass. There is uncertainty as to the actual value of these pieces, or the exact nature of their monetary role, if they were anything more than patterns. The conditions of some of the surviving pewter and brass specimens suggest the likelihood that they may have actually circulated as dollars during the inflationary days of the American Revolution. Benjamin Franklin had a hand in suggesting the designs as executed.

Q. *It is common knowledge that Spanish piece-of-eight silver coins cut into halves, fourths, and eighths circulated in the English colonies of America. Did the colonies originate this practice?*

A. The practice of cutting Spanish pillar dollars into fractional units to serve as small change likely originated on the Caribbean islands, although these "bits" readily circulated in the American colonies and in the post-Revolution era. It should also be mentioned that from about 1180 (during the reign of Henry II) until Edward I (1272–1307), English silver pennies, halfpennies, and farthings were struck with a "voided cross" device on the reverse. This voided cross, essentially a cross with a center grove running the full length of each extension, also enabled the penny to be easily and equally divided into halfpennies and "fourthings."

Q. *A number of the individual states issued their own coinage after independence from Great Britain was achieved. For how long did they have the right to do so?*

A. The states had the right to coin money from July 2, 1776 (the day independence from Britain was declared), until June 21, 1788, when New Hampshire became the ninth of the original 13 states to ratify the Constitution.

Q. *Is it true that the U.S. Congress once authorized the issuing of a "penny" (not a cent)?*

A. On February 20, 1777, Congress proposed a half-ounce standard for an American "penny." That weight was 218.75 grains, which, interestingly enough, approximates the 224-grain weight of brass specimens of the Continental dollar. It is possible that the Continental dollar patterns, which bear no mark of value, were patterns for both a U.S. silver dollar and the only "penny" ever authorized by the U.S. government.

Q. *What is the difference between coins or tokens identified as Colonial issues, Early American issues, and issues of the States of the Confederation?*

A. Colonial pieces were issued before the American Revolution (1776). Early American pieces were issued during the Revolution or during the infancy of the United States (1832 is the generally accepted date for the end of the Early American era). Coinage of the States of the Confederation consists of state-authorized issues that came into being between the Declaration of Independence and the ratification of the Constitution (1788). Colonial and Early American issues typically are of private origin.

Q. *Which was the first of the states to issue an official coinage after the Revolution?*

A. Vermont is recognized as the first state to issue an official copper coinage; its assembly authorized Reuben Harmon Jr. to initiate coining on July 1, 1785. At that time, Vermont was an independent state, and it remained independent until ratifying the Constitution on March 4, 1791, thus becoming the new nation's 14th state. The Vermont coppers initially featured a representation of the Green Mountains on the obverse and the Eye of Providence on the reverse. In 1786 the designs were changed to a laureate head for the obverse and the figure of a seated woman on the reverse, thus deliberately giving the coppers a distinct resemblance to the English halfpenny, which greatly facilitated their acceptance throughout the Confederation.

Q. *What is the metallic composition of William Wood's underweight "Bath" metal Rosa Americana coinage, which American colonists refused to accept?*

A. Bath metal is an alloy of 75 percent copper, 24.7 percent zinc, and 0.3 percent silver.

Q. *Most of the tokens struck by or for England's colonists in America bear the "pence" denominations of the English coinage system. Spanish coins were the favored currency of the colonists. Weren't any tokens struck in denominations of the Spanish system?*

A. Low-denomination coppers were in the shortest supply in the colonies. What was present were usually English halfpennies, real or counterfeit. In 1688, tin-producer Richard Holt received a British Royal Patent to strike tokens for the English colonies in nearly pure tin, in Spanish style, assigning them a value of 1/24th of one real to facilitate their acceptance in America and the West Indies. The colonists regarded Holt's "American Plantation Token" issues, the earliest authorized coinage for the British colonies in America, as "leaden and pewter farthings" and refused to accept them.

CHAPTER SIX

Early U.S. Mint Coins

Q. *As the American colonies were once British possessions, why did we not adopt the sterling currency system, as did most other countries that subsequently emerged from British domination?*

A. The reason was not, as some have suggested, to disassociate the United States from everything English. The Founding Fathers adopted substantial portions of English law, religious practice, and social and political philosophy, along with weight and measurement standards.

Despite its arbitrary and cumbersome complexities, the sterling standard would quite possibly have been retained had British America remained a colony of the Crown, although efforts to express its value components in terms of the more prevalent Spanish coinage had already created a chaos of intercolony exchange rates. The adoption of a currency system more suited to the economic reality of the colonies/states was facilitated by the philosophical atmosphere of the War for Independence, which conditioned self-reliant men to cast off the shackles of tradition and initiate changes with little nostalgia for customs of the past.

England had never furnished more than token quantities of sterling-standard currency to the colonies. The coins of the colonies were a mishmash of English, Spanish, French, Dutch, and private issues. An effort was made by the various colonial governments to express their values in terms of sterling denominations, but the assigned values varied from colony to colony, making intercolonial commerce a horror of reconciliation and adjustment.

The Spanish dollar, being divided into eight equal parts, contained an inherent suggestion of a more logical system. A decimal currency with subdivisions of 10ths and 100ths, wherein the American and

Spanish dollars would be equivalent units, was both desirable and logical, and the intellectual climate was equitable for the inauguration of change.

Q. *Who formulated the original plans for our system of decimal currency?*

A. In 1780, Gouverneur Morris, a member of the Continental Congress, wrote a series of essays containing suggestions for the projected financial system of the new nation. These proposals attracted the attention of Robert Morris, superintendent of finance under the Articles of Confederation, causing him to appoint Gouverneur Morris to serve as his assistant. Over the following four years, Gouverneur Morris laid the basis for much of the resulting national currency system.

The Morris unit was based on 1/1440th of a dollar, and was calculated to agree with all different valuations of the Spanish milled dollar, as then stipulated by the various states, without a fraction. Thomas Jefferson agreed with the fundamental Morris suggestions, but disagreed with Morris's complicated monetary unit. In 1784, he suggested a simple dollar unit with decimal divisions of 10. In this, he was later supported by President George Washington.

In 1791, Secretary of the Treasury Alexander Hamilton came out in support of the decimal proposal, also calling for the use of both gold and silver in the nation's monetary system. The Hamilton proposals were enacted into law on April 2, 1792, by the Second Congress of the United States; one of the early acts of the First Congress, on March 3, 1789, was a resolution calling for the establishment of a mint.

Q. *Of the various coin denominations that have circulated in this country through the years, which ones were provided for initially?*

A. Congress's Mint Act of 1792 provided "that the money of the United States should be expressed in dollars or units, dismes or tenths, cents or hundredths, and milles or thousandths, a disme being the tenth part of a dollar, a cent the hundredth part of a dollar, a mille the thousandth part of a dollar."

The denominations specified by the act were as follows: gold eagle, or $10; gold half eagle, or $5; gold quarter eagle, or $2.50; silver dollar, or $1; silver half dollar, or 50¢; silver quarter dollar, or 25¢; silver disme, or 10¢; silver half disme, or 5¢; copper cent, or 1¢; and copper half cent, or 1/2¢.

The act further provided that "every fifteen pounds weight of pure silver shall be of equal value in all payments with one pound or pure gold, and so in all proportion."

1793 Liberty Cap half cent. The smallest monetary unit ever issued in the United States was the half cent, minted from 1793 through 1857.

Q. *How long has the United States operated a mint? Where was it first located?*

A. The establishment of the U.S. Mint was authorized by Congress on April 2, 1792, when President Washington signed the enabling act into law. Construction of the first mint, the second building created by the government (the first having been a lighthouse), was underway by early summer in Philadelphia at a site on Seventh Street between Market and Arch streets. Its cornerstone had been laid by the president and others in attendance on July 31, 1792.

Prior to the completion of construction in the fall, the 1792 half disme patterns were struck on equipment acquired for installation at the new mint but held in storage at a nearby location (on Sixth Street above Chestnut Street, and owned by John Harper). Though not actually struck at the nation's first mint, this was the first coin produced under the Mint structure authorized by Congress. By December, the stored equipment had been relocated to the newly completed facility, and during that month several other pattern coins were struck off.

Aside from patterns struck in December 1792, the striking of half cents and large cents began in 1793; half dimes, half dollars, and silver dollars in 1794; dimes and quarter dollars in 1796; $5 and $10 gold in 1795; and $2.50 gold in 1796.

1793 Chain large cent.

Q. *I have often read about a "Chain cent." What is it?*

A. The term "Chain" or "link" cent refers to the first regular-issue cent, struck in 1793. The principal device on the reverse of this cent, a circular chain of 15 links, was intended to symbolize the solidarity of the 15 states then making up the Union. The public, however, thought otherwise, condemning the chain device as being symbolic of bondage. A wreath design replaced the chain type in production for the latter part of 1793. Chain cents are quite scarce and command premiums in excess of two to three times those realized by the wreath type.

Q. *Why are there such a number of die varieties of large cents?*

A. Early dies were individually hand engraved; human imperfection assured that no two dies of any denomination would be exactly alike. While early dies for silver and gold coinages were similarly created, those productions generally mounted to only tens or hundreds of thousands; by comparison, millions of cents were produced annually, meaning the number of dies to be hand engraved to meet production demand was much greater. Today, individual coinage dies are created by a transfer process from a single master die.

Q. *Why was the large cent the only U.S. coin minted during 1816?*

A. A major fire experienced at the Mint in January 1816 damaged much of the coinage-production equipment. Resumption of operations probably concentrated upon production of the large cent because it was essential to a growing commerce and was the only U.S. coin of the time not supplemented by foreign coins that enjoyed legal tender status. The large cent would have been the easiest to produce under emergency conditions, since the cent planchets were purchased outside the Mint and production was not dependent upon the Mint's rolling mill.

Q. *I have noticed that U.S. coins after 1817 have fewer minor varieties in design. Why is this?*

A. Following the 1816 Mint fire, an enlarged, brick building was constructed to house new and improved equipment to replace that which had become worn and damaged over the previous 23 years. The new equipment allowed for better and more uniform die-cutting and hardening, with the resulting, longer-lasting dies produced fewer varieties.

Of particular interest to numismatists, the mechanical screw-type coining presses were replaced by hydraulic presses capable of exerting a greater and more uniformly applied striking pressure. An immediate consequence was the production of Proofs and medals commencing in 1817.

1796 quarter dollar.

Q. *Why are early half dollars relatively easy to obtain, many in quite nice condition, while other coins of the 1790s and early 1800s are hard to find in nice condition?*

A. Free circulation of early U.S. gold and silver coins was greatly hindered by speculators. Worn Spanish dollars of reduced weight were exchanged for newly minted U.S. dollars, with the heavier coin being exported and lost to local commerce. The gold coins were undervalued in relation to the standard of European commercial centers and were melted for bullion. The 1794–1834 coinage of half dimes, dimes, and quarter dollars was negligible. The only U.S. coin readily available for large transactions, bank reserves, and foreign payments was the half dollar. Being regarded as bullion, and being mainly transferred from bank to bank, they were subjected to very little wear, which accounts for the good supply and superior condition of these half dollars today.

Q. *I have an 1818 half dollar with lettering on the edge. Does this edge make it scarce?*

A. Half dollars had FIFTY CENTS OR HALF A DOLLAR lettered incuse on the edge until 1836, after which the edge of the coin was reeded. None of the half dollars of this period are plentiful, but the scarcity of particular varieties is unrelated to the type of edge. Silver dollars minted during this same period (1794–1804) similarly carried HUNDRED CENTS ONE DOLLAR OR UNIT edge lettering. Similarly lettered edges also appeared on early half cents (1793–1797) and large cents (1793–1796)—TWO HUNDRED FOR A DOLLAR and ONE HUNDRED FOR A DOLLAR, respectively—during which time the copper content of these coins nearly equaled their face value.

Q. *What was the idea behind having a lettered edge on coins?*

A. In the day of bullion coinage, many people could not resist the temptation to shave or file a few grains of gold or silver from the edge of each coin that passed through their hands. Lettering, reeding, or ornamenting the edge made the practice more difficult by readily betraying coins that had been depreciated in this common, but unlawful, manner. Silver half dimes, dimes, and quarters, as well as gold quarter eagles, half eagles, and eagles, were minted with reeded edges from the beginning.

The only U.S. coins minted for circulation with lettered edges (in addition to early U.S. half dollars, silver dollars, half cents, and large cents) were the Augustus Saint-Gaudens eagles (46 or 48 raised stars) and double eagles (raised E PLURIBUS UNUM with words divided by stars) introduced in 1907; and the Presidential dollars series introduced in 2007, which incorporated the date and mintmark, along with the legends E PLURIBUS UNUM and IN GOD WE TRUST in incuse lettering on the edge. In 1992 the XXV Olympiad baseball commemorative silver dollar, minted in uncirculated quality at the Denver

Mint, carried the word XXV OLYMPIAD pressed into the edge on a reeded background.

1814 Classic Head large cent.

Q. *What American coin was popularly known as the "Blowsy Barmaid?"*

A. None of the Liberty Head treatments utilized on the large copper cents challenged existing standards of artistic excellence, and they were known by such uncomplimentary names as "Silly Head" and "Booby Head." The public was particularly unappreciative of the 1808 to 1814 Classic Head type, which presented "a sleepy-looking Liberty turbaned with a diaphanous nightcloth" and was promptly dubbed the "Blowsy Barmaid."

Q. *Recently, while viewing the exhibits at a coin convention, I saw a half dime of the late 1700s. It was called Uncirculated and valued in excess of $10,000 although it was obviously defaced, as though someone had filed on it. How can a damaged coin command such a premium?*

A. Many early U.S. coins, particularly the higher-denomination silver and gold issues, bear surface disfigurations similar to those you observed. Some of these disfigurations are actually file marks, as you indicated, and are technically known as "adjustment marks." The coin you saw was probably struck from a planchet inspectors decided was slightly overweight. It was "adjusted" to standard by removing the excess weight with a file.

When the planchet was subsequently struck into a coin, the pressure applied was insufficient to completely obliterate the file markings, which are usually most evident within the detail of the raised design elements. Had the planchet been found to be underweight, it would have been melted.

1792 half disme (top) and disme.

Q. *Were the 1793 cents and half cents the first coins to be struck by the U.S. Mint?*

A. No, but they were the first regular-issue coins produced by the U.S. Mint. The first U.S. coins produced under Mint Director David Rittenhouse, using new equipment acquired for installation at the Mint, were the 1792 half disme and disme. The half disme is generally considered to have been the first pattern piece produced by the Mint. They were struck in the basement of a saw-maker named John Harper on or about

July 13, 1792, at the request of President Washington and on planchets made from silver plate provided by Martha Washington.

It has been speculated that the bust of Liberty featured on the half disme represented Martha Washington, copied in profile by William Birch from a painting by Trumbull, which would distinguish her as being the first American citizen ever to appear on a U.S. coin. While some small quantity of the 1,500 half dismes produced entered circulation, many were distributed by Washington and Secretary of State Jefferson to friends and dignitaries in Virginia and Europe.

The first pieces actually struck at the new Mint building were silver-center cent patterns produced on December 17, 1792, from dies prepared by Henry Voight. These unusual cents had a plug of silver valued at three-quarters of a cent in the center of a copper planchet valued at one-quarter of a cent, the intent being to manufacture a cent of the requisite intrinsic value, but of a smaller size than the huge coppers authorized by Congress. Copper-silver cents were also produced in which the silver was directly alloyed with the copper, in effect producing the billon cent Jefferson advocated.

1792 Birch pattern cent.

Q. *I recently saw an illustration of a large copper piece of the United States which was dated 1792, and had on the obverse a rather attractive Liberty Head and the legend LIBERTY PARENT OF SCIENCE AND INDUSTRY. Is this a coin or a token?*

A. It is a pattern cent prepared in late 1792, shortly after the new U.S. Mint became operational, from dies produced by William Birch, whose name appears on the obverse. One unique variety of this proposed cent carries the abbreviation "G.W.Pt." (George Washington President) directly above the bottom rim on the reverse. The more common type states the value fractionally as 1/100, at it would subsequently appear on the regular issue 1793 cents. The Birch cent patterns come with plain edges (two known) and lettered edge—TO BE ESTEEMED BE USEFUL—varieties (10 total).

1792 quarter dollar.

Q. *Catalogs list the first U.S. quarter as having been struck in 1796. Are any quarter-dollar patterns known that were struck before that date?*

A. Comparatively few pattern pieces are known that were struck before 1836. There is, however, an interesting piece, dated 1792 and attributed to Joseph Wright, that bears a nude female bust on the obverse along with the word LIBERTY; on the reverse it displays an eagle standing on a globe framed by the legend UNITED STATES OF AMERICA. At one time it was thought that this piece was a pattern for a gold half eagle, but its size and the fact that the Mint was planning an early quarter production favors the conclusion that this pattern (actually a die trial with a wide rim) was prepared with the quarter in mind.

1796 Draped Bust dime (left and center); 1809 Capped Bust dime reverse.

Q. *Is it true that the early dimes bore no mark of value?*

A. The face values of the disme and half disme patterns prepared in 1792 were spelled out on the reverses of the coins. From 1796, the first year regular issues were coined, through 1807 the dime carried no mark of value. A value designation first appeared on regular-issue dimes in 1809, when the value was stated as 10 C. A mark of value first appeared on the half dime in 1829—half dime coinage was suspended from 1806 through 1828—and on the quarter dollar in 1804.

Q. *I understand that during the first two decades of the U.S. Mint's existence only about a million dimes were minted. Why weren't more coined?*

A. The demand for minting low-denomination silver coins during the early years of the republic was quite low, with the combined mintage total for 1796 through 1819 being just 1,007,151 dimes. Small Spanish silver coins were in good supply for use in daily trade, and they were not brought to the Mint for re-coining or melting by silversmiths; nor were they exported, because, being excessively worn, the value at which they were accepted in trade significantly exceeded their intrinsic worth.

The quarter dollar was also a denomination seldom requested by those who deposited silver at the Mint for coining. The first quarters weren't struck until 1796, and they were issued in only six different years until 1818, but more or less annually thereafter. The combined mintage for quarters from 1796 through 1819 was 1,155,454 pieces. With the exception of 1835 when nearly two million were struck, it wasn't until 1843 that more than a million examples were struck in any one year.

Half dollar production, on the other hand, for the years 1794 through 1819 exceeded 17 million pieces, with annual production exceeding one million pieces annually from 1808 through 1814. Annual productions for 1818 and 1819 were in the two-million range. Through the first 20 years of the U.S. Mint's history, the half dollar was in demand as America's preferred coin for large transactions, bank reserves, and foreign payments. As they did not readily circulate in daily trade, even today, 200 years later, the issues of early half dollars remain in relatively good supply in the higher grades.

Q. *I have heard it said that one of the early engravers employed by the U.S. Mint was a slave. Is there any truth in this?*

A. John Reich, assistant engraver from April 1, 1807, to March 31, 1817, was a German bondsman freed by a U.S. Mint official. Although officially Robert Scot's assistant, he redesigned and engraved every denomination of coin issued during his tenure.

CHAPTER SEVEN

One-Cent Coins, 1856 to Date

Q. *What was the reasoning behind the change from the large copper cent to the small cent in 1857, and the accompanying decision to drop the half cent?*

A. The large cent, although a useful denomination, was never popular with the public because of its excessive size and weight; nor with Treasury officials because, in relation to its face value, it was expensive to produce.

The half cent, being essentially an unnecessary coin, was even more unpopular, because its weight and production cost were exactly one-half those of the large cent. Many banks considered the coin a nuisance and refused to stock it.

Q. *I had always assumed that the term "white cents" referred to the steel cents of 1943, but my brother maintains that the term refers to cents of the 1850 and 1860s. Who is right?*

A. Your brother. "White cents" is a term applied to the Flying Eagle cents of 1856 to 1858, and the Indian Head cents from 1859 into 1864. They were struck of a metal which contained 88 parts copper to 12 parts nickel, thus giving them a light or white appearance; in mid-1865 the composition was changed to an alloy of 95 parts copper to 5 parts tin and zinc, which gave them a rose or bronze color.

At the same time the alloy was changed, the weight and thickness of the cent was reduced by one-third, from 4.67 grams to 3.11 grams.

Q. *Where is the "L" located on the Indian Head cents of 1864 and what is its significance?*

A. The "L" is located on the bonnet ribbon of the Indian's headdress, immediately below the last feather. It is somewhat hidden, and can best be seen if the coin is slightly turned so that the Indian faces the observer. The letter is the initial of James Longacre, the coin's designer. This initial was not present when this coin was placed in production in 1859, nor on the copper-nickel alloy cents struck in early 1864. Bronze alloy cents were also struck from dies bearing the portrait without the "L" on the ribbon, but in late 1864 the portrait was reworked slightly to make it sharper, at which time the initial was incorporated. All Indian Head cents minted from 1865 through 1909 were of this revised design.

1909 V.D.B. Lincoln cent.

Q. *I have noticed that the initials V.D.B. appear on the reverse of some 1909 Lincoln cents, and am wondering why they do not appear on all of them, and are not on any of the other dates?*

A. The initials V.D.B. refer to the designer of the Lincoln cent, Victor David Brenner. At the time the new Lincoln cent was released in 1909, public objection to "defacing a coin for personal gain or reputation" was so great that the initials were removed. In 1918 the initials were restored, but in very small and unobtrusive letters at the base of Lincoln's shoulder on the obverse, where they have remained to the present time.

1914-D Lincoln cent.

Q. *How can I determine whether I am looking at a genuine 1914-D Lincoln cent or one with an altered date?*

A. The majority of altered-date 1914-D cents are created by removing part of the first "4" of 1944-D cents. Cents altered in this manner can be detected by placing another cent vertically on the coin being tested, placing the left edge of the vertical cent against the right loop of the "9" of the date. If the 1914-D is genuine, only the upright and the right crosslet extension of the "4" will remain visible. If any portion of the left extension of the crosslet is visible, the 1914-D is an altered 1944-D. There will also be an extra wide space between the "1" and the "9," and the "D" will be larger and positioned higher on an altered 1944-D cent than on a genuine 1914-D.

Altered-date 1914-D cents are also made by adding a "D" to 1914 cents, and by replacing the "S" of 1914-S cents with a "D." In fact any Lincoln cent with a date ending with the numeral "4" and bearing a "D" mintmark—1924, 1934, 1944, and 1954—can be, and has been, altered to a 1914-D. The removal of a mintmark or date component will invariably leave traces of the filing or burnishing; the addition of a detail will always leave traces of discoloration resulting from the application of heat.

Genuine 1914-D cents do not bear the V.D.B. initials which were restored to the shoulder truncation in 1918. Thus, if the date has been altered on any cent minted after 1917, the shoulder truncation may reveal the initials or evidence that they have been removed in some manner.

Q. *According to the Mint report, no 1922 cents were coined at any mint except Denver, but I notice that books and dealers offer 1922 plain, or, I assume, Philadelphia, cents. How can this be?*

A. What is advertised as a 1922 plain cent is nothing more than a 1922-D cent struck from a worn die in which the "D" punch filled in, resulting either in no raised "D" or the faintest traces of one. Many 1922 plain cents are altered from 1922-D cents by removing the mintmark surface in the numismatic marketplace, so beware when making a purchase of this coin.

Q. *I can remember that white wartime cents were easily found in circulation in the 1950s and 1960s. However, I have not seen one during the past few years. Are they not rare and valuable?*

A. While the wartime steel cents are seldom encountered in circulation today, they are not rare, nor is there any reason to suppose they will be within the foreseeable future. Intrigued by its novelty, many non-collectors saved the steel cent during the war and immediate post-war years. Many of these accumulations ended up in the hands of dealers and neighborhood collectors. Brilliant uncirculated specimens could appreciate substantially in value, with only the 1943-S having yet reached a double digit value figure; in Fine condition steel cents are worth a quarter or less. The zinc-placed coin was extremely vulnerable to atmospheric solvents, but the "processed" (chemically shined) steel cent will be in good supply for many years to come and of negligible value.

Q. *I have been told by many collectors that the cents of 1944 to 1946 were struck from metal which was recovered from expended military shell cases. Is this correct?*

A. Yes. The coloring of these coins is a little different from sister issues of 1942 into 1946, tending toward the yellow shades, but the coin proved satisfactory in every respect. These "shell case" cents were popularly received by a public that had rejected the steel cent issues of 1943. The alloy used in "shell cases" did not include the small tin component otherwise present in all cents minted from 1864 to 1942 and 1947 to 1962.

1955 Lincoln cent. Small quantity of 1955 Philadelphia cents were struck from die with doubled obverse, a result of die shifting out of alignment between successive strikes from the master die, or hub.

Q. *I have noticed that on some 1955 cents struck at the Philadelphia Mint, the features on the obverse appear to be double struck. Can you explain why the reverse features do not also appear to be double struck?*

A. The 1955 cent of which you speak is not really a double strike. The coin was struck as a single impression from an obverse die pressed by a misaligned hub on each of the two or more pressings required to produce a finely detailed working or production die. The result is a doubling of features on the working die, which when placed in production produces double-image devices on minted coins. As a reverse die is created independently (though by the same process used to create an obverse die), the reverse features on the 1955 "doubled-die" cents are normal. Any die can exhibit doubling—many coins are struck from dies with minor doubling—but the 1955 cent is an unusual example of major doubling.

Q. *I have noticed that all the Lincoln cents with the memorial on the reverse spell the OF in UNITED STATES OF AMERICA with a small "o." Is this an error?*

A. No. The small "o" was deliberate on the part of the engraver, Frank Gasparro, whose initials appear at the base of the steps to the right of the memorial. This has been done on a number of U.S. coins, including the Franklin half dollar and several commemoratives.

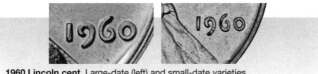

1960 Lincoln cent. Large-date (left) and small-date varieties.

Q. *Is it easy to distinguish between the large and small dates on 1960 cents?*

A. It isn't difficult once you have examined the two coin varieties or seen good illustrations of them. The mental picture most viewers retain is of the chubby compactness of the small date "6" and its shorter tail. Other differences to look for are that the top of the "1" aligns with the top of the "9" in the small-date variety, and the numerals are somewhat closer together in the large-date variety.

1970-S Lincoln cent. Large-date (left) and small-date varieties.

Q. *Can the large- and small-date varieties of the 1970-S cent be readily distinguished? How were the varieties created?*

A. The most obvious difference in the date varieties is that, on the large date, the "0" and the loop of the "9" extend above the "7." According to a spokesman for the Bureau of the Mint, the varieties were created when an engraver sharpened the date features in the master die from which the working dies are produced.

Q. *Is it true that a little Caucasian girl modeled for the Indian head on the Indian Head cent?*

A. One of the more enduring of numismatic legends holds that the model for the cent was Sarah Longacre, the engraver's 12-year-old daughter, wearing the ceremonial bonnet of a visiting Indian chief. However, Longacre's sketches would seem to indicate that his inspiration was the goddess Venus in Indian attire.

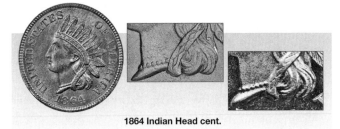

1864 Indian Head cent.

Q. *I have been told that 1864 Indian Head cents with the "L" can be identified without directly verifying the presence of the "L." How can this be?*

A. The tip of the bust is pointed on the variety with the "L," rounded on the variety without it.

Q. *What is meant by Variety 1 and Variety 2 of the 1886 Indian Head cent?*

A. On the Variety 1 cent the last feather of the bonnet points between the "I" and "C" of AMERICA; on Variety 2 it points between the "C" and "A." All Indian Head cents after 1886 are Variety 2.

Q. *Are "cents" and "pennies" the same thing?*

A. It is true that, due to our predominating English heritage, the terms are used interchangeably in the United States, but they are not the same thing. "Cent" is from the Latin "centesimus," meaning "a hundredth part." In our coinage laws the cent is the hundredth part of the dollar. The British "penny" was formerly valued at 240 per pound sterling. Since the British change to a decimal system coinage in 1971, the new pence or "penny" is valued at 100 per pound. At this writing, the pound is worth approximately $2 U.S.

1856 Flying Eagle cent.

Q. *I thought it was required by law that each of the coins of the United States bear "an impression emblematic of Liberty." The word "Liberty" is plainly evident on the large copper cents, the Indian Heads, and the Lincolns. Where is it on the Flying Eagle cent?*

A. LIBERTY does not appear on the Flying Eagle cent, nor is it present on two-cent pieces, silver three-cent pieces, or the Shield nickel. Apparently it was felt that the primary device of the Flying Eagle cent, an eagle in flight, adequately symbolized the idea of liberty.

Q. *I have read that, during the Civil War, citizens hoarded copper-nickel cents, hoping to profit from their bullion value. Is that the only reason why the composition of the cent was changed to bronze in 1864?*

A. A number of other considerations also influenced the decision. Nickel was expensive to procure and difficult to alloy with copper because of its high melting point. Its hardness was very destructive to dies. Treasury official were favorably impressed by the public acceptance of the privately produced and circulated lightweight, low-value copper Civil War tokens, and reasoned that the cent could be made lighter and of a cheaper metal without adversely affecting its acceptance.

Lincoln Memorial cent. Detail shows the Lincoln Memorial statue.

Q. *Is it true that one of the regular-issue coins of the United States carries a representation of the same person on both sides?*

A. The Lincoln Memorial cent has the bold bust of Lincoln on the obverse as introduced in 1909, and a seated Lincoln set within the pillars of the Lincoln Memorial on the reverse. This coin also carries the initials of two engravers: Victor D. Brenner for the obverse and Frank Gasparro for the reverse.

Q. *Why were only 1,000 Flying Eagle cents minted in 1856, the year the type was first struck?*

A. As authority for producing the Flying Eagle cent wasn't forthcoming until February 21, 1857, the 1856 issue is truly a pattern coin, although it is widely collected as the first year of issue for the short-lived series. The quantity produced, which was at least 1,000 and perhaps as many as 2,500 (ostensibly to provide members of Congress with specimens for evaluation of the proposal to change coinage standards and authorize the small cent), makes it the most common pattern. Some small quantity of those produced did actually find their way into circulation.

Q. *I have always thought the Flying Eagle cent to be one of the most attractive coins ever issued by the United States. Why was it discontinued so abruptly?*

A. It would appear that the public didn't share your appraisal of this truly venturesome coin, the design of which was adapted from the powerful flying eagle of the 1836 to 1839 Gobrecht pattern dollars. Allegedly, production ceased after two years because of official objection to the coin being popularly known as the "Buzzard" cent.

Q. *Wasn't Lincoln the first real person to be depicted on a regular-issue coin of the United States?*

A. Lincoln's appearance on the cent in 1909 marked the first appearance of an identifiable person, and the first appearance of a U.S. president, on our regular-issue coinage, although Christopher Columbus's portrait on the 1892 World's Columbian Exposition commemorative half dollar was the first appearance of an identifiable person on a non-pattern U.S. coin.

Q. *Which of the branch mints was the first to mint coins that were not made of silver or gold?*

A. The San Francisco Mint began striking bronze Indian Head cents in 1908, and the Denver Mint not until 1911; both San Francisco and Denver began minting nickels in 1912, the last year of the Liberty Head issue.

1982 Lincoln cents. Small date, 1982, bronze (left); large date, 1982, plated zinc.

Q. *When were the first copper-plated zinc cents struck and placed in circulation?*

A. The first zinc cents (dated 1982) were struck on December 17, 1981, at the U.S. Mint's satellite facility at the West Point Bullion Depository. As these pieces are without mintmark, they are indistinguishable from those sub-sequently produced at the Philadelphia Mint. The first of this new gener-ation of zinc cents began entering circulation in mid-January. Late in 1982, cent production at the Denver Mint was also converted from the old cop-per-based standard to the new zinc-based issue. Commencing in 1983 and continuing through today, all cents have been struck from pure copper-plated planchets with a core of 99.2 percent zinc and 0.8 percent copper.

The 1982 cents struck on bronze planchets at the Philadelphia Mint come in large and small date versions, as do those struck on the zinc-based planchets. While the Denver Mint cents struck on zinc-based planchets come in both large- and small-date versions, the bronze version is known in only one variety. On the large-date varieties, the top of the "1" in the date does not align (it is a bit lower) with the top of the remaining digits in the date, while on the small-date varieties all four digits are in top alignment.

Q. *How can you tell the difference between the bronze and zinc cent strikes of 1982?*

A. There is a perceptible difference in the weight of the two versions: the bronze cent weighs 3.11 grams, or 24.2 percent heavier than the 2.5 grams weight of the copper-plated zinc cents. This difference can actually be detected when the coins are individually held in one's hands. Several inexpensive balance-beam-style devices were developed and marketed to the collector community to facilitate identification by weight as well. Also, the copper-plated zinc cents, particularly those minted through the first few months, often carry dark surface discoloration and may display surface bubbling, both of which are uncharacteristic of their bronze sisters.

Q. *Were Proof cents of 1982 struck on both bronze and copper-plated zinc planchets?*

A. No, all 1982 Proof cents were struck on bronze planchets; commencing in 1983, all Proof cents were struck on copper-plated zinc planchets.

Q. *I understand there are both large and small date varieties of 1982 cents. Can I identify bronze and copper-plated zinc cents of that year by a study of this feature?*

A. Only in that 1982-D small-date cents were struck on copper-plated zinc planchets. Large-date 1982-D cents were struck in both metals, as were both large- and small-date 1982 Philadelphia offerings. All Proofs were struck from large-date dies.

Q. *Can you tell me how many basic types of small cents there are, and the years they were minted?*

A. Flying Eagle — 1857–1858

Indian Head (copper-nickel, Laurel Wreath reverse) — 1859

Indian Head (copper-nickel, Oak Wreath reverse) — 1860–1864

Indian Head (bronze) — 1864–1909

Lincoln Head (bronze, Wheat Ears reverse) — 1909–1942, 1946–1958

Lincoln Head (zinc-plated steel, Wheat Ears reverse) — 1943

Lincoln Head (shell-case bronze, Wheat Ears reverse) — 1944–1946

Lincoln Head (bronze, Memorial reverse) — 1959–1982

Lincoln Head (copper-plated zinc, Memorial reverse) — 1982–2008

Lincoln Bicentennial (copper-plated zinc, four designs) — 2009

Lincoln Head, "Union" (copper-plated zinc) — 2010

About the images in this book: In general, coin denominations of 50 cents and higher are pictured at actual size; denominations below 50 cents and coins that are unusually small (e.g., gold dollars) are generally pictured at 150 percent of their actual size. Paper money is typically pictured at page width. Other items, such as medals, encased postage, and so on, may be enlarged for visibility. Appendix B lists the actual sizes of U.S. coins and currency.

CHAPTER EIGHT

Nickels, 1866 to Date

Q. *Why did the United States begin producing nickel five-cent coins in 1866 when they had been, and still were, coining silver half dimes?*

A. The onset of war, with its requirement of vast expenditures of money and the orientation of priorities for non-consumer goods, traditionally creates inflationary monetary conditions. Early in 1862, all metallic currency began to disappear from circulation. Citizens, anticipating an increase in bullion values, began hoarding gold and silver coins and even the lowly cent, whose metal content was 88 percent copper alloyed with 12 percent nickel. In 1864 the weight of the coin was reduced by one-third, and it was given a new alloy: 95 percent copper and 5 percent tin and zinc (the standard for the cent until 1962, when the tin was eliminated, with the switch to a copper-plated zinc planchet being effected in 1982), which effectively reduced the cent's copper content by about 28 percent.

As the silver half-dime was an essential denomination in everyday commerce, it was actually among the first coins to vanish from circulation, despite dramatically increased productions in 1861 and 1862. For the next four years only modest quantities were produced at the Philadelphia Mint, but in quantities five times as great at the San Francisco Mint, as in the far west the coins tended to maintain circulation rather than being withdrawn.

It was determined to introduce a five-cent piece of non-precious metal in 1866 (75 percent copper, 25 percent nickel) of five grams weight (3.75 grams copper; the copper weight of the cent was about 3.58 grams) that would discourage hoarding and satisfy an essential need of commerce east of the Mississippi, specie payment having been suspended as a consequence of the Civil War. The coin was produced in massive quantities for the time—90,864,445—from 1866 through 1869, all at the

Philadelphia Mint, a quantity that is 2-1/2 times as great as cent production over the same period; comparatively, only a combined 1,719,000 dimes, 330,200 quarters and 6,413,100 half dollars were produced in Philadelphia and San Francisco in those years.

Q. *What does the term "racketeer nickel" mean?*

A. The only indication of value on the first Liberty Head nickels minted in early 1883 was a large letter "V" on the reverse. The coin's relatively close similarity in size and weight (21.2 mm diameter vs. 21.6 mm; 5 grams weight vs. 8.359 grams) to a five-dollar gold piece prompted some opportunists to reed the edge with a private tooling device, gold plate the coin, and pass it as a new type five-dollar gold piece. These gold-plated nickels became known to collectors as "racketeer nickels." Later in 1883, the reverse design of the coin was altered by adding the word "CENTS" below the wreath on the reverse to eliminate the confusion. While only about 5.5 million of the "without cents" version were produced, in contrast to slightly over 16 million "with cents," the latter are worth roughly three times as much as the former in all grades, except that "without cents" Proofs are slightly more valuable than those "with," the respective mintages being 5,219 examples of the former and 6,783 examples of the latter.

1913 Liberty Head nickel. Although not an official U.S. coin issue, five specimens of the 1913 Liberty head nickel were struck, all of which are accounted for. Sometimes reported as number six is a copper strike of the 1913 Indian Head type.

Q. *How many of the Liberty Head type nickels were struck in 1913?*

A. No 1913 Liberty Head nickels were *officially* struck. The five known specimens were illegally struck, almost certainly at the Mint and with authentic dies, by private initiative. All five coins are presently accounted for. By established legal precedent, they could be confiscated by the government at any time as unauthorized coinage, as some other coins of similar origin have been, but the right of private ownership has never been challenged in this instance.

Although not an official U.S. coin issue, research has established that specimens of the 1913 Liberty Head nickel were struck clandestinely, all of which are accounted for. While reports of a sixth specimen have been published from time to time, that attribution arises from the fact that at one time the five were housed in a plush six-coin display case, with a copper strike of the 1913 Indian Head type nickel being held in the sixth opening.

1937-D Three-legged Buffalo. Enlarged detail of the missing leg.

Q. *I have been told by some that the three-legged variety of the 1937-D Buffalo nickel was created when the engraver preparing the die made a mistake and omitted a leg. Others have said the variety was created when that area of the die became filled with a foreign material. Who has given me the correct explanation?*

A. The first answer is certainly incorrect, and the second is likely incorrect as well, from the technical perspective. The creation of this error, which caught the fancy of the collecting public, is generally attributed the fact that a Mint workman used a tool to salvage a damaged die, grinding the surface of the die "down to remove injuries sustained during its accidental clash with the obverse die." In addition to the foreleg of the buffalo above the hoof having been removed, certain areas of detail are struck up weakly on genuine specimens as well. Beware that this error can be easily faked by carefully tooling off the foreleg of the buffalo on regular 1937-D strikes. Similar errors exist of other Buffalo nickels, but they are not widely collected because they did not catch the fancy of the collecting community, the 1936-D 3-1/2 legs error being one of them.

Q. *Are the so-called restored date Buffalo nickels considered valuable as collectors' items?*

A. Not by serious collectors. An acid application makes the worn dates temporarily visible. The disappearance of the "restored" date after the coin has been passed off on an uninformed or novice collector can be of no possible benefit to the hobby.

Q. *Why is a coin struck only about 60 years ago, the 1950-D nickel, so hard to find?*

A. The quantity of coins minted for a given mint in a given year is determined by what is required to meet circulation requirements, not collector needs. The 1950-D nickel had the lowest mintage (2,630,030) of any year or mint of regular-issue Jefferson nickel coinage to date, and relatively few entered circulation. With only six exceptions, even annual Proof mintages of nickels since 1961 have exceeded that quantity. When collectors and speculators realized that the mintage of this issue was going to be so small—the Philadelphia Mint produced nearly 10 million of the coin that year, while Denver had produced about 46.5 million in 1949 and would produce about 20.5 million in 1951—a significant percentage of the mintage was set aside in uncirculated rolls, so few specimens ever reached circulation. That accounts for the tight spread in values between the circulated and uncirculated grades; while the 1950-D mintage was by far the lowest among issues of the first 13 years of the Jefferson series, it is one of the most common in uncirculated condition. It was the subject of a great speculative boom in the early 1960s, which collapsed in 1964.

1942–1945 Jefferson nickels.

Q. *What is a "silver nickel?"*

A. This term is applied to the wartime five-cent piece (1942–1945) composed of 56 percent copper, 35 percent silver, and 9 percent manganese. Because nickel imparts great strength and corrosion resistance when alloyed with steel, and because the United States must import most of its nickel, with the onset of World War II it was decided to reserve the stockpile of that metal normally employed in the production of five-cent pieces for use in war industry. Indicative of the resulting alloy change for the nickel, the mintmark was made larger and placed above the dome of Monticello, and for the first time in the nation's coinage history, the letter "P" was used to designate domestic coins struck at the Philadelphia Mint.

Q. *I have a 1944 silver nickel without a mintmark. Is it valuable?*

A. It is undoubtedly a counterfeit that originated in New Jersey. The numismatically ignorant counterfeiter evidently prepared his mold from coins of two different dates, using the reverse of a prewar nickel struck at the Philadelphia Mint, thus producing a passable copy of a nonexistent coin.

Q. *Is it true the Jefferson nickel was designed in open competition outside the Mint?*

A. The design for the Jefferson nickel resulted from a completely open competition for a $1,000 prize. The winning design was submitted by Felix Schlag, a rather obscure sculptor at the time, but it was extensively modified by the engraving staff at the U.S. Mint in Philadelphia. While Schlag's Jefferson portrait rendering for the obverse was retained, with only the lettering style of his original changed, his reverse representation of a three-quarter view of Monticello was rejected in favor of a flat frontal view. The designer of the coin was anonymous to the public from 1938 through 1965, with his initials "FS" being added below the truncation of Jefferson's bust on the obverse starting with the coins struck in 1966, remaining there until Schlag's obverse was abandoned when the third issue in the "Westward Journey" commemorative series came out in 2005. When the regular issue Jefferson nickel series resumed in 2006, an architecturally strengthened representation of the Monticello view first minted in 1938 was reinstated.

Q. *I recently found a naturally dark (not tarnished) Jefferson nickel. What caused the unusual color? Is it valuable? Is it real?*

A. Off-color Jefferson nickels are not uncommon, and are known in hues ranging from smoky blue through deep purple to black. The natural discoloration is caused by an incorrect alloy mix containing significantly too much copper. These dark nickels generally originated from the Philadelphia Mint, which experienced much difficulty with the atmospheric operation of its annealing ovens from 1946 through the 1950s, being particularly prevalent from 1951 through 1955, and again in 1957 and 1958. Nicely struck examples of these dark coins appeal to some collectors who prefer darkly toned uncirculated or Proof coins, and they will pay a small premium for them.

Q. *Is the Indian on the Indian Head or Buffalo nickel a real person?*

A. Actually, it is a composite of three of them as created by sculptor James Earle Fraser. It is generally agreed that Chief Two Moon, a Cheyenne, modeled the forehead; Chief John Big Tree, an Iroquois, the nose and mouth; and Chief Iron Tail, a Sioux, the chin and throat. Black Diamond, a bison then in captivity at the New York Zoological Gardens, served as the model for the "buffalo" on the coin.

1913 Indian Head / Buffalo nickel.

Q. *Why is the buffalo standing on a mound on some 1913 nickels, and on a straight ground line on others?*

A. Soon after the new design was placed in production, it was realized that the "mound" design was causing striking difficulties, would be subject to rapid wear in circulation, and provided a coin that tended not to work well in early mechanical vending machines because of its thickness. Both deficiencies were corrected by recessing the surface of the coin below the top of the "mound" on which the buffalo stood, dropping the value statement in and beneath the "straight ground line," which essentially became a protective bar that inhibited the wearing down of the denomination line.

Q. *I have some nickels dated 1942, 1943, 1944, and 1945 that appear to be of a much darker color than normal. Each of these coins also has a large letter above the dome of Monticello on the reverse. Are these coins rare?*

A. Your coins are not rare, but circulated examples of them are significantly more valuable than most other Jefferson nickels immediately preceding and following them. The reason they are more valuable is that they contain a substantial percentage of silver, the same property that makes them darker in color. Nickels of these years struck with this silver content, in substitution for nickel, are distinguished by the presence of the large letters P, D, or S mintmarks over Monticello's dome on the reverse, this being the only instance when a U.S. coin minted at Philadelphia has carried a mintmark.

Nearly 60 percent of the nickel production of 1942 consisted of coins bearing a 35 percent silver content (0.05626 ounces of silver) and 9 percent manganese in replacement of the 25 percent nickel content utilized from earlier in 1942, back to 1866, silver being less valuable than nickel at the time. The new alloy, which reduced copper content from 75 percent to 56 percent, was then utilized for all nickel coinage for 1943, 1944, and 1945. This new alloy was arrived at as a technical substitute for the old one, because it created a coin with identical electrical conductivity qualities, which was important for the functioning of vending and slot machines, subway turnstiles, and a host of other devices attuned to weight or magnetism. This change perhaps had more to do with boosting the morale of the public during wartime than the need for nickel for war purposes, as it has been calculated that only a little more than 800 *thousand* pounds was saved from coinage due to the change, while about 180 *million* pounds were produced that were available to Allied countries over the same period.

When the bullion value for silver hit the 90-cents-per-ounce range in the early 1960s, these nickels started trading at a premium based on the value of their metal content, and people quickly found it to their advantage to remove them from circulation for recycling as bullion. As a "wartime nickel" contains approximately 0.011252 ounce of silver per one-cent of face value, while the 90 percent silver fractional coins minted from 1873 to 1964 contain approximately 0.007234 ounce of silver per one-cent of face value, they bear approximately 55 percent more silver value per one-cent of face value, so they became subject to Gresham's Law—bad money drives good money from circulation—several years before the 90 percent fractional coins did.

Q. *When did the motto "In God We Trust" first appear on the nickel?*

A. The first use of the motto occurred on the 1866 to 1883 Shield nickel. The shield featured on the obverse of this issue was actually a loose adaptation of that presented on the two-cent piece (1864–1873), both offerings having been the work of Mint engraver James B. Longacre. It did not subsequently reappear on either the Liberty Head or the Indian Head (Buffalo) nickels, but was reintroduced in 1938 with the appearance of the Jefferson nickel.

1867 Shield nickel (with rays).

1867 Shield nickel (without rays).

Q. *I have noticed that the nickels of 1867 come in two types, one with 13 rays positioned between the 13 stars encircling a large numeral 5 on the reverse. While this design does not appear attractive to me, is there a reason why the rays were removed?*

A. Various reasons have been advanced. One opinion holds that the rays produced a cluttered effect which the public found unattractive, but there is no evidence to support that possibility. Another, and more logical and likely sole reason is that the hardness of nickel planchets caused dies to break after about 20,000 strikes, so the rays were removed to prolong the life of the working dies. Documentary evidence exists in support of this being the sole likelihood.

Q. *When authority to mint a nickel five-cent piece was legislated in 1866, was the coin a needed and logical substitute for the silver half-dime?*

A. A non-silver five-cent coin was required at the time to serve as a replacement for the silver half-dime which, along with other gold and silver coins, had been driven from circulation by the post-Civil War suspension of specie payment. A five-cent coin that would remain in circulation was also required to speed the retirement of unpopular fractional currency notes of ten-cent and lower denominations. Logically, a nickel five-cent piece was a curious coin to produce in the aftermath of a successful campaign to mint cents of bronze instead of copper-nickel (1856–1864) that had been largely based on the argument that striking hard copper-nickel cent planchets had worn out the Mint's coin presses and prematurely broken a fantastic number of expensive working dies. Making the nickel of copper or of a bronze composition would have made more sense.

Westward Journey nickels of 2004 and 2005.

Q. *Why were the first two issues in the four-coin "Westward Journey" commemorative nickel series rendered with the old Felix Schlag obverse portrait of Jefferson, while the two subsequent issues of 2005 feature a different, bolder, and tightly cropped portrait?*

A. As it was quite late in 2003 when the law authorizing the "Westward Journey" commemorative series was passed, the U.S. Mint was not left with much time to get the first coin in the series in production. Thus, Mint sculptor Norman E. Nemeth quickly adapted an old Indian Peace Medal of 1801 design for the reverse of the first coin, celebrating the 1802 Louisiana Purchase, and it was decided that the Schlag design would be utilized unchanged for that coin. With that precedent, it was determined to maintain the design for the second coin as well, which featured a Lewis and Clark keelboat representation executed by Mint sculptor Al Maltesky. An open competition under the aegis of the U.S. Mint's Artistic Infusion Program was conducted for the 2005 designs, with the obverse being the work of Joe Fitzgerald, while the American Bison reverse was executed by Jamie Franki and the "Ocean in View" reverse by Joe Fitzgerald. While the American 5-Cent Coin Continuity Act of 2003 had provided for five special reverses to be employed on the nickels of 2004 to 2006, only four were actually produced.

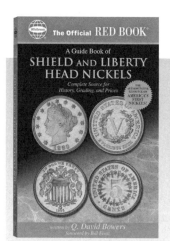
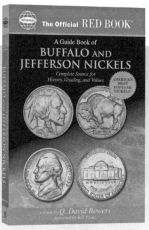

For more information: Consult the *Guide Book of Shield and Liberty Head Nickels* and the *Guide Book of Buffalo and Jefferson Nickels* (Bowers).

CHAPTER NINE

Discontinued Denominations

Q. *Is it possible to distinguish between the large and small motto two-cent pieces of 1864 without the aid of a magnifying glass?*

A. A difference in the shape of the letters "O" and "D" in the motto IN GOD WE TRUST can be readily detected without the use of visual aid enhancement. On the small motto variety, the inside space of these letters is wider and relatively rounded in shape. On the large motto, the space is perceptibly narrower and oval-like in shape.

Q. *People have told me that the three-cent denomination was introduced into our coinage system because of the postal situation at the time. Could you explain this for me?*

A. There were two principal reasons for the introduction of the three-cent piece, or "trime" as it came to be referenced in Treasury documents. One of the reasons was the fact that the basic letter-rate postage fee was reduced from five cents to three cents in 1851. It was thought that purchases of three-cent stamps could be facilitated with the presence in circulation of a three-cent coin, as opposed to having to pay with three of the large copper cents of the day. The cent had a diameter of 27.5 mm and a weight of 10.89 grams, in contrast to trimes' diameter of 14 mm and weight of just 0.8 grams.

Then there was the discovery of gold in California in 1848, which dramatically increased the supply of that precious metal, resulting in a drop in the price of gold in relation to that of silver. This development caused the intrinsic value of silver coins to rise above their face value; that is, they became worth more as bullion than as money. This caused all silver coins to be hoarded or exported, to the detriment of trade. The first three-cent pattern coins were produced in early 1849, with another added in 1850. None of these patterns resemble the coin ultimately issued in 1851, a year for which no additional three-cent patterns are recorded.

When the silver three-cent piece was introduced, it was produced to a lower silver fineness and fine silver weight standard, representing an intrinsic value of 86% of the nominal face value to discourage hoarding and to provide a coin for trade, with a convenient transaction value between the cent and half-dime. Initially it was issued as a .750 fine silver coin with a net silver weight of about 0.6 grams, significantly below the proportional net silver weight of a half-dime, which was 0.7236 grams. Commencing in 1853, when the Act of February 21, 1853, mandated a standardization of silver coin fineness and weight standards, the .900 fine silver weight of the three-cent piece was adjusted to 0.675 grams.

Q. *I have seen in advertisements references to three types of silver three-cent pieces. How do you distinguish between them?*

A. The type of 1851 to 1853 has no lines bordering the large six-pointed star on the obverse, and does not have an olive sprig above, nor a bundle of arrows below the Roman numeral III inside the large "C" on the reverse. The type of 1854 to 1858 has three outlines to the star, olive sprig above the numeral III and bundle of three arrows below. The type of 1859 to 1873 has two outlines to the star, along with the olive sprig and arrows treatment similar to the type of 1854 to 1858. The first type has a weight of 0.80 grams and silver fineness of .750, while the second and third types have a weight of only 0.75 grams, with the silver being .900 fine.

Q. *My teacher told us that the first copper coins produced at the U.S. Mint weren't coins at all, but tokens. Is she right?*

A. The coinage bill enacted on April 2, 1792, provided for a "token coinage" of copper cents and half cents. Minor copper coins weren't accorded legal tender status until April 22, 1864, when the cent was made legal tender in amounts up to ten cents and the two-cent piece up to twenty cents. Thus, technically, all the cent and half-cent "coins" minted from 1793 to 1864 were really "tokens" from the legal perspective, though they were accepted as money without distinction.

1875 twenty-cent piece.

Q. *What is the history surrounding the short life of the twenty-cent piece?*

A. The why of the twenty-cent piece has long and often been debated. It was envisioned on the one hand as a means of preventing short-changing that resulted from the Western tradition of pricing items according to the Spanish "bit" (12-1/2 cents). On the other hand, its appearance has been attributed as the first step in the implementation of a proposal by Senator Sarent to mint all coins above the nickel in units of tens; that is, to mint twenty-cent and forty-cent coins, eliminating the quarter and half dollar. It was also viewed as an attempt by the senators from the silver states to legislate another guaranteed market for silver.

The coin's short life can at least in some significant measure be attributed to the fact that while its value was prominently stated, and while the eagle on the reverse was left facing and the edge of the coin was plain, in contrast to the right facing eagle and reeded edge on the quarter, it was in practice easily confused with the quarter dollar, as its 22mm diameter was very close to the 24.3mm diameter of the quarter. Introduced in 1875, it was minted for general issue only that year and in early 1876; Proof specimens were struck in 1877 and 1878, after which time the issue was discontinued. Of the roughly 1.35 million minted for circulation, approximately 96.5% were produced at the western mints in San Francisco and Carson City.

Q. *If the half-cent was "unnecessary," why was it initially included in the nation's coinage program?*

A. When the U.S. Mint became operational, the most widely used currency along the eastern seaboard was the Spanish dollar and its subsidiary parts, which remained legal tender until 1857. Although both the Spanish and

U.S. dollars during this time were equivalent to 100 cents, U.S. standard, their minor coins were computed by different fractional standards. That is, while 2-reales Spanish equaled 25-cents U.S., the 1 real was equal to 12-1/2 cents, and the 1/2 real had an accepted value at the retail level of 6-1/2 cents, as contrasted to its 6-1/4 cents value based on the real system. Alexander Hamilton proposed the half-cent piece to prevent the poor from being systematically bilked when making purchases with Spanish real coins and receiving change in U.S. cent coins.

Silver three-cent pieces (trimes). No lines around star (1851–1853); olive sprig and bundle of arrows (added for issues of 1854–1873); three outlines to star (1854–1859); two outlines to star (1859–1873).

Q. *Can you tell me why the tiny silver three-cent piece was popularly called a "trime?"*

A. Not really. Although the authorizing legislation specified a "three-cent" piece, the term "trime" was used in some Treasury documents of the period. The word isn't in *Webster's Collegiate Dictionary*, but the word "trine" is. The definition of trine is three-fold or triple. My best guess would be "trime" originated as a misspelling of "trine," which caught on with the public as a consequence of official reference.

1877 nickel three-cent piece.

Q. *Why did the United States stop minting a three-cent piece?*

A. Three-cent pieces were introduced in 1851 as silver coins under the same March 3, 1851, law that cut the nation's basic prepaid letter rate postage from five cents per half-ounce to three cents. An anomaly in a decimal-standard coinage, it was intended as an issue that would facilitate stamp purchases. Never a popular issue, with the onset of the Civil War silver three-cent pieces all but totally disappeared from circulation. While this coin remained in production until 1873, when it was eliminated by law, only modest quantities had been produced annually from 1863 on. In 1865 three-cent coinage was reintroduced on a large scale as a nickel coin that would circulate alongside and replace a fractional currency note issue of like denomination. Although the minting of nickel three-cent pieces continued until 1889, the quantities produced annually were quite small after 1876, with the exception of 1881 when more than a million examples were struck. The base postage rate had been revised downward again in 1883.

Q. *Why was the nickel three-cent piece introduced into our coinage while silver three-cent pieces were still being minted?*

A. The hoarding of metallic currency during the Civil War forced the government to issue fractional currency notes. Early in 1863, silver three-cent pieces that had been minted in quantities averaging in excess of 3.5 million pieces from 1851 through 1862 began rapidly disappearing from circulation as the public hoarded them for their silver content. When that happened, the government produced a large issue of three-cent notes to serve the commercial sector. The nickel interests in 1864 viewed this development as an opportunity to push for the production of a nickel three-cent piece, which would possess a low intrinsic value, to discourage hoarding and as a replacement for redeeming the three-cent notes. More importantly to their interests, this would replace some of the demand for nickel that was eliminated with the discontinuance of nickel as part of the alloy for the cent in 1864. The nickel three-cent piece was introduced in 1865. The first four years (1865–1868) of three-cent nickel production resulted in the minting of 23.35 million pieces, in contrast to the 101.755 million one-cent pieces produced in the last four years (1861–1864) of copper-nickel production, reducing the U.S. Mint's nickel demand by approximately 60 percent.

Q. *Can you tell me why the Philadelphia Mint struck more than one million nickel three-cent pieces in 1881, while the quantities produced in 1880 and 1882 were only around 20,000 each?*

A. This is a real mystery that has been puzzling numismatic scholars for well over a century. It has generally been assumed that a heightened demand for the coin was created by a postal rate change, as a reduction in prepaid letter rate from five cents to three cents per half ounce in 1851 had provided the basic argument for introducing a three-cent piece in 1851. That certainly would not have been the case, however, as the next change in the basic letter rate came in 1883 when the rate per half-ounce was reduced from three cents to two cents. The upshot of this high mintage for collectors was the creation of the most commonly encountered and inexpensive type coin in the series in all grades ranging from good to uncirculated, although the issue does command a bit of a higher premium in the choice uncirculated range than any date after 1868.

1864 Two-cent pieces. Details show large and small motto varieties.

Q. *The two-cent piece of 1864 to 1873 had a short production run and comparatively small mintages. Why was it introduced?*

A. The two-cent piece was issued in 1864 in an attempt to alleviate the exasperating coin shortage caused by the hoarding of coins in the Civil War years. While it served that need briefly and was readily accepted, the need for it diminished with the end of hostilities, and the coin was discontinued. Of the approximately 44.88 million two-cent pieces produced for circulation, nearly 75 percent were minted in the first two years (1864–1865), and 98 percent in the first six years (1864–1869), with only Proofs being produced in the last year of issue.

Q. *When did the motto IN GOD WE TRUST first appear on our coinage?*

A. The two-cent piece of 1864 was the first U.S. coin released to circulation bearing this now-familiar motto. Pattern two-cent pieces bearing the motto, and also two similar mottoes—GOD OUR TRUST and GOD AND OUR COUNTRY—were prepared in 1863, while half dollar and $10 gold patterns bearing the GOD OUR TRUST motto were also prepared in 1861 and 1862.

Q. *What was the smallest coin the United States ever minted?*

A. The silver three-cent piece (1851–1873) was the smallest in physical size—14 mm diameter and 0.80 or 0.75 grams weight—but the half-cent piece (1793–1857) had the lowest face value of any U.S. coin.

Q. *What is the difference between a half dime and a nickel?*

A. The principal difference is one of metallic content. Half dimes were made of .8924 fine silver from 1794 into 1837, and of .900 fine silver thereafter until the denomination was discontinued in 1873. Nickels have from the beginning in 1866 been made of an alloy of 75 percent copper and 25 percent nickel, with the exception of the emergency silver wartime nickels of 1942 to 1945. The nickel was made substantially larger (21.2 mm) and heavier (5 grams) than the half dime (15.5 mm diameter, 1.24 grams weight) from 1853 to 1873.

Half dime reverses.

Q. *I have an 1872 half dime that doesn't carry the mottoes IN GOD WE TRUST and E PLURIBUS UNUM. Is this true of all types of the half dime?*

A. No half dimes carried the IN GOD WE TRUST motto. Half dimes of the Draped Bust–Heraldic Eagle type of 1800 to 1805 carried the E PLURIBUS UNUM inscription, on the ribbon the eagle holds in its beak, as the Liberty Cap type of 1829 to 1837 did boldly on a ribbon above the head of the eagle.

CHAPTER TEN

Dimes, 1837 to Date

Q. *How did the 1844 dime gain the tag "Orphan Annie?"*

A. Only 72,500 dimes were minted in 1844, but nobody noticed at the time, as coin collectors were then as rare as Greeley's union printers and there were no speculators wearing slide rules calibrated to predict instant and infinite profits. Attrition, abetted by collector neglect, took a great toll of the small mintage over the next 80 years or so. In 1930 (so the story goes) a collector in Kansas City discovered that the 1844 dime was even rarer than its mintage indicated, and that this rarity wasn't reflected by its market premium. He dubbed it "Orphan Annie" because "the coin had no buyers, and was just an orphan in the coin world." Today, it commands the highest premium by far, in the lower circulated grades, of any pre-Civil War era Liberty Seated dime struck at the Philadelphia Mint.

Dimes. Arrows at dates.

Q. *Can you explain the significance of the arrows near the date on some 1853 dimes?*

A. The arrows were added by the date on dimes of 1853 to 1855 to denote a decrease in the weight of the dime from 41.25 to 38.4 grains. Proportional changes in the weights of half dimes, quarters, and halves were denoted in the same manner. The arrows were again employed from 1873 to 1874 to denote a slight increase in the weight to 38.58 grains. Dimes struck early in 1853 at the Philadelphia Mint to the heavier standard do not have arrows at the date. The 1853 change resulted in the fine silver weight in the dime being reduced from 37.125 grains to 34.56 grains.

1942/1 Winged Liberty Dime. Enlarged details show Philadelphia (left) and Denver overdates.

Q. *Can you explain what is meant by a 1942/41 dime? Is it a dime struck with a dual date?*

A. Two major "overdate" Mint errors exist for 1942, one from the Philadelphia Mint and one from the Denver Mint. Both were produced when production dies in the preparation process were first sunk with a 1941-dated hub die and then, by accident, finished with 1942 hub dies. The result was working dies with a "2" sunk over the "1" of the date. An unknown number of dimes were struck with the production dies before the error was detected. The Philadelphia Mint overdate is the more distinct and scarcer of the errors, with the "1" closing the loop on the "2." On the Denver Mint overdate, the "1" is barely discernible. On both errors doubling of the "4" in the date is reasonably discernable as well, and in the latter instance is the most discernable feature evidenced. While both errors are relatively equal in value in circulated grades, in choice condition the Philadelphia error carries a significantly higher premium than does the Denver error.

Detail of Micro-s-mintmark variety of 1945-S dime.

Q. *What is meant by the term "Micro S 1945-S dime?"*

A. The "S" mintmark on some of the 1945-S dimes is significantly smaller than that appearing on normal 1945 dimes struck by the San Francisco

Mint. This was caused by the "S" having been stamped into the working die with a much smaller type punch than normally employed. There are a number of other mintmarked dimes in the Mercury dime series that boast large and small mintmark varieties—the 1928-S, 1934-D, and 1941-S, in particular—as well as quarters and half-dollars of the same era.

Q. *I have always held the opinion that the Roosevelt dime was introduced in 1946 to commemorate the passing from the scene of the president who had the longest tenure in the history of the country. Is this the accepted theory?*

A. Popularity is greatness to one's contemporaries, but not to history. Greatness is neither chance nor destiny. It is a "compound product in which genius of the man is one element, and the sphere opened to him by the character of his age and the institutions of his country, is another."

Roosevelt was elected president at the darkest hour of the Great Depression, at a time when the people had lost faith in the ability of their leaders and in the capacity of the free enterprise system to provide the greatest good for the greatest number of citizens. He was wise enough to recognize the need for drastic and immediate change, and to perceive that the national mood provided the sphere for it. He initiated the change, gave it direction and impetus, and by so doing irrevocably altered the industrial, economic, and sociological philosophy of the nation.

His refusal to imitate, his willingness to improvise and initiate, surely earned him a dime's worth of recognition by a nation that was founded and developed by men of similar courage and resourcefulness. As Roosevelt lived his adult life as a victim of infantile paralysis, or poliomyelitis, and given the development of the March of Dimes to focus attention on the need to fight the scourge of polio, it was quite natural that a decision would have been made following his passing in early 1945 to memorialize his standing in our history with the launch of the new dime in 1946.

1964 Roosevelt dime. The initials "JS" lie just to the left of the date, below Roosevelt's neck.

Q. *A friend has told me that the initials "JS," which appear at the base of Roosevelt's shoulder on modern dimes, were placed there by an undercover Russian agent who worked in the U.S. Mint to show his allegiance to Joseph Stalin. Is this true?*

A. As true as the moon is made of Wisconsin cheddar cheese. The initials are those of John R. Sinnock, who designed the coin, and in the tradition of numismatic sculptors signed the work with his initials. Two years later Sinnock was also credited for his design work on the Franklin half dollar, but his full initials "JRS" appear thereon. That didn't fit the conspirator theory either, as Stalin's middle name was Vissarionovich.

The appearance of the Kennedy half-dollar in 1964 prompted a similar outpouring of hysterical patriotism when the ornate "GR" signature of designer/sculptor/engraver Gilroy Roberts was interpreted as the Communist hammer and sickle symbol.

Q. *Can you explain the contradiction of the Mercury dime bearing both the portrait of a pagan god and a motto stating national trust in the Christian God?*

A. There is no contradiction. "Mercury dime" is a misnomer, for the ancient god Mercury is not depicted on the coin. Designer Adolph Weinman created a representation of Liberty, as coinage law required, placing wings on the Liberty Cap to symbolize freedom of thought.

Q. *What is the meaning of the word "dime?"*

A. "Dime" is derived from the Latin "decimal," meaning "tenth part." The coin was originally authorized as a "disme," which the Law of April 2, 1792, defined as the "tenth part of a dollar."

Q. *During the years 1837 to 1964 when the dime contained 90 percent silver, what was the other 10 percent?*

A. Copper, to increase the hardness, and therefore the wearing qualities of the largely silver coin.

Early dime reverses.

Q. *An eagle appeared on the reverse of all dimes until 1837, when it was replaced by a wreath. Was the change the decision of Christian Gobrecht, the designer of the Liberty Seated dime?*

A. No. The first coinage act (April 2, 1792) mandated that an eagle be represented on the reverse of all gold and silver coins. A revision of the nation's coinage law enacted on January 18, 1837, eliminated the requirement for an eagle to be represented on the reverse of the silver dime and half dime.

Q. *Is it true, as I have been told, that all 1923-D and 1930-D dimes are counterfeits?*

A. While such dimes have been reported occasionally, officially, the Denver Mint did not produce dimes in either 1923 or 1930. For whatever the rumor is worth, dimes of either year bearing the Denver "D" mintmark are likely counterfeits of unknown origin, or were altered from 1928-D, or 1936-D or 1939-D issues, respectively.

Q. *In the exhibit area of a coin convention, I saw an 1859 Liberty Seated dime that didn't have anything on it to identify it as a U.S. coin. How could this happen?*

A. When the Liberty Seated dime first appeared in 1837, the obverse design included only the figure of Liberty seated with the date below. In 1838 the design was enhanced with the addition of 13 stars around the rim framing the seated figure. On both versions the country name—UNITED STATES OF AMERICA—appeared on the reverse encircling the central wreath. Commencing in 1860 the country name was moved from the reverse to the obverse, supplanting the stars, with a bolder wreath of agricultural products replacing the former wreath of laurel on the reverse.

In preparing for this change, the engraving department at the Philadelphia Mint created patterns mating the 1859 dated obverse die with the 1860 reverse die, neither of which included the national identity. These "transitional pattern" dimes were struck on regular dime planchets in very limited numbers. Similar "transitional pattern" half dimes of the same type and origin were also struck in very limited numbers dated both 1859 and 1860. It is believed that the Mint director at the time caused these "nationless coins" to be deliberately struck for sale to collectors. Thus, while these three coins were not struck for circulation, and are of substantial rarity, they are considered part of the Liberty Seated series by some specialists.

Q. *Why did the San Francisco Mint ever bother to strike a mere 24 dimes in 1894?*

A. The reason isn't known with certainty. A 1905 explanation, attributed to the Mint, maintains that they were struck at the end of the fiscal year when it was discovered that $2.40 in struck coins was needed to balance the books of the branch mint. Another opinion holds that the 24 dimes were struck arbitrarily by the Mint superintendent to give to friends. Only about 10 of the 1894-S dimes are known to exist. In October 2007, a PF-64 specimen sold for more than $1.5 million.

Q. *What U.S. coinage tradition came to an end with the appearance of the so-called "Mercury" or Winged Liberty Head dime in 1916?*

A. From the inception of U.S. regular-issue coinage, the dime had always carried the same obverse device as the higher fractional silver denominations.

That tradition ended dramatically in 1916, with the introduction of A.A. Weinman's Winged Liberty Head dime and Walking Liberty half dollar, along with H.A. MacNeil's Standing Liberty quarter.

Q. *Is there any symbolic significance in the bundle of sticks appearing on the reverse of the Winged Liberty Head dime?*

A. Weinman intended the "bundle of sticks," a fasces enfolding a battle-axe and entwined by an olive branch, to symbolize unity (bound fasces), preparedness (battle-axe), and love of peace (olive branch).

Q. *Can you tell me how many basic types of dimes there are, and the years they were minted?*

A.
Draped Bust (Small Eagle)	1796–1797
Draped Bust (Heraldic Eagle)	1798–1807
Liberty Cap	1809–1837
Liberty Seated (No Stars on Obverse)	1837–1838
Liberty Seated (Stars on Obverse)	1838–1860
Liberty Seated (Arrows at Date)	1853–1855
Liberty Seated (Legend on Obverse)	1860–1891
Liberty Seated (Arrows at Date)	1873–1874
Liberty Head (Barber)	1892–1916
Winged Liberty	1916–1945
Roosevelt (Silver)	1946–1964
Roosevelt (Clad)	1965–Date

About the images in this book: In general, coin denominations of 50 cents and higher are pictured at actual size; denominations below 50 cents and coins that are unusually small (e.g., gold dollars) are generally pictured at 150 percent of their actual size. Paper money is typically pictured at page width. Other items, such as medals, encased postage, and so on, may be enlarged for visibility. Appendix B lists the actual sizes of U.S. coins and currency.

CHAPTER ELEVEN

~

Quarters, 1838 to Date

Q. *I have noticed that some 1853 quarters are different from all other Liberty Seated quarters, in that there are arrows by the date on the obverse and rays radiating around the eagle on the reverse. The latter feature makes for a very unusual and attractive design. Why was it not continued?*

A. The arrows and rays were added to the design of the quarter in 1853 to denote a decrease in the weight of the quarter from 103.5 grains to 96 grains. This change was made subsequent to the enactment of February 21, 1853, legislation, prior to which a relatively small quantity of 44,200 quarters had been minted for circulation to the old Philadelphia Mint standard; subsequently, more than 15.2 million were struck to the new standard at the Philadelphia Mint and 1.3 million at the New Orleans Mint. This law made half dimes, dimes, quarters, and halves all subsidiary to the silver dollar; that is, they were now proportionally lighter in weight, thus intrinsically worth less than their face value. While the rays were incorporated on the reverse of the quarter only in 1853—halves were similarly treated that year as well—the arrows remained beside the date on the quarters of 1854 and 1855 as well. While this was the only appearance of rays on the reverse of Liberty Seated quarters, the arrows beside the date were again employed in 1873 and 1874, that time to denote a slight increase in weight to 96.45 grains.

1916–1917 reverse designs of the Standing Liberty quarter.

Q. *I have a 1917 quarter that does not have any stars below the eagle, and all of the other Standing Liberty quarters in my collection have three stars below the eagle. Is this a pattern coin?*

A. No, more than 12 million coins of the type you describe were minted in 1916 and 1917, of which 8.74 million were produced at the Philadelphia Mint in 1917, along with about 1.51 million in Denver and 1.95 million in San Francisco. The 1916 issue, all of which were minted in Philadelphia with only 52,000 struck, is a great rarity. The design of the initial Standing Liberty quarters of 1916 to 1917 portrayed Liberty with a partially unclad bust (a treatment that offended puritanical tastes), also featuring 13 stars placed along the rim to either side of the eagle.

In changing treatment of the obverse design in 1917 by covering Liberty's torso with a chain-mail corselet (designer Herman MacNeil's original preference), it was also determined to modify the reverse as well. While MacNeil's flying eagle rendering was retained, it was repositioned upward; the lettering along the upper and lower rims and above the eagle was restyled; and the 13 stars, originally split unevenly along the rim to the left (7) and right (6) of the eagle, were evenly displayed 5-and-5 to the sides, with three placed in the field below the eagle. These are known as varieties 1 and 2 of the Standing Liberty quarter; a third minor variety was created in 1925 when the pedestal date area on which Liberty stands was recessed to provide a more durable display of the date.

Q. *What were the forces which deemed it proper that Washington be featured on the new quarter introduced in 1932, when in his lifetime Washington is said to have rejected the idea of having his image featured on a coin?*

A. It isn't unusual for posterity to ignore a man's preference when they design to honor him. Confucius was a teacher who professed no knowledge of a god or hereafter; his disciples reacted after his death by making his teachings a religion, and him a god.

A precedent for a numismatic commemoration of the 200th anniversary of Washington's birth existed in the Lincoln cent, which had been introduced in 1909 to observe the 100th anniversary of Lincoln's birth. The Washington quarter was introduced as a one-year commemorative, but it proved so popular with the public that, following a one-year lapse in mintage, it was decided in 1934 to continue the coin as a regular issue. The conversion to presidential portraiture on our circulating coinage continued in 1938 with the introduction of the Jefferson nickel and in 1946 with the introduction of the Roosevelt dime, being concluded in 1964 with the Kennedy half supplanting the Franklin half introduced in 1948.

Q. *How many commemorative quarters have been issued by the U.S. Mint?*

A. Just three prior to the initiation of the 50 State Quarters® Program in 1999. The first was the 1893 Isabella quarter, struck for sale by the Lady Board of Managers of the 1892–1893 Columbian Exposition. The second was the Washington Bicentennial quarter of 1932, which resurfaced in 1934 as a regular issue. The third was the "Drummer Boy" American Revolution Bicentennial quarter of 1976, it having been in production during both 1975 and 1976 bearing 1776–1976 dual dating.

About the images in this book: In general, coin denominations of 50 cents and higher are pictured at actual size; denominations below 50 cents and coins that are unusually small (e.g., gold dollars) are generally pictured at 150 percent of their actual size. Paper money is typically pictured at page width. Other items, such as medals, encased postage, and so on, may be enlarged for visibility. Appendix B lists the actual sizes of U.S. coins and currency.

1917 Standing Liberty quarter.

Q. *Who was the model for the Standing Liberty depicted on Hermon MacNeil's beautiful quarter?*

A. MacNeil acknowledged that his rendition of a standing or striding armed Liberty was inspired by Roty's early 20th century "sowing Marianne" of the French silver coinage. The actual model was 22-year-old Miss Dora Doscher (later Mrs. H.W. Baum), who also posed for New York City's Pulitzer Memorial Fountain and the famous "Diana" that reposes in the Metropolitan Museum of Art, both figures by Karl Bitter.

Q. *Is it true that the Standing Liberty quarters struck from 1917 through 1930 were illegal, or were illegally struck?*

A. That could be said. The authorizing legislation for the Standing Liberty quarter specified: "No change shall be made in the emblems and devices used," providing only that "the modifications shall consist of the changing of the position of the eagle, the rearrangement of the stars and lettering and a slight concavity given to the surface." Nevertheless, when variety 1 was supplanted by variety 2 in 1917, it was immediately obvious that substantial unauthorized, therefore illegal, changes had been made to the "emblems and devices" on the obverse, including the "dressing" of Liberty's breast with "chain-mail."

Q. *What was the reason for the introduction of a new type quarter dollar, the Seated Liberty in 1838, after the minting of the Capped Bust type had already gotten under way?*

A. While the weight of the quarter was reduced from 6.74 grams to 6.68 grams and the fineness increased from .8924 to .900 by a law enacted in 1837, the minting of Capped Bust quarters to the old standard continued into 1838. Thus, the better question would be why coinage of the Capped Bust type quarter was continued on the old standard into 1838, when the switch to the new standard for dimes and quarters was made in 1837, at which time Seated Liberty designs were introduced. On the other hand, the switch to the new standard for half-dollars was made in early 1837, with the Capped Bust design being retained until 1839. Obviously, the new type quarter would have facilitated the identification of quarters struck to the new standard, just as was the case with half-dimes and dimes, in an era when the bullion content of coinage was of paramount importance, even when the differential was small.

1913 Barber / Liberty Head quarter.

Q. *What unusual and seldom-noticed innovation did Barber introduce to the coinage of the United States with the appearance of his quarter and half-dollar designs of 1892?*

A. The stars on the obverses of both coins are six-pointed, while those on the reverses are the first five-pointed stars to appear on U.S. coins.

Q. *When did the motto IN GOD WE TRUST first appear on the quarter dollar?*

A. The motto was added to the reverse side, displayed on a banner above the eagle, on the Liberty Seated Quarter in 1866. It has been retained on the quarter since that time.

Washington quarter. Compare the obverse of 1932–1998 (left) to that of 1999–2008.

Q. *Is it true that one of the current regular-issue coins of the United States has also served as a commemorative coin?*

A. The Washington quarter was first issued in 1932 to commemorate the 200th anniversary of George Washington's birth. When regular coinage of the quarter was reintroduced in 1934—the last Standing Liberty quarters were produced in 1930, with no quarters being minted in 1931 or 1933—the Washington quarter commemorative had been so favorably received as the nation's second presidential coin that it supplanted its predecessor as a regular-issue coin. It again became a commemorative during 1975 and 1976 when the "Drummer Boy" Bicentennial commemorative design was adapted to the reverse. The designs reverted to John Flanagan's originals commencing in 1977, continuing through 1998, at which time the obverse design was modified to incorporate the country name and denomination which previously appeared on the reverse.

Q. *Copper-nickel clad coins were introduced in 1965. What was the first denomination to be struck in this new coinage material?*

A. The Washington quarter was the first clad coin to be placed in production (August 23, 1965) and the first to be released to circulation (November 1, 1965).

Q. *Which of the branch mints was the first to strike quarter dollars?*

A. The New Orleans Mint began striking Liberty Seated quarter dollars in 1840. The San Francisco Mint followed in 1855. The only other mint to produce quarters, other than Denver, which first minted quarters in 1906, was Carson City, which produced modest quantities annually from 1870 through 1878, with the exception of 1874.

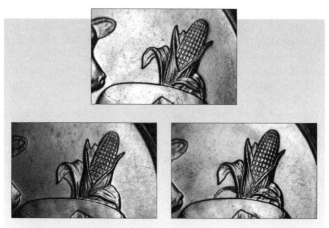

2004 Wisconsin quarter. Enlargements of the ear of corn on the normal, Extra Leaf High, and Extra Leaf Low varieties.

Q. *What's the story of the 2004 Wisconsin quarter "Extra Leaf" varieties?*

A. These are minting errors rather than design varieties. There are actually two distinct die flaw error varieties, resulting in what appear to be extra leaves on the ear of coin adjacent to the wheel-of-cheese design element, the origins of which are still being debated. On the one variety the extra leaf appears high and relatively straight under the left curl of the peeled-back husk on the corncob, while on the other the extra leaf appears low and curved. It has been variously posited that the "extra leaf" features on these coins resulted from die or hub clashing, or that they were tooled into a working die, intentionally or unintentionally, before the dies were hardened for press installation following the hubbing process. Both varieties command substantial premiums in choice grades, with the high-relief variety generally commanding 50 percent to 75 percent more than the low-leaf variety. While there are other error varieties in the 50 State Quarters® Program, these are the only ones that enjoy general popularity.

Q. *Can you tell me how many basic types of quarter dollars there are and the years they were minted for circulation?*

A. Draped Bust (Small Eagle)   1796

Draped Bust (Small Eagle)	1796
Draped Bust (Heraldic Eagle)	1804–1807
Liberty Cap (E PLURIBUS UNUM motto)	1815–1828
Liberty Cap (Without Motto)	1831–1838
Liberty Seated (Eagle Reverse Without Motto)	1838–1866
Liberty Seated (Arrows and Rays)	1853
Liberty Seated (Arrows, Without Rays)	1854–1855
Liberty Seated (Motto Added to Reverse)	1866–1891
Liberty Seated (Arrows at Date)	1873–1874
Liberty Head (Barber)	1892–1916
Liberty Standing (No Stars Below Eagle)	1916–1917
Liberty Standing (Stars Added Below Eagle)	1917–1924
Liberty Standing (Recessed Date)	1925–1930
Washington (Silver)	1932–1964
Washington (Clad)	1965–1998
Washington (Clad, American Revolution Bicentennial)	Dated 1776–1976
Washington (.400 Silver, American Revolution Bicentennial)	Dated 1776–1976
Washington (50 State Quarters® Program)	1999–2008
Washington (DC and U.S. Territories Quarters Program)	2009

CHAPTER TWELVE

~~

Half Dollars, 1839 to Date

Q. *Why do arrows appear alongside the dates on certain issues in the Liberty Seated half dollar series?*

A. In 1853 arrows were placed at the date on the obverse, and rays on the reverse, to denote a decrease in weight from 206.25 to 192 grains. The rays appeared only on 1853 dated halves, but the arrows remained through 1855. Arrows, but no rays, were again incorporated on halves in 1873 and 1874 to denote a slight weight increase to 192.9 grains.

Q. *Is there any explanation for why the New Orleans half dollar of 1861 is not worth more than its present valuation, when the U.S. Mint report officially reports that only 330,000 were struck? Other coins of the period with similar mintages are valued much higher.*

A. In addition to the "official" U.S. mintage, another 1,240,000 1861-O half dollars were struck in the name of the government of Louisiana after it seceded from the Union, with the Mint having been seized by the state militia on Jan. 31, 1861, at the beginning of the Civil War. Two months later the Mint was turned over to the Confederate States of America, under whose control 962,633 additional halves were subsequently struck between then and May 31, 1861, when continued operation of the facility as a mint was discontinued due to a lack of bullion. Thus, the combined mintage total was 2,522,633. All three mintages were struck utilizing regular U.S. dies prepared for and received by the Mint prior to the secession, and cannot be distinguished from the much smaller quantity struck as U.S. issues.

Q. *Through the years I've set aside a lot of 1964 Kennedy halves, every one I've come across, as I once heard that they are quite valuable. Can you tell me how much my coins are worth?*

A. Your coins are probably not particularly valuable. Highly cherished as keepsakes when they were first issued, and for many years regarded as the most respected tip an American traveling overseas could extend, that fascination with 1964 Kennedy's has now largely passed. Actually, regardless of their grade, they are probably worth less than any of the predecessor Franklin type halves which you could have been putting away to somewhat greater advantage during this time. In 1964 more than 277 million halves were struck at Philadelphia and 156 million at Denver, a figure which more than quadruples the previous high half dollar coinage total for a given year. In the circulated grade range, their *worth* is based on the bullion value of their silver content, while most Franklin halves in the upper circulated grades command modest collector premiums. In the uncirculated grade range, Franklin halves generally command premiums at least triple those enjoyed by 1964 Kennedy's; for Proofs, multiples of five or more.

Liberty Bell on the Franklin half dollar. Detail shows the "Pass and Stow" inscription.

Q. *I have often heard that the Franklin half carried the advertising of a private firm, but I have never been able to locate such a reference on the coin. Can you explain where it is located, and how it is possible for this to be?*

A. The words "Pass and Stow, Philada., MDCCLIII" are inscribed on the Liberty Bell at the upper extremity of the crack running up from the rim. This inscription "advertises" the name of the firm that in 1753 recast the bell after it cracked while being tested for tone at the time of its original installation. The inscription was ordered by the Philadelphia Assembly as a courtesy to Pass and Stow. The history of the bell is that the first one cracked upon being tested; the second proved to be defective; the third announced the signing of the Declaration of Independence, but cracked as it was being tolled for the death of Chief Justice John Marshall in 1835, thus resulting in the state of the bell as represented on the Franklin half. Fortunately, the nation was made of sterner stuff than its celebrated Liberty Bell.

Kennedy half dollar.

Q. *A friend told me the slight bulge along the line of Kennedy's neck on the half dollar is intended to represent the point at which the bullet from the assassin's rifle hit our late president. Is that true?*

A. Absolutely not. On many specimens of the coin, the feature you are calling attention to, which appears on the truncation of the bust just above the word WE in the "In God We Trust" legend, appears quite indistinct. It represents, however, the stylized initials of the coin's designer, Gilroy Roberts, then chief sculptor-engraver at the U.S. Mint in Philadelphia. It should also be mentioned that a conspiracy theory sometimes advanced maintains that this is a representation of the Soviet Union's hammer and sickle symbol.

Q. *I'd like to add a 1970 half dollar to my collection, but I don't want to pay the price dealers are asking for the uncirculated and Proof versions. Why don't they offer circulated specimens of this issue?*

A. This is a coin that was never released to the public, so any specimen not uncirculated or better would be a mishandled collector coin or one which was accidentally placed in circulation. Actually, in this particular case, a collector encountering a circulated specimen of this coin would have himself a truly rare coin, although its value would certainly be less than that of a reasonably well preserved uncirculated or Proof specimen.

Only 2,150,000 regular issue half dollars were struck in 1970, all at the Denver Mint, to provide a half-dollar for inclusion in the Mint Sets of uncirculated coins assembled for sale to collectors. None of the 1970-D half dollars were released to circulation because of the inability to maintain even a half dollar of only 40 percent silver content in circulation, even though bullion value of the coin did not exceed its face value until silver approached the $3.40 per ounce level. The production of half dollars for circulation was suspended from 1969 to 1971, when enactment of the Law of December 31, 1970, authorized the production of the cupro-nickel clad half dollar to the like standard of dimes and quarters. Nicely preserved examples of the 1970-D uncirculated half dollar command a somewhat higher premium than do 1970-S Proof specimens, of which a somewhat greater quantity of 2,632,810 were struck.

1897 Liberty Head half dollar (left) and Barber's inspiration.

Q. *The Liberty Head appearing on the obverse of the 1892 to 1915 Barber half dollar has a familiar look. Has it been employed elsewhere?*

A. Charles E. Barber is reputed to have loosely modeled the handsome Liberty Head of his half-dollar, quarter-dollar, and dime series after the Liberty Head appearing on the French Second Republic silver coinage of 1849 to 1851.

About the images in this book: In general, coin denominations of 50 cents and higher are pictured at actual size; denominations below 50 cents and coins that are unusually small (e.g., gold dollars) are generally pictured at 150 percent of their actual size. Paper money is typically pictured at page width. Other items, such as medals, encased postage, and so on, may be enlarged for visibility. Appendix B lists the actual sizes of U.S. coins and currency.

Liberty Walking mintmarks.

Q. *Where is the mintmark located on the 1916 Liberty Walking half dollar?*

A. The Denver and San Francisco mintmarks on 1916-dated halves, and the early portion of their 1917 productions, are located on the obverse immediately below the IN GOD WE TRUST motto. This marked the first appearance of mintmarks on the obverse of the half dollar since the 1838 and 1839 Liberty Cap issues struck at the New Orleans Mint carried its identifying "O" immediately above the date. In 1968 the Kennedy half dollar became the third coin of that denomination to bear a mintmark on its obverse, at which time mintmarks were also moved to the obverse of nickels, dimes, and quarters as well.

Q. *I enjoy using my coins as conversation pieces when I entertain guests. Is there anything interesting I can say about the rather common Kennedy half dollar?*

A. Few modern coins are more suited to your purpose. Only 24 days elapsed between the time President Lyndon B. Johnson asked Congress to authorize the striking of Kennedy half dollars and the first dies were completed at the Philadelphia Mint for Proof coinage production. Two skilled Mint engravers collaborated to design the Kennedy half dollar, neither of whom had time to create an original design for his side of the coin. Chief Engraver Gilroy Roberts modeled his likeness of Kennedy for the obverse after that of the Treasury Department Presidential Medal. For the reverse, Assistant Engraver Frank Gasparro adapted a rendering of the Presidential Seal that had been featured on the Kennedy issue in the Treasury's U.S. Presidents medal series.

The Kennedy half dollar bears the initials of the two engravers, Gilroy Roberts' GR monogram being presented on the truncation of the bust on the obverse and Frank Gasparro's initials between the left talon and the tail feathers of the eagle on the reverse. While many U.S. regular coins carry the initials of the artists who rendered the designs, Roberts became only the third designer to sign his work with a monogram, the others being Anthony De Francisci on the Peace dollar and Augustus Saint-Gaudens on the double eagle. In his participation as designer of the reverse of this coin, Gasparro for the second time shared his signature on a coin with another designer, having become the first to do so in 1959 when he designed the Lincoln Memorial reverse introduced on Victor D. Brenner's cent in tribute to the 150th anniversary of Lincoln's birth.

Although it is a relatively recent addition to the more than two-century-old regular-issue coinage of the United States, the Kennedy half dollar has already garnered several distinctions within the run of half dollar production which commenced in 1794. Just over 10 years into its existence, it was employed as a commemorative in 1975–1976 when the Bicentennial-theme representation of Independence Hall designed by Seth Huntington was mated to the Roberts obverse. Thus far, the Kennedy half dollar has been issued in three metallic varieties—as a .900 fine silver issue in 1964, and also since 1992 in the silver Proof sets; as a silver clad composite netting out to .400 fine silver from 1965–1970, along with 11 million uncirculated and 4 million Proof examples of the 1776–1976 Bicentennial issue; and cupro-nickel clad copper since 1971—and with mintmarks appearing on both the reverse (1964 only) and the obverse (since 1968). More examples of the Kennedy half dollar were produced during the first nine years of its existence—in excess of two billion—than the total combined production of half dollars through the previous 170 years.

1952 Franklin half dollar.

Q. *Can you tell me why the very small eagle is incorporated in the reverse design of the Franklin half dollar? It looks like an afterthought.*

A. It was an afterthought, one that was required to make the coin legal. Chief Mint Engraver John R. Sinnock prepared the designs for the Franklin half dollar in the mid-1940s. His reverse design, being an adaptation of the reverse of the Sesquicentennial of American Independence commemorative half dollar he had executed in 1926 (modeled after a sketch by John Frederick Lewis), did not include an eagle. Sinnock passed away before the tooling workup for minting the Franklin half dollar was prepared. After his death, Mint officials had second thoughts about the wisdom of ignoring a provision of the law of 1873 proscribing that the figure of an eagle appear on the reverse of all silver coins above the denomination of 10 cents, a requirement that has been embodied in every primary coinage law enacted since 1792. Sinnock's successor, Gilroy Roberts, added a small eagle to the right of the Liberty Bell at the direction of Mint officials. That action satisfied the spirit of the law but was criticized by the Commission of Fine Arts, which found the eagle to be "insignificant and hardly discernible."

Liberty Walking half dollar. The incused initials "AW" are near the right-hand end of the branch.

Q. *I have a 1941 Proof set on which the designer's initials (AW) are missing from their usual place on the reverse of the half dollar. I have never seen another set like this, and am wondering if it is unique?*

A. A substantial number of 1941 Proof sets were minted with this error. It probably resulted from the accidental removal of the initials, which appear lightly incused in the coin's surface, from the die. When the die was polished during the production process it is likely that the raised die surface, which created the incuse feature on a finished coin, was polished off.

Q. *Has anyone who wasn't a president ever been portrayed on a U.S. coin?*

A. Many non-presidents have appeared on U.S. commemorative coinage. Benjamin Franklin, later joined by 19th century women's rights activist Susan B. Anthony and Shoshone Indian guide Sacagawea, was the only non-president political figure to appear on a regular-issue U.S. coin through the first 186 years of the country's coinage history. Incidentally, the appearance of the Franklin half dollar marked the third time that a likeness modeled after a bust by Houdon appeared on a regular-issue coin of the United States, the other instances being the Washington quarter and the Jefferson nickel.

Q. *Why are there so many varieties of halves listed in catalogs for the years 1805 to 1836?*

A. There are four basic reasons. First, the half dollar was the highest denomination silver coin in production at the Philadelphia Mint. Second, the quantities produced annually vastly exceeded the quantities for half dimes, dimes, and quarters. Third, the die preparation process during this era was a highly manual, as opposed to mechanized process. Fourth, early on collectors undertook to extensively collect the series by varieties.

The reason halves were produced in large numbers over that 30-year period is that President Thomas Jefferson had suspended the minting of silver dollars in 1804. During 1800 to 1803 the production of silver dollars had exceeded that of half dollars by roughly two to one. That step was taken because the newly minted coins, which were heavier in weight than the worn Spanish milled dollars alongside which they circulated on a part value basis, tended to flow out of the country to cover the purchase of imported goods, or were melted down for bullion.

With the absence of silver dollars for use in large transactions within the country—$10 gold pieces were also discontinued from 1804 to 1838, though half eagles remained in production throughout the period, and quarter eagles were minted only sporadically in very small quantities— half dollars became the desirable coin for the settlement of substantial transactions, bank reserves, and foreign payments. As the halves seldom circulated in the traditional sense, but were principally transferred from bank to bank, they survived in relatively large quantities in better than average condition for coins of the period.

Q. *Can you tell me how many basic types of half dollar there are, and the years they were minted?*

A. Flowing Hair   1794–1795

Flowing Hair	1794–1795
Draped Bust (Small Eagle)	1796–1797
Draped Bust (Heraldic Eagle)	1801–1807
Liberty Cap (First Portrait Style; 50 C.)	1807–1808
Liberty Cap (Second [Remodeled] Portrait Style, 50 C.)	1809–1833
Liberty Cap (Third [Modified] Portrait Style, 50 C.)	1834–1836
Liberty Cap (Motto Removed, 50 CENTS, Reeded Edge)	1836–1837
Liberty Cap (Motto Removed, HALF DOL., Reeded Edge)	1838–1839
Liberty Seated (Without Motto)	1839–1866
Liberty Seated (Arrows and Rays)	1853
Liberty Seated (Arrows, Without Rays)	1854–1855
Liberty Seated (Motto Added to Reverse)	1866–1891
Liberty Seated (Arrows at Date)	1873–1874
Liberty Head (Barber)	1892–1915
Liberty Walking	1916–1947
Franklin Head	1948–1963
Kennedy Head (.900 Silver)	1964
Kennedy Head (.400 Silver)	1965–1970
Kennedy Head (Clad Metal)	1971–Date
Kennedy Head (Clad, American Revolution Bicentennial)	Dated 1776–1976
Kennedy Head (.400 Silver, American Revolution Bicentennial)	Dated 1776–1976

CHAPTER THIRTEEN

Silver Dollars

Q. *Why is there such a multitude of varieties of the U.S. silver dollar series from 1794 to 1803?*

A. During the 1790s and the early 1800s, U.S. coinage dies for all denominations were individually hand engraved, with the inevitable result that no two dies of any design type were truly identical. The difficulty of striking the large coin also resulted in excessive die wear and breakage, so on the average significantly fewer dollar coins could be successfully struck from a die than, say, quarters. During this period, the dollar was the only silver coin minted in appreciable quantities. Thus, the relatively short-lived hand-crafted dies, coupled with an early emphasis on dollar production, could only translate into infinite die varieties.

1804 dollar. The King of American Coins also demands kingly prices. In 1999, one specimen sold for $4,140,000.

Q. *What is the real story behind "The King of American Coins," the silver dollars of 1804?*

A. Proclaimed the "King of American Coins," the prestigious dollar of 1804 is an impostor. It is known to exist in fifteen examples, not a one of which was actually struck in 1804.

The fifteen known examples are segmented into three classes. Eight so-called "originals" form the first class. Seven are so-called "restrikes," six of which are categorized as class three. They are struck on regular planchets with lettered edges. The single specimen of class two is a piece with a plain edge struck over an 1857 Swiss Shooting Thaler, and it reposes in the Smithsonian collection. Their common bond is that all are impostors, but their combined value in today's marketplace likely exceeds $50 million.

The originals were created in 1834 and 1835 when the secretary of state ordered two complete sets of the nation's coinage prepared for presentation to the King of Siam and the Imaum of Muscat. At that time, the silver dollar had not been minted since production was suspended in early 1804, after 19,570 coins had been produced utilizing 1803-dated dies. Apparently, it was reasoned at the time that the 1804 production had been struck utilizing 1804-dated dies. The first specimen of the coin of record to collectors was acquired from the Mint in 1843 by a prominent collector of the day.

It is believed that the restrikes were created clandestinely in 1858 or 1859 for the personal profit of Mint employees, but due to a Mint scandal were concealed until 1869.

It has been said that "'The King of American Coins' is an impostor, but the originals were made for a king." The truth of that observation certainly pertains today, as only a king can afford to own one.

1836 Gobrecht dollar.

Q. *Are the Gobrecht silver dollars of 1836 to 1839 considered to be regular issues?*

A. The famed Gobrecht dollars were prepared in anticipation of a reduction in the fine silver weight standard of the silver dollar that would permit issuing the denomination for the first time since 1804. In view of the fact that the majority of Gobrecht dollars are dated 1836—and that the law reducing the weight of the silver dollar wasn't enacted until January 18, 1837—numismatic authorities consider the coins to be pattern dollars. The government, however, lists them as regular issues, having been struck and released in December of 1836 and March of 1837 (though all were dated 1836). The quantities produced—a combined 1,600 released—and condition of many of the surviving specimens is consistent with the belief that they served as a circulating medium of exchange.

Q. *Why was the coinage of silver dollars suspended from 1804 through 1839?*

A. Speculators, upon learning that in the West Indies the U.S. dollar was accepted at par with the heavier Spanish dollar, shipped the U.S. dollars to the Indies to be exchanged for their heavier counterpart. The Spanish dollars were then turned in to the Philadelphia Mint as bullion to be re-coined into a greater quantity of the lighter U.S. dollar. This abuse prevented the U.S. dollars from circulating and caused President Jefferson to suspend minting of the coin in 1804, although he had no constitutional authority to do so.

1878 Morgan dollar. Reverse details shows parallel top arrow, slanted top arrow, and 7 over 8 tail feathers.

Q. *I understand some of the silver dollars of 1878 have eight tail feathers on the eagle, while all subsequent Morgan dollars have only seven. Why was this change made?*

A. The eight-feather type was made in error, as Morgan's original patterns had seven. To correct this deviation from the approved design, it was necessary to make a new master die with seven feathers. At least one of the working dies that had been made with the eight-feather master die was directly altered by the engraver's hand, thus creating a 7 over 8 tail feathers variety.

There are actually four distinctly different die varieties known for 1878 Philadelphia Mint issues: the eight-feather variety, the 7 over 8 feather variety, and the seven-feather version with both parallel and slanted arrow-feather treatments of the bundle of arrows held in the eagle's claws. While only about 750,000 of the eight-feather variety were minted against a combined quantity of nearly 9.76 million for the other three varieties, all are of relatively equal rarity—except in the upper Mint State range, where the 7 over 8 and seven-feather with slanted arrow-feather varieties command premiums roughly double those for the eight-feather and seven-feather parallel arrow-feather varieties.

1878 Morgan / Liberty Head dollar.

Q. *Is it possible to account for the fact that the 1895 Philadelphia Mint silver dollar is available only in Proof, when the Mint report shows that 12,000 production pieces were struck?*

A. Morgan dollars were coined in amounts fantastically in excess of circulation requirements, as Congress had mandated by law that the Treasury purchase newly mined silver in large quantities in support of Western silver mining interests. Many of the issues were bagged and stored in Treasury vaults for years, with Silver Certificate issues being circulated in their stead. Other supposedly scarce issues (1898-O, 1903-O, and 1904-O) were similarly stowed away in large quantities for over a half-century, but eventually started appearing in quantities when released to banks to satisfy a demand for shiny new dollars to be given to children on Christmas.

Many supposed at the time that the 1895 dollars were similarly tucked away in the Treasury, to eventually surface as inventories depleted. Others believed that they had been melted and re-coined under the provisions of the 1918 Pittman Act, which mandated the melting of silver dollars from Treasury coffers, with more than 270 million being melted down between then and 1921 when the coinage of silver dollars was resumed. Once the Treasury-held reserve of silver dollars was largely dispersed in a series of mid-1970s sales conducted by the government's General Services Administration—at that point about 3 million dollars remained, including large quantities of several Carson City Mint issues—the melting theory seemed to be the obvious answer. Subsequent research has established, however, that the reported 1904 Philadelphia Mint silver dollar production for circulation was of 1903-dated coins, although Proofs dated 1904 were produced.

Q. *Why was there a suspension of silver dollar coinage from 1905 through 1920?*

A. Coinage of silver dollars was suspended in 1904 because the supply of bullion for its minting, which was supplied under the provisions of the Sherman Act of 1890 requiring the Treasury to purchase 4.5 million ounces of newly mined silver per month to be purchased with Treasury Notes. The coinage of silver dollars was suspended from 1904 to 1921 due to a lack of demand. Coinage of silver dollars was resumed in 1921 under provisions of the Pittman Act of 1918, which provided for the melting of minted silver dollars into bullion for the settlement of certain international payments, but also mandated keeping silver dollars in reserve against Silver Certificate circulation.

About the images in this book: In general, coin denominations of 50 cents and higher are pictured at actual size; denominations below 50 cents and coins that are unusually small (e.g., gold dollars) are generally pictured at 150 percent of their actual size. Paper money is typically pictured at page width. Other items, such as medals, encased postage, and so on, may be enlarged for visibility. Appendix B lists the actual sizes of U.S. coins and currency.

1921 Peace dollar.

Q. *I have been told that the Peace dollar represents the first instance where the word "Peace" was used on a coin of any nation. Could this possibly be true?*

A. Yes, unfortunately. But it is not a commemorative coin, though it celebrates the return of peace following World War I, rather than the universal ideal of peace.

In 1920 the American Numismatic Association advanced a proposal for a coin of peace-motif design to commemorate the cessation of hostilities between the Imperial German Government and the people of the United States. Although an enabling resolution for this purpose was allowed to die in Congress without coming to a vote, the peace motif was adopted for the silver dollar under the terms of the Act of 1890, which permits design change without congressional approval in the instance of a coin that has been minted for 25 years.

Q. *Is there more than one variety of the Peace dollar?*

A. There are two major varieties of this coin. The 1921 dollars were struck with concave fields and high relief on the Liberty portrait and the at-rest eagle. The 1922 to 1935 dollars were struck with flat fields and shallower relief on the features. While some 35,000 silver dollars of the high relief variety were minted in early 1922, most if not all of them were subsequently officially melted; 1922 Proofs do exist in both the high and low relief varieties, with the low relief being of greater rarity. The high relief coins have eight rays below the eagle's tail and four below the "N" of ONE. The low relief coins have six rays below the tail (seven have been reported on some of the later dates) and three below the "N."

Q. *I have a silver dollar on which there is a mistake in the lettering. It is a 1922 Peace dollar, and I have noticed that the word "Trust" in the motto "In God We Trust" is misspelled TRVST. How much is such an error worth?*

A. The spelling of the word "Trust" as TRVST is not an error. It is so spelled on all Peace dollars, and on Liberty Standing quarters as well. The substitution of a "V" for a "U" has been extensively employed in inscriptions appearing on public buildings and monuments, and on other coins as well, although much less frequently.

The immediate precedent of this usage will be found in Old English, where the letters "U" and "V" were used interchangeably until the 15th to 17th centuries, the latter being used as the printed form, and the former as the cursive or written form wherein the letters of a word are joined. The distant precedent will be found in Latin, where "V" was first used as a vowel interchangeable with "U," and only later as a consonant.

Q. *Was the minting of silver dollars suspended from 1928 until 1934 because the Treasury was overstocked with them?*

A. Overstocking of unnecessary silver dollars was a normal condition during the reign of the powerful Western Silver Lobby. The Pittman Act, which authorized the melting of reserve silver dollars and sale of the bullion to Britain, also provided that the dollars disposed of be replaced with dollars coined from newly mined silver. Satisfaction of this stipulation was achieved by April of 1928, at which time the minting of silver dollars ceased. The 1934 and 1935 mintages were carried out under an executive proclamation.

Q. *Why is it that no traditional silver dollars were coined for circulation after 1935?*

A. Throughout its long and vexatious history, the U.S. silver dollar was never essential to the welfare of the domestic marketplace. In our nation's early days, it was principally utilized to ship abroad in quantity to pay for imports. In the latter part of the 19th and early part of the 20th centuries it served chiefly as a subsidy for the Western silver mines. Subsequently, it was justified solely by the Silver Certificate redemption pledge which stipulated: ". . . there has been deposited in the Treasury . . . One Silver Dollar payable to the bearer on demand." When that obligation was changed after 1935 to read, ". . . One Dollar in Silver payable to the bearer on demand," that need vanished, for thereafter (until 1967 when the tie between silver and our circulating currency was completely severed) silver bullion on deposit became legally sufficient backing.

1977-S Eisenhower dollar.

Q. *I often hear people refer to the Eisenhower dollar as a silver dollar, but am wondering if that is correct terminology, as any circulated examples of this coin that I have encountered appear to be made of a similar metallic composition to that used for dimes, quarters, and halves?*

A. Actually, that terminology could be considered technically correct, as the enabling legislation passed in 1970 stipulated the coin be minted of both silver and cupro-nickel clad copper, but with only the latter intended for circulation. While Eisenhower dollars have the same physical diameter (38.1mm) as traditional silver dollars, they are somewhat lighter in both versions. The traditional silver dollars, minted from 1840 through 1935, were struck of .900 fine silver with a total weight of 26.73 grams, the pure silver weight of each being 0.77344 ounce. From 1971 through the 1975–1976 issue, the Eisenhower silver dollars were struck of a clad silver composite with a .400 fine silver content, the pure silver weight of each being 0.3161 ounce. The cupro-nickel clad Eisenhower dollars were minted from 1971 through 1978, the weight of these pieces being just 22.68 grams. Silver versions of the Eisenhower dollar were struck and sold to collectors in both uncirculated and Proof qualities. The silver Eisenhower dollar issues through 1975–1976 (Bicentennial) stand as the last hurrah of the Western Silver Lobby, their champion being Senator James McClure of Idaho.

Q. *Until the mid-1960s I was always able to obtain like-new silver dollars from any local bank to give out as birthday, anniversary, and Christmas gifts, but they never seem to have any now. What happened to the onetime plentiful supply of these?*

A. In 1964, an upsurge of interest in silver dollars—stemming from the belief that no more of them would be coined, and the awareness (caused by the release in 1962 of some hitherto rare issues) that uncirculated dollars of desirable dates were available—resulted in a raid on the Treasury's remaining inventory. This development became known as the "Great Treasury Raid of 1964," which depleted Treasury stocks by 25 million coins. At that point the Treasury suspended distribution of the remainder to formulate a plan for selling them at a premium. That development was followed closely by a rise in the bullion price of silver, causing the government to abandon traditional silver coinage in 1965, which drove all silver coins (including silver dollars) out of circulation.

1794 Flowing Hair dollar.

Q. *Is it true that the silver dollars of 1794 and part of those struck in 1795 comprise an unauthorized issue?*

A. Technically, yes. The standard for the first U.S. silver dollar, as determined by an analysis of Spanish dollars culled from circulation, proved deficient to full-weight Spanish dollars in weight and fineness. Acting on his own, but in anticipation of passage of remedial legislation then before Congress, Mint Director David Rittenhouse increased the silver content of the dollar, striking 1,758 1794 dollars and 203,033 in 1795 to this illegal standard. While the legal standard called for 371.25 grains of silver content in a 416 grains coin, resulting in a fineness of 0.8924, the coins actually contained 374.75 grains of silver, for a fineness of 0.900.

Q. *Why was the decision made to strike the Eisenhower dollar in two metallic varieties?*

A. The decision was a compromise to end an 18-month stalemate between the pro-silver Senate and the anti-silver House of Representatives. The compromise bill authorized a clad cupro-nickel dollar for general circulation and a limited collector issue of 150 million .400 fine silver pieces to be offered as uncirculated and Proof specimens at $3 and $10, respectively.

Q. *Is it true that the dollar coin was resurrected after the death of President Eisenhower specifically to provide a medium for an Eisenhower commemorative?*

A. At the time of Eisenhower's death, a "non-silver dollar" for commerce had already been proposed. The timing of the two proposals was certainly a convenience, in that it enabled Congress to avoid the usual controversy that prevailed at the time, when the government stridently opposed design changes on coins struck for circulation and the offering of commemorative coin issues.

Q. *I recently read that the Eisenhower dollar was intended to be a quarter. Is this true?*

A. There were a number of proposals for creating a numismatic recognition of the life and achievements of President Eisenhower. Congressman William J. Scherle of Iowa introduced a proposal calling for an Eisenhower quarter dollar on March 31, 1969, just three days after Eisenhower's death. In the following weeks there were other proposals introduced, including one for a one-dollar Eisenhower note.

Q. *I have heard that Peace dollars were minted in 1964. What's the story?*

A. On August 3, 1964, President Johnson authorized the minting of 45 million .900 fine silver Peace dollars. At some point during the first half of 1965, 30 trial pieces, 76 die adjustment coins, and 316,000 1964-D dollars were struck of the Peace dollar design. Congressional criticism and a general lack of enthusiasm within the Treasury Department for the striking of silver dollars caused the minting order to be rescinded on May 25, 1965. Mint officials maintain that all of the struck coins were subsequently melted and the dies destroyed. Skepticism in numismatic circles maintains that a small quantity of at least seven of the 1964-D Peace dollars escaped the melting pot, but none have surfaced after more than 40 years, perhaps due to the likelihood that if one were to be displayed or offered at auction, it would likely be confiscated by federal authorities.

Q. *A collector friend maintains that the reason no silver dollars were coined from 1874 through 1877 was the new Mint law of 1873 did not make a provision for the coining of a silver dollar. This does not seem reasonable to me, so I would like to have your opinion?*

A. Your friend knows the coinage laws. The clumsy and involved revision of coinage laws in 1873—in some quarters referred to as the "Crime of '73"—dropped the regular-issue silver dollar entirely, in effect placing the country on a gold standard. The same law authorized the minting of a heavier trade dollar, which initially did not enjoy legal tender status within the country.

1874 trade dollar.

Q. *What is the difference between a standard silver dollar and a trade dollar, and what was the purpose for which the trade dollar was intended?*

A. Aside from the obvious difference in design, the trade dollar contained 420 grains of .900 fine silver, which was 7-1/2 grains more than the 412.5 authorized for the regular-issue dollar, providing the coin with a 1.8 percent greater fine silver content than that of the Liberty Seated silver dollars of 1840 to 1873. This heavy dollar was issued for the benefit of importers dealing with merchants in China and was intended to compete in the Orient with the favored Mexican silver dollar, which the lighter regular-issue U.S. dollar had been unable to do.

The coinage law provisions of February 12, 1873, extended domestic legal tender status to trade dollars in amounts not exceeding $5, a step which effectively based the country's monetary standard on a gold basis going forward. This action effectively placed the face value of the coin greatly in excess of its bullion value, and as silver prices fell in the West, they began to flood into circulation. This negative economic impact led to the enactment of legislation on July 22, 1976, revoking the legal tender status. Minting of the coins in substantial quantities continued through 1878 for the Orient trade—trade dollars are frequently encountered with oriental "chop marks" that served to certify their value in that trade—when the act of February 28, 1878, authorized resumption of production of the 412.5 grains .900 fine silver dollar as a legal tender coin. The minting of Proof trade dollars continued through 1883, with the law authorizing trade dollars being repealed in 1887 and the Treasury authorized to redeem all trade dollars that were not "mutilated."

Q. *Why am I having so much trouble locating 1973 Eisenhower dollars for the sets I am putting together for my great-grandsons?*

A. The 1973 Ike dollars are the keys to the series among the regular issue offerings. While the 1971, 1972, 1976 (Bicentennial), 1977, and 1978 issues were struck in large quantities at both mints for circulation issue, in 1973 the U.S. Mint found that the nearly 285 million dollar coins it had produced the previous two years had pretty much filled the coffers of the nation's banking system. As a result, it was determined that the only dollars minted in circulation quantity that year would be for inclusion in official Mint sets, with 2,000,056 being produced at Philadelphia and 2,000,000 at Denver. As only 1,767,691 Mint sets were officially produced, the balance of both productions was destroyed at the Mint.

Aside from one variety of the 1972 cupro-nickel clad Ike produced for circulation, the "King of the Ikes" is the 1973-S silver clad Proof, of which only 1,013,140 examples were struck, and the 1976-S (Bicentennial) silver clad uncirculated, of which about 11 million were struck, from a value perspective. With the exception of that one minting variety of the 1972 issue, all clad Ikes in circulation condition are nominally priced. Those in uncirculated condition, with the exception of the 1973 offerings, generally command premiums in the range of five times face, while San Francisco minted cupro-nickel clad Proofs generally command premiums double that level, as do silver clad Proofs with the exception of the 1973-S issue.

Q. *The law of April 2, 1792, established the dollar as the "unit" of the U.S. decimal system of coinage. What is meant by "unit" in this instance?*

A. In the era of bullion coinages, the "unit" of a nation's coinage system was the standard from which the bullion values and denominational indices of all other coins in the monetary system were calculated.

Q. *Where did George Morgan place his initial on the Liberty Head dollar he designed?*

A. In two places, both cleverly concealed. His initial "M" can be found at the tip of the hair scroll on the truncation of the neck on the obverse, and inside the left loop of the wreath bow on the reverse.

Q. *Isn't there something unusual about the appearance of IN GOD WE TRUST on Morgan's Liberty Head dollar?*

A. Morgan engraved the motto with Old English or Gothic lettering, the first use of this kind of lettering style on a U.S. coin.

Q. *I have been told that an 1885 Proof specimen of the U.S. trade dollar that sold in 2004 for over $1 million was illegally struck. Could this be so?*

A. The origin of the ten 1884 and five 1885 Proof trade dollar specimens that are known to exist will probably remain one of the mysteries of numismatics. The Mint has no record of Proof trade dollars being struck during those two years, the first knowledge of their existence not unfolding until nearly 25 years later. It is believed these valuable rarities resulted from private enterprise at the Mint. If the latter theory is correct, the coins are illegal.

Q. *Is it true that it was once possible to buy silver dollars from the U.S. Mint for less than face value?*

A. Yes. This opportunity was provided by America's only unwanted and unhonored coin—the only coin of the United States ever to be demonetized—the infamous U.S. trade dollar.

Anyone who so wished could purchase trade dollars from the Mint for 378 grains of silver and a coining charge. When it was first issued in 1873, a trade dollar in the United States was worth about $1.05 in gold. Over the following three years, the price of silver declined dramatically, making it possible for holders of bullion to have it coined into trade dollars at a total cost of less than the declared legal tender face value of the coins. When the legal tender status of the trade dollar was revoked in 1876, the gold value of the silver it contained had tumbled to 83 cents. There was, of course, a catch to it. When the merchants realized that the banks wouldn't accept trade dollars for deposit at face value, they began discounting trade dollars tendered to them for payment of goods by 10 percent and more.

Q. *I have seen U.S. trade dollars advertised as "free of chop marks," or "three neatly spaced chops on obverse." What is meant by this reference to "chop marks?"*

A. The chop marks frequently found on the obverse and/or reverse of trade dollars that traveled to the Orient and back were put there by Chinese merchants at a time when a silver dollar was expected to contain a dollar's worth of silver. The presence of a chop mark indicated that the merchant identified by the Chinese character stamped on the coin had tested it and found its weight and fineness to be as represented. The presence of this mark enabled him and others to accept the coin without the bother of testing should a future trade transaction return it to him.

Many collectors consider chop-marked trade dollars to be defaced or damaged, and therefore less valuable as a collector item. Others appreciate their historical significance. A device reminiscent of the Britannia of Roman coins struck on American silver and "defaced" by an Oriental moneychanger provides a numismatic combination that span three disparate civilizations.

1976 Ike Bicentennial dollar. Details show bold and delicate lettering on reverse.

Q. *What distinction did the appearance of the Bicentennial commemorative Eisenhower dollar bring to Frank Gasparro, designer of the regular-issue Eisenhower dollar?*

A. Adoption of the Bicentennial dollar reverse designed by Dennis R. Williams marked the third time Gasparro's signature initials had appeared on a U.S. coin with those of other designers. The first two instances were the Lincoln Memorial cent reverse that appeared in 1959, which he shared with Victor D. Brenner as designer of the obverse portrait introduced in 1909, and the Kennedy half dollar reverse, for which Gilroy Roberts designed the obverse.

Q. *Can you tell me how many basic types of the traditional silver dollar coin there are and the years they were minted?*

A. Flowing Hair 1794–1795
Draped Bust (Small Eagle) 1795–1798
Draped Bust (Heraldic Eagle) 1798–1803
Gobrecht (generally considered to be a
    pattern issue) 1836–1839
Liberty Seated (Without Motto) 1840–1866
Liberty Seated (With Motto) 1866–1873
Trade Dollar 1873–1885
Liberty Head (Morgan) 1878–1921
Liberty Head (Peace) 1921–1935
Eisenhower Head (Copper-Nickel Clad) ... 1971–1974, 1977–1978
Eisenhower Head (.400 Silver Clad for
    Collectors) 1971–1974, 1977–1978
Eisenhower Head (Bicentennial Reverse;
    Copper-Nickel Clad) .... Dated 1776–1976
Eisenhower Head (Bicentennial Reverse;
    .400 Silver Clad) .... Dated 1776–1976

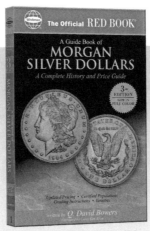

For more information: Consult the *Guide Book of Morgan Silver Dollars* (Bowers).

CHAPTER FOURTEEN

Anthony, Sacagawea, and Presidential Dollars

Q. *What was the first official act in the drive to put Susan B. Anthony on the dollar coin?*

A. House Bill No. 12728, calling for the new small-size dollar coin and providing for the effigy of Susan B. Anthony to be represented thereon, was passed by a 6 to 1 vote on July 23, 1978, by the Historic Preservation & Coinage Subcommittee of the House Committee on Banking, Finance & Urban Affairs.

Q. *Why did the Mint make the mistake of making the Anthony dollar almost the same size as the quarters?*

A. The principal reasons were economy, and the feeling that the public would not respond to a bulky, cumbersome coin of the old dollar size. They were right about the second reason, but the public rejected the coin anyway, at least in part because it was readily confused with the quarter. The coin was originally envisioned as a multi-sided coin—11 short facets, which were ultimately represented on the border with a perfectly round circumference—but what resulted was a round coin, as it was concluded that the round shape was preferable for vending machine applications, which likely adversely influenced user confusion and its acceptance. A contributing factor may also have been the coin's reeded edge. The quarter is roughly equally larger than the nickel, which has a plain edge, but since both quarters and Anthony dollars have reeded edges, many of the latter were unknowingly tendered as quarters, so when received in change they usually were returned to the banks, rather than maintained in circulation.

Q. *Is there a difference between the clad metal composition of the Anthony dollar and that employed on dimes and quarters as introduced in 1965?*

A. The inner core of clad Roosevelt dimes, Washington quarters, and Kennedy halves is uniformly of pure copper, and the clad outer surfaces are of the same composition (.750 copper and .250 nickel), but the clad layers are significantly thicker on the Anthony dollar. Also, trial strike Anthony dollar pieces were prepared in an alloy consisting of .820 copper and .180 nickel.

Q. *Didn't the Post Offices and the Army get involved in trying to make the Anthony dollars circulate?*

A. Although, when the Anthony dollar was first released, the U.S. Post Office system was enlisted as a primary outlet to get the coins into circulation by passing large quantities in the conduct of business, that effort only delayed the inevitable trip back to the bank. The Defense Department also tried to force service personnel stationed in Europe to use the coins in place of paper dollars, but that initiative collapsed as well because the coins were seldom accepted for exchange into other currencies and when they were, it was generally at a discounted value.

The logic behind circulating a dollar coin in favor of a paper dollar is sound—as this answer is being drafted, three of the eight quarters in my pocket change date from the 1970s, and it is not at all untypical for me to find a 1965, 1967, or 1968 dated quarter in such an assortment. A typical clad metal coin will enjoy an active circulating life of at least 25 to 30 years, as opposed to just a few months greater than one year for a paper dollar. The real reason that the Anthony dollar coins did not gain a foothold in circulation is the fact that the effort was undertaken without discontinuing production of paper dollars.

When our Canadian neighbors introduced their Loon Dollar in 1987 and their bi-metallic Polar Bear $2 coin in 1996, following a limited transition period the comparable notes were systematically retired from circulation. That was similarly the case in Great Britain in 1983 when a circulating one pound coin was introduced, followed by a two pound coin in 1986. There are a number of other examples, including Australia in 1984 and 1988 with one and two dollar coins, New Zealand in 1990 with one and two dollar coins, South Africa with the one rand in 1977 and the two rand in 1989, and other countries both large and small around the globe.

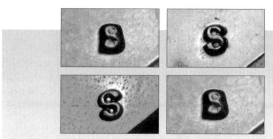

Four types of "S" mintmarks. Left to right, from top: Type 1 "Blob" discontinued July 1979; Type 2 geometric design introduced in July 1979; Type 1 (1981) created with the same master introduced in July 1979, but now deteriorated; Type 2 (1981) irregular curves design introduced July 1981.

Q. *I see references to varieties of Anthony dollars—identified as Type I and II—for both 1979 and 1981. What are they?*

A. All six of the Proof coins of those years—cent through dollar for both years—feature one of two different "S" mintmarks. In both instances the mintmark punch broke mid-year, requiring the introduction of new punches which differed slightly in their treatment. Also in both cases, the second (Variety II) mintmarks have the greater value, as all six of those varieties have relatively low mintages of less than one million, as opposed to 2.5 million to 3 million of Variety I.

Q. *What can you tell me about the differences between the "narrow" and "wide" rim varieties of the 1979 Anthony dollar?*

A. For starters, the "wide" rim variety was introduced into production only at the Philadelphia Mint late in the year, with all issues in subsequent years at all mints being of that style. Thus, only the "narrow" rim variety is encountered on coins struck for circulation at the Denver and San Francisco mints, and on the year's Proof production as well. On the "narrow" rim variety, the date is widely separated from the rim, while on the "wide" rim variety the feet of the date characters rest very close to the rim.

Q. *What were the cost comparisons on the manufacture of an Anthony dollar compared to a paper dollar?*

A. At the time of authorization, paper money costs ran about 1.8 cents per note, while the Anthony dollars cost was about three cents apiece to mint. The savings was to be in the difference in survival rates. While a dollar bill enjoys a circulation life average of only about 18 months, a metal coin was calculated to have a minimum life of 15 years in circulation. In fact, were it not for the attrition factor of coins being lost or otherwise retired from circulation, the true circulating life of a clad Anthony dollar would have been more like 30 years.

Q. *Was there a standard number of Anthony dollars in a roll?*

A. There were at least three standards. They included the old 20 dollars to a roll unit for the Morgan, Peace, and Ike dollars. Another popular unit size was 25 to a roll, and some banks even wrapped them 40 to a roll, just like quarters.

1979 Anthony dollar. Details of the near-date (left) and far-date varieties. Notice the distance between the "1" and the edge on each.

Q. *Can you explain why there is such a great price differential between the "near" and "far" date varieties of 1979-P Anthony dollars?*

A. This being the only major variety in the Anthony dollar series, there is some mystery about the ongoing rarity of the "near" date 1979-P variety, as Mint officials have estimated that "up to" 160,750,000 dollars were struck with the date closer to the rim, which is only marginally less than half of that year's production at the Philadelphia Mint. As more than 95 percent of Anthony dollars struck for circulation issue over the 21-year life of the issue were minted in 1979 and 1980—quantities from just these two years greatly exceeded the resulting demand—it is believed that nearly all of the "near" date variety may even today remain buried in Federal Reserve bank vaults. The "near" date variety is also alternatively revered to as the "wide" rim variety, while the "far" date variety also finds designation as the "narrow" rim variety. The "near" date, "wide" rim variety displays the date much closer to the rim than does the "far" date, "narrow" rim variety.

Q. *Why was the switch made to the Sacagawea dollar coin just 21 years after the Anthony dollar had been introduced? I thought U.S. coin designs could not be changed more frequently than every 25 years?*

A. While the Secretary of the Treasury is prohibited from changing circulating coin designs more frequently than every 25 years, Congress can mandate such changes. In this instance, a 1997 law stipulated that dollar coins be struck of a new design representing a new American woman and of a new composition. This action was taken with the intention of creating a dollar coin that would circulate "alongside" the paper dollar. Promoted as the "Golden Dollar," the new coin was struck in a new metal comprised of a manganese-brass composition— .770 copper, .120 zinc, .070 manganese, and .040 nickel—of a golden hue, layered on a pure copper core, so it would possess the electrical and magnetic coin discrimination properties of the Anthony dollars. It was believed (wrongly, as it turned out) that a coin possessing that appearance, and boasting a plain edge—rather than a reeded edge, like the Anthony dollar—would be favorably received by the public, as it would be clearly distinct from the similar sized quarter. While more than 1.4 billion of the Sacagawea dollars were produced for circulation in the first two years—2000 and 2001—a quantity about two-thirds greater than the first two years of Anthony dollar production, the coin is still only infrequently encountered outside the banking and collector communities.

Q. *I understand that in addition to the annual Proof examples of the Sacagawea dollar, there was a special "Presentation Finish" edition produced of the 2000-P issue. What can you tell me about this piece?*

A. Artist Glenna Goodacre, who was responsible for the obverse design depicting Native American Shoshone Sacagawea carrying her infant son Jean Baptiste on her back papoose style, received payment for her contribution in the form of 5,000 coins of a special finish. She privately marketed these pieces, which are high quality uncirculated specimens, not Proofs, and now command a hefty premium. In fact, one could purchase one example of each uncirculated and Proof version of the coin produced through the first eight years of the series for approximately half of what a single example of the Goodacre presentation pieces commands.

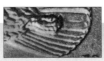 

2000 Sacagawea dollar. Tail feather details.

Q. *Are there any varieties of the Sacagawea dollar?*

A. The only true variety documented to this point is a rare Philadelphia Mint variety of 2000, on which the tail feathers of the eagle are boldly detailed. This variety is also sometimes referred to as having 13 tail feathers rather than 12. The die for this production was prepared from a prototype hub, which also prepared the die employed for the production of a small quantity of 22-karat gold specimens struck at West Point in mid-1999 using 2000-W dated dies. While 39 of these gold specimens were struck, 27 were subsequently melted, with the 12 remaining being carried into space on the July 17, 1999, Columbia shuttle mission. Controversial in origin, these "gold" Sacagaweas are of questionable legal status and have subsequently reposed in the Fort Knox bullion depository. There is also a Mint error variety of the Sacagawea dollar, a quantity of specimens with the Sacagawea obverse displaced by a 50 States Quarter® obverse, mated to the soaring eagle reverse of the Sacagawea.

Q. *How did it happen that Glenna Goodacre was engaged to prepare the designs for the Sacagawea dollar?*

A. Glenna Goodacre was selected in a national competition from among 120 submissions that were considered by a selection panel appointed by Treasury Secretary Robert Rubin. She was, however, only responsible for the obverse design of the piece, her model for the portrait being a Native American student at the University of New Mexico, Randy'L He-dow Teton, as no image of Sacagawea exists. The reverse was prepared by U.S. Mint sculptor and engraver Thomas D. Rogers Sr. The obverse representation was intended to exemplify the spirit of liberty, peace, and freedom shown by Sacagawea in her conduct as interpreter and guide to explorers Meriwether Lewis and William Clark during their Louisiana Purchase Expedition of 1804 and 1805.

Anthony (left) and Sacagawea reverses.

Q. *It seems unusual to me that the reverse of the Sacagawea dollar depicts the soaring eagle in a circle of 17 stars, in contrast to the 13 stars that encircle the Flame of Liberty on the Bicentennial quarter, beneath Independence Hall on the Bicentennial half and on both the obverse and reverse of the Anthony dollar. What's the story?*

A. The 17 stars represented on the reverse of the Sacagawea dollar represent the number of states in the Union—the original 13 states, plus Vermont (1791), Kentucky (1792), Tennessee (1796), and Ohio (1803)—at the time of the Lewis and Clark Expedition. Silver and gold coin issues of the 1790s were produced from dies featuring various arrays of 13, 15, and 16 stars on both the obverses and reverses, depending on the number of states in the Union at the time they were created. Subsequent to that time, practice was to feature just 13 stars representing the original 13 states on regular issue coins.

In the interim no circulation issue coins carried more than 13 stars in a given representation, although the Missouri (24) and Alabama (22) commemorative offerings of 1921 did, while the Kennedy half dollar with its representation of the presidential seal on the reverse did feature 50 stars. Interestingly, the reverse of the Lewis & Clark Bicentennial silver dollar of 2004 was also rendered with a field of 17 stars arrayed above a representation of the clasped hands Indian Peace Medal. Also, the 2000 New Hampshire issue in the 50 States Quarter® series carried just nine stars, the 2001 New York issue 11 stars, and the Indiana issue 19 stars, representing their respective orders of admission.

CHAPTER FIFTEEN

Commemoratives, Past and Present

Bicentennial coins. The quarter, half dollar, and dollar each got a new reverse design for the Bicentennial, and a new dual date for the obverse.

Q. *What is a commemorative coin?*

A. All coins are commemoratives to the extent that by their existence they affirm and recall the beginning and development of art and metallurgy, the rise of nationalism, the development of monetary theory, etc.

Our present regular-issue presidential-theme coinage honors the achievement of past presidents who left indelible marks on our nation and society.

However, by definition and practice, the official commemorative coins of the United States have been issued supplementary to and concurrent with the regular-issue coinage to specifically honor a person, place, or event—generally in celebration of an anniversary. They were struck by the U.S. Mint with authority from Congress and, though generally sold for a premium, they are legal tender for their face value.

Regrettably (and this caused their suspension in 1954) most U.S. commemoratives have been commercially—as well as historically— motivated and their issuance facilitated through political connections. Rather than being released to general circulation, the early issues of the classic commemorative period (1892–1954) were generally sold to the sponsoring commemorative commissions at face value, to be resold to the public at a premium. The modern commemorative issues (since 1982) have generally been sold as a U.S. Mint program, with designated proceeds from sales being earmarked for the benefit of organizations tied to the event, place, or person honored.

Commemoratives were issued intermittently from 1892 through 1954 in 157 distinct varieties, including mintmarks and dates. That total includes 48 major types of half dollars, creating 143 varieties; one silver dollar; one quarter dollar; six major types of gold dollars forming nine varieties; two 2-1/2 gold pieces; and two $50 gold slugs.

Commemorative designs were adapted to our circulation issue quarter, half dollar, and dollar coinage in 1975 and 1976 in commemoration of the Bicentennial of the American Revolution.

In 1982, following a 28-year lapse, the matter of special-issue commemoratives was renewed with the introduction of a single coin: a half dollar marking the 250th anniversary of George Washington's birth. Over the subsequent 25 years (through 2006) the number of modern commemorative issues vastly eclipsed the number of types and varieties issued over the 63-year period from 1892 through 1954. The 49 commemorative issues over that time (an average of two per year) have embraced 95 types, of which 26 were offerings tied to the Olympic Games. Of the 95 types, 16 were half dollars, 54 were silver dollars, 20 were $5 gold pieces, and five were $10 gold pieces. Inclusive of mintmark varieties, the number of distinctive issues is 134, without considering the various uncirculated and Proof editions that were offered of some types, bringing to 197 the grand total of varieties. And there is no end in sight! Even more commemoratives have been issued in recent years.

2000 Library of Congress $10 gold.

Q. *What do you consider to be the most significant issues within the modern commemorative series?*

A. I would probably point to five: the 1982 George Washington 250th anniversary half dollar issue, the 2000 Library of Congress $10 piece, the 2001 American Buffalo offering, the 2002 West Point Bicentennial silver dollar, and the 2006 San Francisco silver dollar and $5 gold piece set. Each of these represents truly significant additions to the series.

The 1982 Washington half dollar is a truly unique coin within the series. Struck of .900 fine silver, in addition to being the first .900 fine coin struck by the U.S. Mint subsequent to 1964, it is the only one of 16 half dollar types struck during the modern era that has a .900 fine silver content, as opposed to the customary cupro-nickel clad composition. Featuring a classic representation of George Washington astride his horse on the obverse, with his Mount Vernon home depicted on the reverse, it was designed and sculpted by Elizabeth Jones during the time she was on the Mint's engraving staff.

The 2000 Library of Congress $10 piece provides another purely unique ingredient for the series. In addition to being the only the second $10 commemorative coin ever issued, the other being the 1984 Los Angeles Olympiad commemorative, it is the only bimetallic coin ever struck by the U.S. Mint for circulation. It is comprised of a platinum disk set within a gold ring. This coin can claim some kinship to the famous 1792 silver center cent pattern, which was struck with a small silver plug in the center of a copper planchet roughly the size of the half cent introduced in 1793.

The 2001 American Buffalo silver dollar commemorative is an intriguing offering, one that resurrected, with slight modification, the James E. Fraser Indian or Buffalo nickel design of 1913. Five years later that original design, with fewer modifications, was also subsequently adapted to the $50 American Buffalo .9999 fine gold one ounce bullion piece.

The 2002 West Point Bicentennial silver dollar from a design standpoint is a rather mundane offering. The West Point Bullion Depository, built as a major repository for the Treasury's silver inventory and operated by the U.S. Mint, under legislation enacted on October 18, 1973, was converted to coinage operations as of July 29, 1974, producing cents and quarters over the next ten years utilizing dies indistinguishable from those employed at the Philadelphia Mint. All of the U.S. commemorative gold coins of the modern series have been struck at the West Point minting facility, with the exception of some quantities of the 1984 Los Angeles Olympiad issue and the 2006 San Francisco Old Mint offering, and bear the "W" mintmark of the facility, as do eight of the silver dollar varieties and one of the 1993 Bill of Rights half dollar varieties.

My final candidate for the most significant list would be the 2006 San Francisco Old Mint issue, consisting of a silver dollar and a five dollar gold piece. This is a very meaningful numismatic offering, as the obverses of both pieces present rendering of the old Mint which survived and was instrumental in San Francisco's recovery from the disastrous earthquake and fire of 1906. The reverse of the silver dollar reproduces the Morgan dollar type minted from 1878 to 1921, while the five dollar gold piece reproduces the Liberty Head gold half eagle of the type minted from 1856 to 1908 with the motto "In God We Trust."

Q. *I have a rare Columbian half dollar. It was found in my grandfather's estate. How much is it worth?*

A. The Columbian half dollar is historically significant in being the first U.S. commemorative coin, but it is neither rare nor particularly valuable. In fact, in basic uncirculated condition, both the 1892 and 1893 dated issues command a modest premium, the lowest by about two-thirds of all issues from the classic commemoratives series, with the exception of type coins of the 1946 to 1954 Booker T. Washington and Carver/Washington issues.

It was issued in conjunction with the World's Columbian Exposition in Chicago in 1893, the theme of which was the 400th anniversary of the first voyage of Columbus to the Americas. In lieu of a requested $5 million appropriation to help defray the cost of the exposition, Congress authorized the striking of 2,500,000 souvenir half dollars from subsidiary silver coin held by the Treasury. They were sold at the exposition for $1 each.

A delay in the opening of the exposition—the intended October 1892, opening was delayed to May 1, 1893—resulted in two date varieties of the coin, 1892 and 1893. As a substantial number of the coins remained unsold when the exposition closed on October 30, 1893, about 2.5 million of the four million 1893 strikes were melted, leaving net mintages of slightly more than 1.5 million 1893 dated strikes, against the 1892 production of slightly less than one million. The unsold stocks of the 1892 strikes were released into circulation by the Chicago banks holding them as par security against loans. The Columbian half is one of the few classic commemorative issues frequently encountered in circulated condition.

1900 Lafayette dollar.

Q. *Is it true that we issued a silver dollar in honor of Lafayette?*

A. Yes. The commemorative Lafayette silver dollar of 1900 was issued in conjunction with the erection of an equestrian statue of Lafayette in Paris during the Exposition of 1900. Both the statue and the enabling coin were an expression of gratitude to the French nation for Lafayette's contribution to the rebel cause during the American War for Independence. It is numismatically significant in being the first U.S. commemorative of one-dollar denomination and the only silver dollar in the classic commemorative series. It was also the first authorized U.S. coin to bear the portrait of one of our presidents (Washington), jugate on the obverse with that of Lafayette.

This coin was sold by the Lafayette Memorial Commission for $2 each with the profits, augmented by contributions ($50,000) from American schoolchildren, going toward the Lafayette statue. The inscription on the reverse records the role played by the schoolchildren in bringing the memorial project to fruition. The act authorizing the Lafayette dollar also specified that the issue would serve as a commemoration of the centennial of Washington's death; all were struck during a 10-hour press day on December 14, 1899, the exact day of the centennial of Washington's death.

Q. *What is the Isabella quarter? How valuable is it?*

A. The Isabella quarter, bearing the portrait of Queen Isabella I of Spain, was the second commemorative coin issue of the United States. It was also the first and only 25-cent issue in either the classic or modern commemorative coin series. It must be mentioned for the record, however, that the 1932 Washington quarter was initially intended to be a commemorative, but was continued as a regular issue in 1934, and that the "Drummer Boy" Bicentennial quarter of 1975/76 was produced as a regular issue commemorative.

Pressure upon Congress by Susan B. Anthony and the suffrage movement led to a provision for a coin to benefit the efforts and pay tribute to the participation of the Board of Lady Managers at the Columbian Exposition. Part of the money allotted to them to promote their interest in the exposition was generated from the striking of 40,023 Isabella quarters intended for sale as souvenirs at $1 each. Ultimately, slightly more than 24,000 were issued, with nearly 16,000 being melted following the close of the exposition. Not surprisingly, Isabella quarters command much higher prices than do Columbian halves.

1920–1921 Pilgrim Tercentenary half dollar.

Q. *Does the Pilgrim half dollar commemorate one or two events?*

A. The Pilgrim Tercentenary commemorative half dollar was issued in 1920 to commemorate the 300th anniversary of the landing of the Pilgrims. It was reissued in 1921 with the addition of the 1921 date in the obverse field to the left of the portrait that represents Governor William Bradford of the Pilgrim Plantations. There is an opinion that the 1921-dated issues commemorate the 300th anniversary of the founding of Plymouth, but it is by no means a unanimous one. It is more likely that the presence of the 1921 date is in keeping with legal requirements of the Mint Act of 1873, stipulating that U.S. coins must be dated in the year of their production. With an authorized production of 300,000 pieces, 200,000 were minted in October 1920, with the Pilgrim Tercentenary Commission ordering the remaining 100,000 struck in July 1921.

1921 Alabama 2x2 half dollar.

Q. *Why is a "2x4" sometimes appended to listings of the Missouri commemorative half?*

A. The reason can be found in your pocketbook. The "x" stands for a five-pointed star inserted between a 2 and 4 that appears on the obverse of about a fourth of the Missouri Centennial half dollars. This feature was added to this issue deliberately to create a "variety" to lure the dollar of the collector haunted by the notion that his devotion to the hobby is measured by the completeness of his collection. The first 5,000 halves were minted with this feature, which was incuse in the field, being raised on the die; thereafter the feature was ground off the die, and another 25,000 were struck without it. While all 5,000 of the 2x4 pieces were sold, nearly 30,000 of the 45,000 struck without were eventually melted down, while the legislative authorization was for 250,000 specimens.

The numerals, in combination with the star, were intended to indicate that Missouri became the 24th state in the Union. Similarly, a 2x2 was added to the Alabama Centennial commemorative halves, which were struck in 1921 following the Missouri issue, although this issue had actually been authorized for 1919 to honor the 100th anniversary of Alabama's statehood. In 1922 when the Grant commemoratives were struck, a star was added to the field of both the half dollar and the gold dollar offerings. In this instance the star was of no particular significance, beyond the objective of selling a pair of coins, be they silver half dollars or gold dollars, to the then eager collector universe. Alabama was successful in selling all 6,000 of its with star coins, but for the Grant issue only 4,250 of the 5,000 struck sold.

1922 Grant Memorial. Obverse without star at left.

Q. *Why was a star added to the Grant Memorial half dollar and gold dollar issues?*

A. Unlike in the cases of the Alabama and Missouri statehood commemorative issues, the star added in the field was of no particular significance, beyond the objective of selling a pair of coins to the enthusiastic hobby community. Buyers of these varieties should exercise great caution, as private initiative has been known to engrave this star feature on "without star coins," which particularly in the instance of the Grant half dollars command a substantially lower premium. None of the subsequent classic period commemoratives were similarly treated from the marketing perspective, although mintmark and dating variations were offered up for eight issues.

Q. *How scarce is the Hawaiian commemorative half dollar?*

A. On the 150th anniversary of the discovery of the Hawaiian Islands by Captain James Cook, 10,058 commemorative half dollars (including eight reserved for assay along with 50 sandblast Proof specimens) were issued for the Captain Cook Sesquicentennial Commission, and sold through the Bank of Hawaii, at $2 per coin—the highest sale price for any commemorative half dollar up to that point—with half of the production earmarked for Hawaii and the other half in the mainland "States." The low mintage, even distribution, and theme of the commemorative combined to make it a popular coin. It has commanded a substantial premium from inception and today carries one of the highest catalog values of any classic era commemorative half dollar, regardless of condition.

Q. *Is the 1936 Arkansas Centennial commemorative coin, with the portrait of Joseph Robinson, the only U.S. coin to bear the portrait of a living person?*

A. It is neither the only nor the first. The first living person to be portrayed on a coin of the United States was Governor Thomas E. Kilby of Alabama. His portrait and that of William Bibb, the first governor of Alabama, appeared on the 1921 Alabama Centennial half dollar. However, the Arkansas coin projects other unusual features. Although it bears the date 1936, it was not issued until 1937. The enabling act passed on June 26, 1936—regular Arkansas halves were first minted in 1935 and continued to be minted annually through 1939—stipulated a change of design on the reverse of the coin, with the side bearing the coining date, as opposed to the date of the commemoration, which was 1936, specifying that side as the obverse. Collectors have generally been unimpressed with that bit of legalese . . . they generally refer to the portrait sides of both versions as the obverse.

1938 Oregon Trail half dollar.

Q. *What commemorative half dollar do you consider to be the most artistic?*

A. When one assesses "artistic" quality you are entering the realm of personal opinion rather than technical presence. An object assessed as being beautiful in the eyes of an individual can be measured, weighed, analyzed, and defined, but the quality of beauty is a chimera having neither permanence nor universal validity.

The Oregon Trail is outstanding in its concept, treatment, and symbolic representation. The reverse of an Indian clad in ceremonial bonnet and dignity, standing before a map of the United States with arm outstretched toward the east in the futile posture of primitive defiance, eloquently depicts the age-old conflict between the free nomad and the tinkers and farmers who flowed across the land like a sea of tar, felling the forests and furrowing the plains, rooting more firmly than the oak and pine whose shadow they brush from the hills. On the obverse, a Conestoga wagon rolls irrevocably toward the setting sun, conquering with oxen and wheel, prevailing through numbers.

Q. *What details can you provide me on the Booker T. Washington half dollar?*

A. Booker T. Washington is associated with two commemorative half dollars: the Booker T. Washington coin issued from 1946 through 1951, and the Washington-Carver (George Washington Carver) coin issued from 1951 through 1954.

The Booker T. Washington commemorative was the first U.S. coin to bear the likeness of an African American, and the first to be designed by one (Isaac Scott Hathaway). It was issued to commemorate the black educator's work in behalf of black education and the Tuskegee Institute, which he founded and fostered to vibrant life. This theme is augmented on the 1951–1954 coin by a concurrent commemoration of George Washington Carver's experiments and advocacy of diversified farming that revolutionized the agriculture of the post-bellum South.

The intent of the Booker T. Washington Commission was to sell the initially authorized BTW mintage of five million commemoratives to the nation's 15 million African Americans at $1.00 each. The plan failed when only about 3 percent of the African American population responded to the project, and the coin collecting community quickly tired of the annual sets made up of Philadelphia, Denver, and San Francisco issues. Congressional approval was provided by an act dated August 7, 1946, which carried an expiration date five years hence, by which time only 3.166 million had been minted, of which roughly half were subsequently melted down, leaving a net mintage of 1,574,369 over six years between the three mints. When the five-year deadline for the BTW authorization expired, the commission was successful in getting a new bill passed by Congress, on Sept. 21, 1951, that authorized the minting of up to 3,415,631 of the Washington-Carver commemoratives, with 2.422 million ultimately being coined, of which about 1.1 million were melted, leaving a net gross mintage of 1,330,802 over four years between the three mints.

The excesses to which this pair of commemoratives were subjected by the issuing authority—multiplicity of date and mintmark varieties, as well as allegations of financial improprieties in their merchandising, paralleled the abuses that characterized the long-lived Arkansas, Boone, Oregon Trail, and Texas issues of the 1930s—created a legislative and administrative environment that led to a 28-year interruption of the U.S. commemorative coinage tradition (1955–1981). As most of the annual sets in both series were minted in modest quantities by today's standards, they command reasonable premiums as collector items today. As quantities of the individual BTW 1946, 1946-D, 1946-S, 1950-S, and 1951 issues, along with the Washington-Carver 1951, 1952, 1953-S, and 1954-S issues, were produced greatly in excess of demand, with some being released to circulation, these are modestly priced type coins for the series.

Q. *Does the motto "In God We Trust" appear on all of the commemorative coins of the United States?*

A. Nearly all. The motto does not appear on the Isabella quarter dollar, the Columbian and Missouri Centennial half dollars, or the Lafayette dollar. It appears on the Philadelphia Sesquicentennial quarter eagle ($2.50) but on no other gold commemoratives, other than the two varieties of the Panama-Pacific $50 gold "slug." The Columbian and Missouri Centennial half dollars are the only commemoratives of that denomination to lack all three statutory inscriptions; LIBERTY, E PLURIBUS UNUM, and IN GOD WE TRUST.

Q. *I understand an Indian is depicted on six of our commemorative coins. Can you tell me which ones they are?*

A. The 1921 Missouri Centennial, 1926–1939 Oregon Trail and 1934–1939 Daniel Boone Bicentennial half dollars, the 2001 American Buffalo silver dollar, and the 2007 Jamestown silver dollar and gold $5.

Commemorative designs featuring Indians. Oregon Trail 1926–1939, Daniel Boone 1934–1938, Arkansas 1935–1939, Long Island 1936, American Buffalo 2001, Jamestown 2007.

1935 Boone half dollar. The enlargement shows date details.

Q. *I have a 1935-dated Boone Bicentennial commemorative half dollar that also carries the date 1934 in small numbers to the right of the figure of the Indian represented on the reverse. Can you tell me why that second date is present on my coin, but not on other 1935-dated Boone halves that I have seen?*

A. The purpose was really to sell more coins to collectors. This exploitative action contributed measurably to the late 1930s rejection of the flood of commemorative issues being produced during that era. The Daniel Boone Bicentennial commemorative issue was introduced in 1934 in celebration of the birth of the famous trapper, frontiersman, and explorer, with 10,000 coins being struck at the Philadelphia Mint. This issue was modestly well received by the public and the collecting community.

In early 1935, an additional 10,000 pieces were minted at Philadelphia, along with 5,000 each at the Denver and San Francisco mints. Apparently due to sluggish sales of these issues, the issuing authority sought authorization—granted by law on August 26, 1935—to add the date 1934 in the field to resurrect the presence of "the commemorative date of 1934" so as to not confuse the public; 10,000 more pieces were produced at Philadelphia and 2,000 each at the Denver and San Francisco mints. The latter pieces, however, were marketed only in pairs as "rare" varieties priced at $3.70 for the pair, as contrasted to the $1.10 price attached to the Philadelphia offering.

In 1936, the Boone was produced in a quantity of 12,000 pieces at Philadelphia and 5,000 each at Denver and San Francisco, with the price of the latter pieces being dropped to $1.60 each. When it came time to produce 1937-dated Boones, 15,000 were struck at Philadelphia, 7,500 at Denver, and 5,000 at San Francisco. The Philadelphia coin was initially priced individually at $1.60, but later was available only in pairs with Denver specimens at $7.25 per pair. The San Francisco was initially offered individually at $5.15, but later only in three-piece sets for $12.40. With large quantities of all three being subsequently melted, the net mintages became 9,800 for Philadelphia and 2,500 each for the other two mints. The final mintages in 1938 were 5,000 for each mint, with the net falling to 2,100 after melting, and the issue was available only in sets of three at $6.50.

When relatively few of the 87,100 Boone commemoratives produced were sold to the public—out of an authorization of 600,000—so ended the exploitation of the collector market, with no new commemorative issues being introduced until the Iowa Centennial and Booker T. Washington issues in 1946, although the Oregon Trail and Arkansas Centennial issues continued in sharply curtailed issue quantities for 1939.

Q. *I notice that some of the U.S. commemorative half dollars that I have purchased do not incorporate the word LIBERTY into their designs. Can you tell me which issues do not include that national proclamation?*

A. The word "Liberty" is incorporated into the designs of all modern era commemoratives as a statutory requirement, but the classic era half dollars which do not include that feature, of which there are 18, are the Alabama Centennial (1921), Albany Charter (1936), Boone Bicentennial (1934–1938), World's Columbian Exposition (1892–1893), Elgin Centennial (1936), Grant Memorial (1922), Hawaiian Sesquicentennial (1928), Hudson Sesquicentennial (1935), Huguenot-Walloon Tercentenary (1924), Lexington-Concord Sesquicentennial (1925), Maryland Tercentenary (1934), Missouri Centennial (1921), Monroe Doctrine Centennial (1923), Oregon Trail (1926–1939), Panama-Pacific Exposition (1915), Pilgrim Tercentenary (1920–1921), Fort Vancouver Centennial (1925), and Vermont Sesquicentennial (1927).

None of the classic era gold commemoratives incorporate the word "Liberty" in their designs, as is also the case with the Isabella Quarter (1893) and the Lafayette Dollar (1900). While "Liberty" was rather inconspicuously placed on many of the classic era halves, it is typically prominently displayed on most of the issues of the modern era.

Q. *When did the practice of issuing commemorative coins begin?*

A. Commemorative coins are nearly as old as coinage, which began about 700 B.C. The first commemorative coin of record was issued by Anaxilas of Rhegium in 280 B.C. to commemorate his chariot victory at the Elis Olympic Games, which he won driving a biga of mules.

Q. *Why did the United States wait until 1892, a century after the establishment of the U.S. Mint, before issuing its first commemorative coin?*

A. Until 1892 the United States followed the custom inaugurated during the War for Independence of issuing national medals as commemoratives. However, the 1,389 1848 quarter eagles minted from the initial shipment of California gold to reach the East Coast, counterstamped "CAL." above the head of the eagle on the reverse, while not technically designated a commemorative, was one in reality.

Q. *Is it true that when the statue of Lincoln in the Lincoln Memorial appeared on the reverse of the cent in 1959, Lincoln became the first person to have his likeness on both sides of a U.S. Coin?*

A. It is true of regular-issue coinage. A likeness of Marquis de Lafayette can be found on both sides of the 1900 Lafayette commemorative silver dollar.

Q. *How much money did the Los Angeles Olympics effort receive from the sale of the Olympics commemoratives?*

A. The amount turned over by the Treasury Department was $73.4 million, which was shared equally by the U.S. Olympic Committee and the Los Angeles Organizing Committee. The payments were generated from a $10 premium per coin charged on the sale of each silver dollar and $50 each on the gold pieces.

1982 George Washington half dollar.

Q. *How do the quantities of issue for the 1982 George Washington 250th anniversary of birth commemorative half dollar compare with the quantities struck of earlier U.S. commemoratives?*

A. The Washington coin was produced in far greater numbers than any of the earlier commemorative issues. The combined production of uncirculated and Proof specimens exceeded 8.45 million pieces; with nearly 1.5 million unsold specimens being melted in 1986 net mintage came in at just over seven million, 2,210,458 uncirculated and 4,894,044 Proof examples. The uncirculated version originally sold for $8.50 and the Proof for $10; prices were subsequently increased to $10 and $12 each, respectively. Unlike subsequent modern era commemorative issues, this first offering generated profits of more than $36 million to the Treasury Department, being paid into the general fund to reduce the national debt. Commencing with 1984 Los Angeles Summer Olympic Games, subsequent issues have earmarked designated surcharge profits to benefit projects favored by politically connected interests.

Prior to the Washington commemorative, the 1952 Philadelphia Mint version of the Washington-Carver commemorative half dollar had enjoyed the largest sales, with a net issuance of 2,006,292 examples. Only eight other U.S. commemoratives had been issued in quantities of more than 200,000 examples, the 1892 Columbian (950,000), 1893 Columbian (1,550,405), 1923-S Monroe Doctrine (274,077), 1925 Stone Mountain (1,314,709), the 1946 (1,000,546 struck, with an estimated 500,000 having been melted) and 1946-S (500,279 struck, an estimated 300,000 melted) Booker T. Washington, and the 1950-S (512,091 struck, an estimated 235,000 melted) and 1951 (510,082 struck, an estimated 230,000 melted) issues of the same series.

Historically, the total coinage of U.S. commemoratives from 1892 through 1954 had numbered approximately 12.28 million pieces, more than 5.5 million of these from the 1946–1954 production of the Booker T. Washington and Washington-Carver series. Actual sales of the 1982 Washington commemorative (7,104,502 pieces) exceeded the total number of all commemorative issues sold (under 6.8 million) from the 1892 Columbian Exposition offering, the first, through the Iowa Centennial issue of 1946, the last, excepting the BTW and Washington-Carver issues.

Q. *How many coins must a person acquire to have a complete set of the 1983-1984 Los Angeles Olympiad commemorative coinage?*

A. A complete type set would consist of just three pieces: silver dollars dated 1983 and 1984, and the 1984 ten-dollar gold piece. A complete set featuring all of the mintmark and striking varieties would consist of 13 coins: 1983 and 1984 silver dollars struck in uncirculated at the Philadelphia,

Denver, and San Francisco mints, and in Proof only at the San Francisco Mint; 1984 $10 gold piece struck in uncirculated only at the West Point minting facility (the first appearance of the W mintmark) but in Proof both there and at the Philadelphia, Denver, and San Francisco mints.

Q. *Is the Eisenhower dollar a commemorative?*

A. Technically it was not introduced as a commemorative issue in 1971; the enabling act proposed it as a replacement for the suspended Peace dollar. Semantics aside, the Eisenhower dollar is, by the historical significance of its theme, a dual commemorative. The obverse bears witness to the nation's appreciation of the contributions of general and president Eisenhower to the national accomplishment. The reverse commemorates the initial moon landing on July 20, 1969, being an adaptation of the official Apollo 11 insignia.

Other commemoratives that are not, strictly speaking, commemoratives are the Bicentennial dollar, half dollar, and quarter, first issued in 1975 in anticipation of the nation's 200th anniversary in 1976. The three coins, with special reverse designs, bear the dual dates 1776–1976. In that respect they are true commemoratives, drastically changed from regular circulation coins. But they were struck for circulation (no single dated dollars, halves, or quarters were produced for either 1975 or 1976) and the large mintages executed for each puts them in the realm of everyday circulating coins. Perhaps they should be called our first "circulating commemoratives," while in more recent years (1999 through 2008) the 50 States Quarter® series would be added to that category.

1997 Roosevelt $5 gold.

Q. *What was the purpose for the issuance of the 1997 Franklin D. Roosevelt commemorative $5 gold coin?*

A. To sell it to coin collectors. Aside from that result, and the fact that a $35 surcharge from the sale of each coin was designated to benefit the Franklin Delano Roosevelt Memorial Commission, there was no really compelling merit for the issue. The issue was a real misfit in the modern commemorative series. The year 1997 is of no significance where Roosevelt was concerned. He was born in 1882, so that was the 115th anniversary of his birth. He became president and suspended the minting and paying out of U.S. gold coins in 1933, so it was the 64th anniversary of those events. He passed away in 1945, so it was the 52nd anniversary of his death. Thus, there is no logical tie between Roosevelt, the year of the coin, and the fact that it was a gold issue. Only roughly 41 percent of the 100,000 authorization limit contained in Public Law 104-329 were actually minted—11,805 as uncirculated examples and 29,233 as Proofs—making it the lowest mintage commemorative of the modern era, which has translated into the coins realizing substantial value increases in the secondary market.

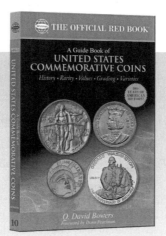

For more information: Consult the *Guide Book of United States Commemorative Coins* (Bowers).

CHAPTER SIXTEEN

Gold Coins of the U.S. Mint

Q. *I have seen early U.S. gold coins that appear to be bigger than gold coins of like denominations of later years. Did they at one time have more gold in them?*

A. The gold coins of the 1790s and early 19th century were larger in diameter and thinner than gold coins of later years, although there was not a significantly higher amount of fine gold in these early coins. This was the case with most denominations of silver coins as well. The half eagles ($5 gold) of 1795 to 1829, for example, had a diameter of 25 mm and a fine gold weight of 8.02 grams, with the diameter being reduced to 23.8 mm from 1829 to 1834, then to 22.5 mm from 1834 through 1838, with the fine gold weight being 7.517 grams for 1834 to 1836 and 7.524 grams for 1837 to 1838, with the diameter being reduced to 21.6 mm and the weight adjusted to 7.523 grams or .24187 ounce commencing in 1839, which standards were maintained thereafter. The one exception to this was the gold dollar, minted from 1849 through 1889, the Type I issues of 1849 to 1854 being smaller (13 mm diameter) and thicker than subsequent gold dollars of 1854 to 1889 (15 mm).

Q. *What is an "Eagle" as the term applies to U.S. coins?*

A. A 10-dollar gold piece. Alexander Hamilton, a strong advocate of decimal denomination coinage, proposed that establishing a monetary system comprised of 100 units to a dollar and 10 dollars to an eagle would enable the average citizen to more easily understand its mathematical structure. The term was never used on the coin itself to denote its value, but the 10-dollar gold coin has been known as an "Eagle" down through the years. The term has also been applied to the divisions and multiple of the 10-dollar gold piece: quarter eagle for $2.50, half eagle for $5, and double eagle for $20. Gold coins minted from 1795 to 1807 did not carry an indication of value thereon, indications of value being first incorporated with introduction of the Capped Bust half eagle in mid-1807 and on the quarter eagle the following year. With the eagle not being minted from 1805 through 1837, the $10 denominational value first appeared on the eagles of 1838.

Q. *What makes the early U.S. gold coins so prohibitively expensive?*

A. Their comparative rarity. When the United States, upon the recommendation of Alexander Hamilton, adopted a bimetallic monetary standard in the ratio of 15 (silver) to 1 (gold), that ratio conformed to that in general world usage. But by 1799 the ratio in European commercial centers had broadened to 15-3/4 to 1, giving our gold coins a higher bullion value than their face value. The undervalued gold coins flowed out of the country, or were melted for bullion. This destruction, coupled with the subdued mintage of the time necessarily produced the present imbalance of supply and demand, and consequent high prices.

1860 three-dollar gold piece.

Q. *What was the purpose of the $3 gold piece?*

A. Sometimes referred to as the rich man's three-cent piece, it is widely assumed that the $3 gold piece was issued to facilitate the purchase of three-cent stamps by the hundred. This belief is supported by the fact that the silver three-cent piece was issued to make purchase of the stamp less bothersome for the public, and by the discontinuance of the $3 gold in 1889, the same year the nickel three-cent piece was discontinued, but this is pure conjecture. Never minted in substantial quantities—approximately 62 percent of the total production dates from the first six years, 1854 to 1859, with another 23 percent being inexplicably produced in the years 1874 and 1878—as the coin never enjoyed extensive circulation, it is readily available today in high-grade circulated and Mint State conditions.

One of the great regular-issue coinage rarities of the United States is the 1870-S three-dollar gold piece. Only one example of that coin is known to exist, part of the collection formed by Harry W. Bass Jr., which is on display at the Edward C. Rochette Money Museum at the American Numismatic Association headquarters in Colorado Springs, Colorado, although another which has never been located is rumored to have been placed in the cornerstone of the old San Francisco Mint. Interestingly, while the San Francisco Mint produced modest quantities of $3 gold pieces in 1855 to 1857 and again in 1860, the only subsequent year of record for the coin at the West Coast mint was 1870.

Q. *Were one-dollar gold coins ever used, or were they just hoarded?*

A. The fact that so many circulated pieces are available today substantiates that they were actively employed as a medium of exchange. Gold coins were a favorite of the business community because they had an intrinsic worth independent of the ability of a government to support its money. Generally speaking, gold dollars were produced in substantial quantities—between three-quarters and 4 million annually from 1851 through 1857, following a combined total of 1.17 million for 1849 and 1850—only at the Philadelphia Mint, although 1.13 million were produced at the New Orleans Mint from 1849 through 1855, with only modest amounts being minted annually at the Charlotte, Dahlonega, and San Francisco mints from 1849 through 1861.

1848 CAL. Gold Quarter Eagle.

Q. *Is the 1848 gold quarter eagle that has CAL. punched in the field above the eagle on the reverse a private or territorial gold issue?*

A. Although the story of this unusual, and unusually valuable, gold piece is part of the history of the territory of California, it is an official coin of the United States that was struck at the Philadelphia Mint. California was not yet a state when Military Governor Colonel Richard B. Mason collected 230 ounces of gold gleaned from early recoveries of the California Gold Rush, believing this tangible evidence of the wealth of the territory would add impetus to the movement for statehood, sending it to Washington by military courier. The courier carried the gold to Washington by way of Peru, Panama, Jamaica, and New Orleans, delivering it to Secretary of War W. L. Marcy. Marcy sent it on to the mint at Philadelphia, suggesting that a portion of it be reserved for medals, and that the balance "be used in striking quarter-eagles bearing a distinguishing mark" to identify the content as being a part of the first shipment to the East from California's gold discovery.

Mint Director R.M. Patterson struck 1,389 quarter eagles from the gold, and to distinguish them from regular issues had "CAL." hand stamped above the eagle. Although struck using an 1848 dated die pair, these coins were likely struck in early 1849, as Mason's gold dispatch did not go forth until December 9, 1848, although the original California gold discovery was made on January 24, 1848, when John Sutter made his discovery at Sutter's Mill on the American River. These coins from the gold discovery that ushered California into the Union have a distinctive brassy color imparted by the high silver content of California gold, with several specimens being possessed of prooflike surfaces.

Q. *Why can't a collector own a 1933 $20 gold piece?*

A. While this was true for 69 years, since late July of 2002 one example of the issue has been legally held in private hands, its owner having paid $7,590,020 for the privilege, that being the highest price ever paid for a single coin. There are also two examples of the issue within the National Numismatic Collection holdings of the Smithsonian Institution. In addition, there are another ten specimens that are presently in possession of the Treasury Department and stored at the Fort Knox Gold Depository, they having been confiscated by the government when tendered to the United States Mint for "authentication."

None of the 1933 $20 gold coins were released to general circulation, President Franklin D. Roosevelt having promulgated an executive order halting the minting and circulation of gold coins immediately following his inauguration in 1933, with those already minted being subsequently consigned to the melting pot. In 1937 the U.S. Mint completed the melting down of the government's gold coin stocks into bars that were transferred to Fort Knox. There were a few, however, that were paid out at the mint's cash window, legally or illegally depending on perspective, but have been subject to confiscation since 1933.

In 1944 one of those coins was licensed for export from the country to King Farouk I of Egypt, it being subsequently withdrawn from the February 25, 1954, sale of the deposed king's collection at the request of the U.S. Treasury for return to the United States government. It was more than 42 years later, however, before the coin returned to our shores and public knowledge, after passing through an undetermined number of hands, following arrests and a confiscation as a result of a Secret Service sting operation. Legal maneuvers that transpired over the next six years led to the monetization of this one coin and its legalized sale by auction in New York City on July 30, 2002, with the proceeds split between the consignor and the U.S. Mint. The status of the ten additional specimens which came to light in 2005 is presently undetermined.

Q. *Are gold coins held in storage by the Treasury Department?*

A. No. All gold held by the government is in the form of gold bullion. Mint Director Nellie Tayloe Ross was given orders on June 29, 1934, to commence the task of melting down all gold coins in the Treasury's inventory at the various mints and assay offices, with the resulting bars to be of .900 "coin" fineness. She issued orders to proceed on August 4, at which time the two 1933 double eagles that ended up in the Smithsonian Institution national collection were reserved. As the melting got underway, a high security facility for storage of the gold bars was under construction at Fort Knox, Kentucky. It was not until early 1937 that the massive gold coin–melt was completed, with records indicating the final shipments of bars arriving at the new gold bullion depository by the end of June.

1920 Saint-Gaudens twenty dollars.

Q. *At a recent coin show I heard the term "Saint-Gaudens Twenty" used. What was being referred to?*

A. Specifically, a $20 gold coin of the design minted from 1907 to 1933. The expression denotes a deserved recognition of the coin's designer, Augustus Saint-Gaudens. The Saint-Gaudens double eagle is universally acclaimed a masterpiece of the medalist's art; in the words of President Teddy Roosevelt, who commissioned Saint-Gaudens to create the designs for the new $10 and $20 gold coins introduced in 1907 and placed into regular production the following year, these coins were "more beautiful than any coin since the days of the Greeks."

Q. *It seems there are a lot of strange terms used in coin collecting. Among them is "Paquet Reverse." What does this refer to?*

A. The term refers to a special reverse design employed on some 1861 dated $20 gold coins, principally on San Francisco Mint strikes. Comparison with the initial piece of this year, and those of preceding and subsequent years as well, will readily reveal that the legends of the reverse proposed by Paquet features taller and bolder letters than otherwise. This reverse derives its name from the designer, Anthony C. Paquet. The dies for 1861 double eagle coinage were prepared at the Philadelphia Mint in late 1860, with additional die pairs being shipped to the mints in San Francisco and New Orleans as well. While the denomination was not placed in production at New Orleans, it was at Philadelphia and San Francisco. At the Philadelphia Mint, the short production run was recalled before any coins were paid out, but two examples are known to have escaped the melting pot. The order to cease production did not reach the San Francisco Mint, however, until after 19,250 coins had been produced and paid out, several hundred of which survive in mint state and circulated grades.

Q. *Where did the U.S. Mint obtain gold for coinage before the California gold strike?*

A. Rutherford County, North Carolina, was the source of most of the nation's newly mined gold from 1790 to 1840. Another lesser source was the miscellaneous gold coins of other nations that flowed into the country during the normal course of commerce.

Gold eagle (left). The Indian head design was used on obverse of U.S. gold eagles ($10) from 1907 to 1933. The design is by Augustus Saint-Gaudens, who also created the double-eagle of the same period. **Gold quarter eagle (right).** Incuse designs (cut into the coin surface, rather than raised) have appeared on only two U.S. coins—the gold quarter eagle (shown) and the half eagle. Both were designed by Bela Lyon Pratt and minted from 1908 through 1929.

Q. *I have a little gold coin that looks like it was made backwards; it says 2-1/2 DOLLARS on the back. What is it?*

A. Your coin, issued between 1908 and 1929, is a $2.50 gold piece (quarter eagle) issued by the U.S. Mint. The reason it appears "backwards" is because the design is incused (sunken) into the surface rather than being bas-relief (raised from) the field as most coins are. The $5 gold coins of this period are of similar design, creations of Boston sculptor Bela Lyon Pratt, a pupil of Augustus Saint-Gaudens, making these series unique among U.S. coins. The minting of gold quarter and half eagles was suspended in 1915 and 1916, being reinstated for quarter eagles from 1925 through 1929 and for half eagles in 1929, but discontinued by a Congressional Act dated April 11, 1930. The 1929 half eagle is the rarest issue in that series; although 662,000 were minted, relatively few were paid out prior to the 1934 to 1937 melting of the Treasury's remaining gold coins into bullion bars.

Q. *Does a gold coin that has been soldered to a chain or one that has a hole in it from having been used on a necklace have a deteriorated value?*

A. Definitely. The state of preservation is a determining factor in arriving at the value of any numismatic item. A piece such as you describe would be considered a jewelry piece, with its value generally based largely on its bullion content. Such coins are often found "repaired" by removing the solder or filling the hole, and would generally be considered collectible only if of a rare type or date of issue.

Gold dollars. Three major types of gold dollars minted in the United States were the Coronet or Liberty Head (1849–1854), small Indian Princess Head (1854–1856), and large Indian Princess Head (1856–1889).

Q. *Why was the Type I gold dollar made larger and thinner in 1854?*

A. A change in material or philosophy is but seldom born of a single cause. One of the reasons for enlarging the gold dollar from Type I (Liberty Head, 13 mm) to Type II (Indian Princess, Small Head, 15 mm) is that skilled but larcenous hands had developed the knack of slicing the thin coin in half, paring a bit of gold from the center, then rejoining the diminished halves with solder. Producing a thinner coin made it more difficult for the achievement of this larcenous objective.

Q. *If the motto E PLURIBUS UNUM was made a mandatory part of coinage design in 1873, where is it on the Saint-Gaudens double eagle?*

A. The Saint-Gaudens double eagle was the only regular issue U.S. coin of the modern era to have a lettered edge, prior to the introduction of the Presidential Dollars series in 2007. The motto E PLURIBUS UNUM appears on the edge of the coin, with stars between the words, as it does on the Presidential Dollars series issues.

1915 Panama-Pacific Exposition fifty dollars.

Q. *What is a gold "slug?"*

A. "Slug" is a nickname given to $50 gold coins of both official and private origin, and for bars or ingots of California gold denominated with values up to $150 for issue. The only $50 gold slugs ever coined for the public by the United States government were the Panama-Pacific commemoratives made in 1915 for the Panama-Pacific Exposition held in celebration of the completion of the Panama Canal. This commemorative was issued in both round and octagonal shape, as were the earlier private slugs issued in California which inspired this unusual issue. Western legend holds that the large, heavy gold pieces received the name "slug" from the practice of wrapping them in a bandana and using the impromptu bludgeon to slug unwary miners before relieving them of their gold dust.

Q. *Is it true that the "official" U.S. price of gold was once as low as $20 an ounce?*

A. In 1834, Congress set the price of gold in the United States at $20.67 an ounce. This price level remained in effect until January 31, 1934, when gold's price was officially raised to $35 an ounce, a move which had the effect of devaluing the dollar 40.94 percent. On February 12, 1973, the official U.S. price was raised to $42.22 an ounce, and the dollar devalued 10 percent. The 1834 Congressional legislation establishing gold's value at $20.67 an ounce also fixed the price of silver at $1.2929 an ounce, that price remaining in effect until July 14, 1967, when the Treasury announced that it would no longer engage in the selling of silver at that rate to maintain an artificially low market level.

Q. *What is the difference between "karat" and "fineness" as they refer to the purity of gold?*

A. "Karat" is a jeweler's term, while "fineness" is a coiner's term for quantifying the purity of the precious metal in an alloy. Fineness denotes the number of parts of gold, or the percent of gold, contained in an alloy. A gold item identified as .750 fine contains three parts of gold and one part of another metal, such as copper, or other metals, and consequently contains 75 percent pure gold. A karat is defined as "a unit of fineness for gold equal to 1/24th part of pure gold to an alloy." A gold item identified as 18-karat gold contains 75-percent pure gold, and consequently has a fineness of .750.

Q. *I have a note by means of which Wells Fargo transferred gold from San Francisco to New York. This document is called a "second exchange" note. What does this mean?*

A. Wells Fargo, and other express companies, transferred money from the West to the East by means of first, second, and third exchanges. The exchanges traveled by different routes. One went by sea around Cape Horn, another by sea with a land crossing of the Panama isthmus, and the other overland. The first exchange to arrive at the destination point was honored, whereupon the other two were automatically voided.

1880 Stella four dollars.

Q. *The four-dollar gold "Stella" bears the motto DEO EST GLORIA. What does this mean?*

A. Had Congress approved issuance of the "Stella," of four-dollar gold coin, it would, in effect, have served as an international trade coin. It was thought that the religious motto adopted for use on U.S. coins—IN GOD WE TRUST—the use of which was associated with the Christian deity, would be inappropriate for coins intended to serve people of all religious faiths. The Latin motto DEO EST GLORIA ("glory to God") was considered to be more readily acceptable to the world community.

1908 Indian Head gold eagle reverses.

Q. *I have a 1908 $10 gold piece that has the words IN GOD WE TRUST on the back, and my buddy has one that doesn't. Why is this?*

A. When the Saint-Gaudens eagle and double eagle appeared in 1907, it was soon discovered that the religious motto had been omitted from them. The motto had been eliminated at the suggestion of President Theodore Roosevelt, who thought that using a coin in promotion of faith in God was sacrilegious, and with the knowledge that an oversight in the drafting of the Coinage Act of 1890 had omitted the requirement for the inclusion of the motto. The motto was restored by Act of Congress in 1908, resulting in two varieties of each coin for that year. While both 1908 varieties of the eagle are similarly valued in the circulated grades, the mintages are at great variance, with the Philadelphia Mint having produced only 33,500 without the motto and 341,370 with the motto, and the Denver Mint 210,000 without the motto and 836,500 with the motto. The same is true for the double eagle, of which 4,271,551 were produced at the Philadelphia Mint without the motto and only 156,258 with the motto, while the totals for the Denver Mint were 663,500 without the motto and 349,500 with the motto. The San Francisco Mint produced only the with motto varieties of both coins.

Q. *Why did President Roosevelt act in 1933 to restrict the ownership of gold by American citizens?*

A. The President moved to require holders of gold to deliver holdings of the metal, except for coins of numismatic merit, to the government for one purpose and one purpose only; to prevent individuals from profiting by the official revaluation of gold from $20.67 per ounce to $35 that was subsequently invoked. Prior to the issuance of Roosevelt's executive order on Sunday, March 5, 1933, the day following his inauguration, gold was being hoarded and exported due to its artificially low monetized value, which led to depositors causing a run on the nation's banking system demanding specie payment, resulting in the specter of broad banking insolvencies. Roosevelt's dictatorial action did not define the term "hoard" or "numismatic merit," nor did legislation subsequently rushed through Congress on March 9, technically terminating the gold standard. A subsequent executive order on April 3, 1933, specified that "gold coins having a recognized special value to collectors of rare and unusual coins" were exempted, a provision which served as the cornerstone of gold coin collecting restrictions for more than 40 years, until unrestricted ownership of gold by American citizens was legalized as of December 31, 1974. Only roughly half of the $571 million worth of gold coin estimated to be held by the public in 1933 was ever turned in.

Q. *Can Americans legally own gold coins today?*

A. American citizens have never been prohibited from collecting or otherwise owning U.S. gold coin issues in any quantity. However, Treasury regulations invoked under the Gold Reserve Act of 1934 prohibited U.S. citizens from holding gold in forms other than those intended for customary industrial and artistic (jewelry) purposes, plus items deemed to be of sufficient numismatic merit. Inclusion of the exception of "gold coins having recognized special value to collectors" can undoubtedly be attributed to the influence of Treasury Secretary William H. Woodin, who had assembled one of the finest collections of U.S. gold coins some 20 years before, and his interplay with President Franklin D. Roosevelt, who was a very dedicated stamp collector. This exclusion included all gold coins dated 1933 or earlier, except the U.S. $20 piece of 1933, plus selected issues of later dated coins of other nations through 1965. The regulations were revised on December 17, 1973, to include all gold coins dated 1959 or earlier, but excluding all issues of subsequent dates.

Q. *I have heard it was once illegal to own foreign gold coins. Is that correct?*

A. It was illegal to own, buy, or sell foreign gold coins dated after 1933— except for specific exceptions—until December 31, 1974, at which time the Treasury removed all restrictions on the ownership of gold by Americans. Executive Order 6102 promulgated by President Roosevelt on April 5, 1933, had provided that special gold import licenses were required to import any gold coins purchased abroad by American citizens, with only a restricted list of issues dated from 1934 through 1959 being allowed.

Saint-Gaudens double eagles. Details show dates in roman and arabic numerals, and the coin without motto and with motto.

Q. *Someone recently showed me a Saint-Gaudens $20 gold piece that does not have a date, nor the motto IN GOD WE TRUST. I thought all United States coins carry a date. What's the story?*

A. What you saw was one of the really rare and popular Saint-Gaudens double eagles. The coin is dated, but in Roman numerals—MCMVII— a variety of which only 11,250 examples were struck. This variety is available in two versions; wire rim and flat rim. The difference in the two is really simply a matter of strike, as on the "wire rim" version the striking process caused a small amount of the metal to squeeze up between the die and collar, creating a raised wire rim. Both versions are relatively equivalent in value. The Roman numeral date appears to the right above the boulder on which Liberty's left foot rests, displayed in the field of rays radiating from behind her, as does the Arabic numerals date appearing on the second variety of the coin produced later in 1907 and through subsequent years. All 1907 Saint-Gaudens double eagles and most of those produced in 1908 do not incorporate the motto IN GOD WE TRUST.

Gold quarter eagle reverses.

Q. *The denomination was indicated as 1/100 and 1/200 on the early copper cents and half cents. Has any other coin of the United States ever had the denomination indicated fractionally?*

A. The denomination of the gold quarter eagle ($2.50) was stated on the coins as 2-1/2 D. or 2-1/2 DOLLARS from 1808 through 1929 on four basic types. The fraction 1/2 also indicated the value on the 1796 to 1797 Draped Bust, Small Eagle half-dollar issues as well. No other gold or silver coins minted up to 1807 carried an indication of value on the coin surface, with the exception of the Draped Bust quarter type introduced in 1806. All gold coins of that era had reeded edges, so they carried no indication of value whatsoever, as was the case for half dimes and dimes as well. Silver half dollars and dollars of the Flowing Hair and Draped Bust types were also not denominated on their surfaces, although their edges were incuse lettered with appropriate indications of value.

Grant gold dollar. Images shown display the Grant gold dollar without a star and the Grant gold dollar with a star added to obverse design.

Q. *Among the coins left in my father's estate is a small gold coin identified simply as a Ulysses S. Grant gold dollar, and dated 1922. Is it a regular U.S. coin?*

A. It is a commemorative gold coin struck as a centenary souvenir of Grant's birth. There are two principal varieties, with star and without; both were minted in exactly the same quantities and generally command like values in any given condition.

Flowing Hair Stella.   **Coiled Hair Stella.**

Q. *I have read that the unusual four-dollar gold "Stella" struck by the United States in 1879 was intended to be a "metric" coin. Can you tell me what is meant by this reference?*

A. A four-dollar gold coin was envisioned by John A. Kasson, U.S. envoy extraordinary and minister plenipotentiary to Austria-Hungary, as an international coin approximate in value to the metric-based coins issued by the European members of the Latin Monetary Union, and which were created as a device to standardize coinage systems. A value of four dollars made the stella approximately the equal of the Italian 20 lire, French 20 francs, Austrian and Dutch 8 florins, and the Spanish 20 pesetas, all of which were gold coins. Patterns were struck in gold, aluminum, copper, and white metal. They were produced in very limited quantities in both flowing and coiled hair types in both 1879 and 1880, with the white metal strikes minted only in 1879. Only the Flowing Hair type of 1879 is relatively common, with upwards of 500 examples believed to exist. If adopted for issue, the stella would have been made of "goloid," a combination, with copper, of gold and silver in equal quantities by value, thus serving to reaffirm America's commitment to bimetallism at a time when the major trading nations of Europe were increasingly favoring a gold standard.

Q. *What is the gold content of my U.S. gold coins?*

A. All U.S. gold coins struck subsequent to the enactment of the law of January 18, 1837, had a .900 fine gold content. The weight of the $20 (double eagle) piece is specified at 33.436 grams, resulting in a pure gold content of 0.96750 ounce. All lower denomination gold coins have a proportional fine gold content. The following table illustrates the value of the gold bullion content in quarter eagles, half eagles, eagles and double eagles at selected incremental bullion market price levels:

	Price of 1 oz. Gold Bullion							
Denom.	$800	$900	$1,000	$1,100	$1,200	$1,300	$1,400	$1,500
$2.50	$38.70	$43.53	$48.37	$53.21	$58.04	$62.88	$67.72	$72.56
$5	193.50	217.68	241.87	266.06	290.24	314.43	338.62	362.81
$10	387.00	435.38	483.75	532.13	580.50	628.88	677.25	725.63
$20	774.00	870.75	967.50	1,064.25	1,161.00	1,257.75	1,354.50	1,451.25

CHAPTER SEVENTEEN

Privately Struck Gold Coins

Q. *What is meant by the term "Private Gold?"*

A. In a simpler time—before the railroads bound the disparate parts of the country into a united whole—much of the country was separated from the financial centers of the East by formidable barriers of distance and primitive transportation. The developing industry and commerce of the remote parts of the country was burdened by a lack of sufficient U.S. coinage. Although no state or territory had the right to coin money, private sources in the gold mining areas of Georgia, North Carolina, California, Oregon, Utah, and Colorado endeavored to fill that need by issuing necessity pieces of various denominations and shapes. These do-it-yourself gold coins struck outside of the U.S. Mint are known as "Private Gold." The issues of California, Oregon, Utah, and Colorado are sometimes alternatively referred to as "Territorial Gold," as these issues preceded statehood.

Q. *What are "California fractional gold pieces?"*

A. California fractional gold pieces are gold coins of small denomination issued by jewelers, engravers, and goldsmiths to satisfy a need for small change that developed in California during the Gold Rush days. These tiny gold pieces were issued in denominations of quarter dollar, half dollar, and one dollar from 1852 to 1882, in both round and octagonal form. Genuine fractional gold pieces generally have a Liberty Head, Indian Head, or Washington Head represented on the obverse; a wreath or beaded circle on the reverse, or eagles on a couple of the half dollar issues. The "coin" issues were minted of gold, but invariably under weight, most being denominated and dated. While the Coinage Act of April 22, 1864, outlawed such private issues, that law was not sternly enforced until 1883. Commencing in the 1870s souvenir "token" issues were produced, most of which were of low gold content or gold plated and not denominated. In circumvention of the law many of the "token" issues from the 1880s on were backdated to the 1850s and 1860s.

California gold. Images displayed show fractional gold coins on the left and souvenir gold pieces to the right. The souvenir California gold coins were struck by the M.E. Hart Company of San Francisco to honor Alaska in the early 20th century.

Q. *Is there an easy way to tell the difference between a genuine California fractional gold piece and a California token or souvenir?*

A. Genuine pieces must bear an actual denominational value reference stated as CENTS, DOL., DOLL., or DOLLAR. An 1882 law provided that the word "dollar" could not be used on any gold piece other than issues of the U.S. Mint. Imitation souvenir tokens made after that date and back-dated to the 1850s and 1860s usually state the value numerically as 1/4, 1/2, or 1, without the word dollar, to avoid the legal requirements prohibiting any form of the word dollar, even though the imitation pieces, not being reproductions of government issues, could not legally be considered counterfeits. Some of the "tokens" made immediately after 1882 were of reasonably good gold and weight, but this does not make them genuine fractional pieces. Pieces carrying only the numeric designations of value are much less valuable than those with the denomination spelled out in full or abbreviated. Souvenir issues of more recent vintage, frequently representing a bear on the reverse, are usually made of gold-plated brass, and have little numismatic value.

Q. *I recently saw an octagonal Washington Head California gold piece advertised that did not bear the word DOLLAR or an abbreviation of it, but did carry the word CHARM. Can such a piece be authentic?*

A. Others have also wondered. These octagonal Washington Head fractional gold pieces containing the proper amount of gold for the half dollar denomination are not uncommon. It is believed that such pieces were correctly dated, and in some instances may have even actually circulated as coin, but most authorities believe them to be exactly what the word indicates, a jewelry charm.

Bechtler gold dollar.

Q. *Who produced the first gold dollar in the United States, the government or a private coiner?*

A. Government-issued gold dollars were first authorized by the Coinage Law of March 3, 1849. It has been established that the first gold dollars were produced in 1831 by Christopher Bechtler, a German metallurgist, and his son August, at the private mint they established at Rutherfordton, North Carolina. The Bechtlers struck gold coins in three denominations—$1, $2.50, and $5—in a significant variety of sizes, weights and finenesses. While none of the Bechtler coins are dated, authorities generally ascribe 28 varieties to the three denomination series: five $1 pieces, eight $2.50 pieces, and fifteen $5 pieces. Some of the pieces carry the designation CAROLINA GOLD, others GEORGIA GOLD, they being minted of gold from mines in the Piedmont region of both states. The most unusual coins in the series are 20-karat (.833 fine) $5 CAROLINA GOLD pieces bearing the date of August 1, 1834, which is a date the Treasury Secretary recommended U.S. coins authorized under a law of that date carry but which was not complied with, but the Bechtlers evidently acted on the recommendation to avoid conflict with Treasury edict.

Q. *Why was the need for gold coins so urgent in Gold Rush California that private minters literally broke the law to provide them while the government obligingly looked the other way?*

A. The discovery of gold at Sutter's Mill caused one of the greatest stampedes of man in history. Tens of thousands of fortune seekers poured into an area few had occupied before. California was too remote for the U.S. Mint to provide it with adequate coinage. Foreign coins passed current everywhere, but there weren't enough of them. Gold dust and nuggets circulated freely, but the U.S. customs house refused to accept payment for duties in those forms, causing badly needed merchandise to pile up in government warehouses for want of an acceptable medium. Need and opportunity were sufficient incentives for enterprising individuals to begin minting gold "coins" and ingots.

1849 Norris, Gregg & Norris half eagle.

Q. *I understand that private firms issued gold coins in California before the United States did. What firm issued the first such coins, and what face value did they have?*

A. The first of the California private gold coins are considered to be the half eagles ($5) issued by Norris, Gregg & Norris in 1849. These coins are mentioned in a newspaper account dated May 31, 1849. Gold coins dated 1849 were also issued in California by the firms of Templeton Reid, Moffat & Co.; Massachusetts & California Co.; Miners' Bank; Cincinnati Mining & Trading Co.; J. S. Ormsby; J. H. Bowie; and the Pacific Co.

Q. *I have read that by the end of 1849, there was a "virtual avalanche" of California private gold, mostly larger denominations. Why, then, are these pieces so scarce and prohibitively expensive?*

A. Though technically illegal, many of the issues were produced in substantial number. The need for them in commerce was so pressing that no action was ever brought against any of the coiners. The reason for the large premiums these coins command is, of course, that few have survived. The issuers generally put enough gold in them to assure that intrinsic and face values would be equal, and the coiners agreed to redeem their issues. In some cases the gold content actually exceeded the face value. Most of the coins were, however, eventually redeemed and melted to recover their gold content, with many ultimately recycled into U.S. coins when the new San Francisco Mint became operational on April 3, 1854, nearly two years after the enabling legislation had passed. The new mint was actually an enlargement of the Moffat & Company structure at which the United States Assay Office of Gold coins were struck from 1851 to 1853, the activities of which were terminated on December 14, 1853, with the expansion and equipment installation resulting in a four month suspension of gold coin in the name of the U.S. government.

1851 U.S. Assayer's $50 gold ingot.

Q. *According to the coin catalogs, the first United States coins weren't struck by a branch mint in California until 1854. What were the fifty-dollar pieces struck in California in 1851 at the United States Assay Office, which was apparently a "provisional government mint," if they weren't U.S. coins?*

A. It is true that in 1851 Augustus Humbert commenced operating as the United States Assayer of Gold in San Francisco, for which enabling legislation had been enacted on Sept. 30, 1850. His office became a coin issuing entity, although the de facto mint was actually Moffat & Company, a minting operation under contract to the government. In 1852 Moffat & Company was dissolved, being succeeded by the United States Assay Office of Gold, with the same owners, Joseph Curtis, Philo Perry, and Samuel Ward. The initial productions of 1851 were limited to $50 gold slugs, of which there are several varieties, followed by a single 1852-dated issue, all of which carried imprints of AUGUST HUMBERT UNITED STATES ASSAYER OF GOLD. In 1852 Humbert received permission to strike $10 and $20 gold pieces, which variously carried MOFFAT & CO. and AUGUST HUMBERT UNITED STATES ASSAYER OF GOLD imprints. Later in 1852 $10 coins and $50 slugs carrying the imprint UNITED STATES ASSAY OFFICE OF GOLD SAN FRANCISCO CALIFORNIA were minted, with similar $10 and $20 offerings being minted in 1853. These coins were readily accepted as legal tender on a par with regular U.S. gold coins, but they were officially recognized as "ingots" as opposed to official U.S. Mint issue "coins."

Q. *In Western movies I have seen "Forty-Niners" paying for goods with "a pinch of dust." Since the dust was raw or unrefined gold, how could anyone really be sure what a particular miner's "dust" was actually worth?*

A. Miners and shopkeepers quickly learned to judge the approximate value of gold dust by its color, which varied with the amount of silver present in combination with the gold. Gold in Sacramento and Stanislaus counties had an average value of $18.60 an ounce. That found in Mono County had such a heavy silver content that it bore a distinct resemblance to silver in color. It had an average value of $11.35 an ounce. The first attempt to arrive at an average price occurred on September 9, 1848, when the price of California gold was set at $16 an ounce, providing it had "good color."

1849 Mormon gold piece.

1860 $5 Mormon gold piece.

Q. *I am intrigued by the devices employed on the private gold coins of the Mormon Territory. Can you explain what they mean or symbolize?*

A. The two devices appearing on the 1849 Mormon gold coins are a capped all-seeing eye and clasped hands. The eye on the obverse symbolizes the all-seeing eye of Jehovah surmounted by a Phrygian crown (cap) representing religious freedom. The clasped hands on the reverse are representative of a normal handshake embodying strength, unity, and friendship. The beehive, a favorite device of the Mormons related to the "State of Deseret," the first name given to the Mormon Territory, is represented on the $5 gold piece of 1860. "Deseret" means "honey bee."

1849 Beaver coins of Oregon.

Q. *Is it true that the gold Beaver coins of Oregon were minted despite the fact that the law authorizing them had been declared unconstitutional?*

A. Yes, but all of the private gold coins were of illegal issue. A February 16, 1849, law of the Oregon territorial legislature providing for a mint and authorizing the striking of five- and ten-dollar coins made of gold without alloy was passed after Oregon had been brought into the Union as a territory by an act of Congress. When the territorial governor arrived two weeks later, he declared the Oregon coinage act unconstitutional.

Eight private citizens acted shortly thereafter to provide much needed coinage by forming the Oregon Exchange Company, providing to strike gold coins of the denominations and standards proscribed in the enacted law. Their names were Kilborne, Magruder, Taylor, Abernathy, Wilson, Rector, Campbell, and Smith, the initials on the obverse—K M T R C S—representing six of the partners, with Abernathy and Wilson not being represented. In the view of collectors, they did their job too well; consequently, Oregon gold coins are scarce and expensive today. When it was discovered that the Oregon gold Beavers contained eight percent more gold than necessary, they were bought up in quantity and shipped to California for profitable recoinage into $50 gold slugs.

1855 Kellogg & Co. $50 gold piece.

Q. *Did the California minters of private gold coins cease operating when the United States established a branch mint in the state?*

A. Only a relative few private gold coins dated after 1850 were produced, with the exception of the quasi-federal issues of the United States Assay Office of Gold, which ceased operation in late 1853. Two minters that did continue operating produced issues that were widely accepted. One of these producers was Wass, Molitor & Co., which produced coins in $5 and $10 denominations dated 1852 and $10, $20 and $50 denominations dated 1855. The other was Kellogg & Co., which produced $20 coins dated both 1854 and 1855, very similar in design to U.S. issues, except the reverse legend read SAN FRANCISCO CALIFORNIA rather than UNITED STATES OF AMERICA, and a $50 issue dated 1855 was produced in limited numbers.

Q. *Is it true that the old time prospectors could tell what other metals were combined with gold in an ore sample simply from its color?*

A. It is believed that gold was carried up from great depths, partly in solution, and later precipitated, in chemical combination with other minerals. In chemical combination, rather than in its "free state," gold can appear to be brown, black, purple, blue, and even pink. Experienced prospectors were adept at "reading color." But it is also true that many of those hunting precious metals had no conception of their appearances as ore. The fellow who discovered the fabulous Comstock Lode shoveled tons of "bluish rock" into a gulch before learning that it assayed $1,600 per ton gold and $5,000 per ton silver!

Tobacco advertising card featuring the "Welcome Stranger" nugget.

Q. *Is there a record of the largest nugget of gold ever found in California during the Gold Rush?*

A. We tend to think of a "nugget" of gold being no larger than a walnut, and usually much smaller. Webster, however, defines a nugget as; "A solid lump, especially a native lump of precious metal." The largest lump of gold found in California was found at Carson Hill. It weighed 195 pounds. Another, found at Magalia, weighed 54 pounds. The largest nugget on record is the "Welcome Stranger," which was found in 1869 in Victoria, Australia, only a few inches deep in a wagon rut. It weighed in at a hefty 208 pounds.

CHAPTER EIGHTEEN

Patterns, Trials, Major Errors

Q. *What is a pattern, and how does it differ from a pattern trial piece?*

A. Doctor J. Hewitt Judd, a noted authority on pattern, experimental, and trial pieces of U.S. coinage, defined patterns as "pieces which represent a new design, motto or denomination proposed for adoption as a regular issue, struck in the specified metal, and which were not adopted, at least in the same year." Pattern trial pieces differ from patterns in being struck in something other than the specified metal.

Q. *What is an experimental piece, and how does it differ from an experimental trial piece?*

A. Again quoting Dr. Judd: "Experimental pieces include those struck with any convenient dies to try out a new metal such as aluminum, a new alloy such as goloid, or a new denomination; those which represent a new shape such as the ring dollars; those which represent a new use of an accepted metal such as nickel for a ten-cent piece; and those representing changes in the planchets for the purpose of preventing counterfeiting, sweating, filling, or clipping the edges of the coins. When struck in the proper metal, where it is specified, these are experimental pieces; but struck in other metals, they are experimental trial pieces."

Q. *What is a die trial?*

A. A die trial or die strike is an impression of an unfinished or completed die in a soft metal to test the die for design detail. The planchet utilized in the trial can be of any size or shape, and is usually struck on one side only, creating a uniface specimen.

Q. *Did the United States ever experiment with holed coins, and if so, what was the intended purpose of them?*

A. The United States struck patterns for perforated coins in 1849, 1850, 1851, 1852, 1884, and 1885. The center holes were of three types: round, square, and denticulated. The denominations were one and five cents, a gold half dollar, and a gold dollar. Of the 13 holed pattern types on record, six were for one-cent pieces, two for five-cent pieces, one for a gold half dollar, and four for gold dollars.

Judging from the historical context of their time, it would appear that the patterns of 1849 to 1852 were efforts to create a smaller coin of more precious metal (a holed billon cent to replace the large copper cent was created in 1851). The perforated gold patterns of 1852 were a direct result of the California gold strike, which caused the hoarding of silver coins by increasing the price of silver in relation to gold. Holed gold half dollar and dollar coins were proposed to alleviate the shortage of circulating coin; the holed center served to increase the diameter of the coins to a more convenient dimension.

Undated Jefferson nickel. Clipped planchets and off-center strikes are not uncommon, but are unusual in combination. Known as a "combo" error, this Jefferson nickel from the 1960s or 1970s was struck 40 percent off center on a planchet that is missing almost 25% of the medal (by weight) due to a clipped blank plachet.

Q. *I have heard the term "double-struck coin." Would you please define it for me?*

A. The double-struck coin results from a simple malfunction of the ejector system of a coin press, the consequence of which is that the coin is left in the collar to receive a second strike. If the position of the planchet is not disturbed, the second strike is imposed directly upon the first, and it is not detectable. Should the planchet rotate between strikes, however, it receives two separate and distinct impressions. The value of a double-struck coin, and off-center errors as well, is directly related to the degree of variation, and the presence of a date thereon, with top value given to a 180-degree variation.

Q. *What is an off-center coin?*

A. An off-center coin is created when a failure in the "layer-on" action of a coin press improperly seats a planchet so that only part of it received the die impression. The value of this type error is directly related to the degree the coin is off-center and the presence of a date. Minor off-centering (one to ten percent) historically occurred with routine frequency.

Q. *Having been a casual collector for many years, I am puzzled by the fact that minting errors that seemed to have been in plentiful supply 20 to 25 years ago are today typically priced near or just above the three-digit level. Why is this?*

A. The short answer is supply and demand. Specifically the supply has tightened parallel with a significant increase in demand. In the late 1990s the U.S. Mint's processing equipment and methods were enhanced to the degree that the emission of gross off-center and multiple strikes, along with clipped planchets and similar defective products, decreased dramatically. At the same time and subsequently, the number of collectors pursuing these minting mistakes increased substantially. Back in the 1960s and 1970s, coins displaying die cracks and breaks were the centerpieces of most collections and were typically priced at $1 or less. Major die breaks took years to climb past the $20 level. Today, almost any highly visible minting error variety has a base value of at least several hundred dollars. With demand far exceeding supply, prices have been driven up dramatically from the perspective of twenty-five years ago.

Q. *Are there such things as "off-metal" coins?*

A. They are among the most coveted of mint errors. Off-metal or off-planchet coins are the inevitable consequence of the same coin press and associated materials handling equipment being used to strike several denominations of U.S. coins, as well as foreign coins. At the end of a minting run, an employee makes a cursory inspection of the coining press hopper, or associated materials handling equipment, to see if any unstruck planchets remain. Occasionally one is overlooked. If the press is then switched to the minting of a different denomination, the result will be an off-metal coin. Examples would be a cent struck on a dime planchet, a quarter struck on a nickel planchet and so forth. Harder to explain are instances where a finished coin is restruck with the dies of a different denomination, such as a Lincoln cent struck with the dies for a Liberty Standing quarter. While off-metal coins are commonly traded, they are technically subject to confiscation, as the government considers such errors to be unauthorized coinage.

1955 Lincoln cent, doubled die.

Q. *Was the 1955 "double-date" cent a double struck coin?*

A. Not in the classical sense of being struck twice in different positions in the coin press. The error was caused by a misadventure in the making of the working or production die. Several blows from a hub or master die are required during the die sinking process that produces a working die. The working die must be removed and annealed between strikes to prevent it from becoming work-hardened. If it is not replaced precisely in its previous position for the subsequent strike from the hub, the resulting impression will be out of register, resulting in a working die with doubled impressions. About 20,000 1955 doubled-die cents were struck with such an improperly prepared die before the error was detected. Doubled-die errors with minor doubling evident when the dates and legends are examined under magnification exist for many dates and denominations, but this instance of major die doubling resulted in both the dates and legends being readily discernible with the naked eye.

Q. *Why do 50 State Quarter® mint error coins generally command much higher prices than do, for example, similar Bicentennial quarter errors of a quarter century earlier?*

A. In two words, popularity and presence. For starters, generally speaking, Bicentennial quarter errors of a particular type are generally available in greater numbers than are 50 State Quarter® errors. This is in part due to the fact that the total production of Bicentennial quarters was somewhat in excess of 800 million at both the Philadelphia and Denver mints, while 50 State Quarter® productions for individual states at one mint generally fell within a range of only a bit above 200 to somewhat over 400 million, with the exception of those issues from the last of 1999 (Connecticut) through the first of 2001 (New York), for which the range was from about 500 million (New Hampshire 2000-D) to nearly one billion (Virginia 2000-P). In addition, quality control at the mints was looser in the 1970s than in the first decade of the 21st century. Then, there is the matter of popularity, with the 50 State Quarter® series issues being subject to a greater intensity of interest than are the Bicentennial quarters.

Q. *I have been told that the 1913 Liberty Head nickels are "pieces de caprice." What is meant by this?*

A. A "piece de caprice" is a coin that was not authorized for production that was created within a mint, for some reason other than as a pattern, experimental or trial piece, to satisfy the whim or avarice of an employee in creating a rarity.

Q. *What is a "clover-leaf" error?*

A. A major error of extreme rarity. It is a combination of major errors in being triple struck with a pair of off-center impressions, the resulting appearance being similar to that of a clover-leaf.

Buffalo nickel. Details show a normal coin and the three-legged variety.

Q. *Can you tell me what is meant by a "Three-legged Buffalo?"*

A. This term is used to describe a major error occurring on certain 1937-D nickels wherein the midsection of the buffalo's right foreleg is missing. It is believed that the error resulted when the die was ground down to remove disfiguring marks that resulted when the reverse die accidentally clashed with an obverse die when the press closed without a nickel blank in the coining cavity. A similar, but somewhat less valuable "3-1/2 legged" 1936-D Buffalo also exists. In the case of the 1937-D, regular nickels of that date and mint have been altered to simulate this prized error. The genuine and spurious errors can be distinguished by the fact that on genuine specimens a line of tiny, rough dots in a gentle crescent extends from the belly of the buffalo to the ground. Also the hoof of the missing leg must be visible on genuine specimens, while altered specimens frequently exhibit an abrupt clean severance line and no hoof.

Q. *What is considered to be the most improbable example of a multiple major error coin?*

A. A double-dated coin would certainly be one candidate for this honor. In 1900, a properly struck 1899-dated Indian Head cent was channeled back into the coining process and fed into the coin press, resulting in an upside down, half-off center restrike bearing two different dates! Was this an accident? We'll never know, but such a coin is highly valued regardless of the suspicions about its origins.

Waffled coins.

Q. *I have heard the term "waffled" coins used. What does it mean?*

A. Commencing in 2003 as an extension of its quality control program and to allow fewer error coins to reach the marketplace, the U.S. Mint instituted the use of machines into which coins screened out of production during the quality control process were fed under high pressure between pairs of rollers, distorted the surfaces of the error pieces into an appearance somewhat akin to that of a "waffle" prior to the scrap being shipped to outside vendors for melting. This process has had the effect of greatly reducing the number of error coins—multiple struck and off-center coins, blank and clipped planchets and other scrap—reaching the marketplace, although waffled examples of all denominations struck for circulation are known for all years from 2003 on, but the Mint has not objected to their being traded because they are not considered coins with legal tender status. The machines for this process were originally developed in Austria, in advance of the conversion to the Euro in 2002, to handle the retirement and recycling of the circulating coins of its predecessor individual national monetary systems.

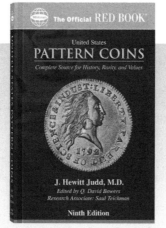

For more information: Consult *United States Pattern Coins* (Judd/Bowers).

CHAPTER NINETEEN

Minor Errors, Oddities, and Varieties

Q. *I am confused by the seemingly endless variety of mint errors. Can you provide me with a breakdown of types?*

A. Minting errors are generally categorized in three major groupings: die/engraving errors, planchet errors, and striking errors. These categories are comprised of the following types:

DIE/ENGRAVING ERRORS

1. Die breaks
2. Die cracks
3. Die gouges
4. Die scratches
5. Die clashes
6. Worn dies
7. Polished dies
8. Double and multiple mintmarks
9. Engraving errors
10. Overdates
11. Shifting
12. Double entry of hub

PLANCHET ERRORS

1. Off metal
2. Wrong planchet
3. Poor alloy mix
4. Clipped planchets
5. Damaged planchets
6. Planchet laminations
7. Split planchets
8. Blank planchets

STRIKING ERRORS

1. Doubling
2. Multiple strikes
3. Collar errors
4. Indented errors
5. Impressed (brockage) errors
6. Off-center strikes
7. Edge strikes
8. Filled die
9. Alien material present
10. Die adjustment strikes
11. Rotated die
12. Misaligned die

Q. *As I was leaving my first coin club meeting, I heard a collector refer to another as a "fido" collector. What did he mean?*

A. The term FIDO is a coin word that was once widely applied to mint errors, but that has fallen out of use since the 1960s. It is only infrequently used today. The term is formed from the first letter of each of four words applicable to coins that deviate from normal strikes: Freaks, Imperfections, Defects, and Oddities.

Q. *Can you account for the upsurge of interest in recent years in mint errors?*

A. Major mint errors—overdates, off-center strikes, and multiple strikes—have long been of great interest to most collectors. Some of the more significant mint errors—die breaks, double dates, and clipped planchets—have also enjoyed a small but enthusiastic following for many years.

The tremendous expansion which occurred during the past few years, an interest which caused the formation of national error clubs, the appearance of regular error columns in the hobby press, and development of comprehensive cataloging of mint errors, is to at least a significant extent due to the mid-1960s phenomenon of the switch to clad metal coins and the disappearance of traditional silver coins from circulation.

Coin collecting attracts devotees from all levels of the social structure. Many collectors, particularly youngsters and those of modest financial means, were at the time unwilling to expend substantial sums on their pursuits of coin collecting. They derived their "kicks" from attempting to assemble their date-mint sets with coins encountered in circulation. The silver coin–melting phenomenon narrowed their activity to cents and nickels and the readily available new clad coins. Many turned to errors, particularly Lincoln cent errors, as these errors were relatively plentiful due to the billion coin and larger quantities of annual production commencing with the 1959 introduction of the Memorial reverse type, providing an inexpensive means to continue hobby enjoyment.

The increased availability of error coins of all denominations from the 1960s through the 1990s also inadvertently exposed and attracted more collectors to the error field. During this time the tremendous production increases greatly increased the incidence of errors through overuse of dies and the physical impossibility of detecting all errors by the inspection procedures then employed. Quality control enhancements introduced in more recent years have greatly reduced the quantities of error coins that escape detection and recycling. Thus, the combination of greater collector interest and reduced availability are combining to drive the price of both major and minor errors to levels that would have been undreamed of in the 1960s.

Q. *Are oddities and varieties in current coinage of the United States considered to be good collector items?*

A. Any valid minting oddity or variety is considered to be a "good" collector item by those interested in the field. The true hobby collector, whatever his interest, however, does not confuse desirability with market value. If by "good" you mean market value or investment potential, it must be remembered that on a relative rarity basis, neither minor nor major errors are likely to ever command the premiums or growth potentials of similar non-error coins. While a very firm market has developed for major error coins—most die and planchet, and some striking errors—and a relatively firm market exists for minor error coins—doubling, filled dies, die scratches, and damaged planchets are some examples—as the great preponderance of U.S. collectors are not mint error buffs, their interests and dollars do not provide support for the mint error market. By and large, mint errors are still priced at moderate levels compared to non-error coins of like quality.

Q. *Recently, while checking an accumulation of cents, I found a number of examples on which various numerals and legend letters appear to be filled, particularly the loops of the Bs, 9s and 6s. What caused this, and is it a common occurrence?*

A. This type of error is created when a small portion of the working die becomes fatigued and breaks away, leaving a hole into which the coin planchet metal is forced by the impact of striking, producing a raised, irregular feature on the coin surface. Die break errors of this type are very common today, and while they make interesting displays they generally command relatively modest premiums.

BIE of Liberty.

Q. *My father gave me a 1966-D Lincoln cent he received in change on which "Liberty" is misspelled LIBIERTY. Is this an engraver's error? Is it valuable?*

A. Your cent is an example of the popular striking oddity known as the "BIE" error. It was caused when a portion of the die between "B" and "E" broke away, leaving a sharply delineated depression in the die, which raised what appears to be an additional "I" in LIBERTY. The BIE error is quite common in its cruder expression; that is, with the extra "I" being generally featureless and of less than full height. They are of little value. However, examples where the I is attractively formed, such as the 1959-D BIE cent have commanded substantial premiums. Such defective die varieties of cents, nickels, dimes and quarters typically command valuations in the $10 to $25 range.

Q. *I am familiar with the "Godless" coins of Canada, but what is an "atheist cent?"*

A. The "atheist cent" is a major, and valuable, example of a die break error. A portion of the rim of a 1970-S cent die broke away, raising a "cud" on the coins—planchet metal flowing into the die to the height of the rim—that obliterated WE TRUST of the motto IN GOD WE TRUST. The popularity of this particular error causes it to command a premium in the range of three to five times that of a typical defective die variety.

Franklin "Bugs Bunny" half dollar (left) and Roosevelt mustache.

Q. *What is the cause of such unseemly oddities as the 1954 Roosevelt dime with the handlebar or Hitler mustaches, and the 1955 Franklin "Bugs Bunny" half dollar?*

A. These curious oddities were created by unusual die deterioration which allowed the coin planchet metal to form unintended but humorous blobs on the surface of the coin; in the instance of the 1955 half dollar, giving Franklin a neat set of buckteeth. This error was more popular and commanded a substantially higher premium in the 1960s than it does today. The 1954 dimes were notorious for die deterioration defects, resulting in fangs, warts, cowlicks, broken noses, and occasional combinations of such defects, in addition to the mustache varieties.

Q. *At a coin show I saw a small exhibit labeled "The Wandering Ds of '56." It consisted of a large number of 1956-D cents on which the D mintmark was erratically positioned. Some were left, right, up, down, even tilted and doubled. Can you explain the erratic positioning of the mintmarks?*

A. Historically, mintmarks were applied to working dies as a hand operation subsequent to their preparation in the hubbing process. All dies were manufactured at the Philadelphia Mint, with the mintmarks of branch mints being applied just prior to their shipment to those facilities. This hand operation led to human error with respect to the specific placement of the mintmarks in total conformation to its intended positioning. In 1990 and 1991 the process was changed, with the mintmarks being applied to the production hubs—which are employed in the creation of the working dies—which brought a halt to the wandering mintmark phenomenon.

Double or multiple mintmarks resulted from the punch being applied more than once with improper alignment with the initial punch impression. Doubled vertical mintmarks are of little value unless the doubling is bold. Rare examples that combine a vertical and horizontal mintmark, or consist of the mark of one mint being struck over the mark of another, are considered major errors and command substantial premiums.

Q. *I have a number of 1943 steel cents on which the "4" of 1943 is either weak or missing. What caused this?*

A. The missing or weak numeral (or letter) error is generally caused by the concerned area of the die filling with dirt, grease, or metal particles which harden and prevent coin planchet metal from flowing into that area of the die as intended, which softens or eliminates the intended raising of the numeral or letter. Weak and small numerals and letters, and missing minor details, can also be caused by a portion of the die being removed or weakened when the die was polished or by a die becoming excessively worn through overuse.

Q. *I have seen coins that appear to have a bit taken out of them. How did this occur, and what is their value?*

A. These "bitten" coins are called "clips," or clipped planchet coins. They occur during the blanking operation, where a group of circular cutters punch planchets from a strip of metal. If the strip of metal fails to advance properly as it feeds through the blanking press, each punch in the first line of the group may overlap the last, with the consequent blanks appearing to have a bite taken out of them. If the strip is moved sideways out of alignment with the punch grouping, or if the punching proceeds to the very end of the strip being blanked, a flat or edge clip will result. While the value of small clips, and other minting errors, is mainly determined by how badly someone wants it, large clips, multiple clips, and clipped coins of older types and higher denominations command greater premiums. All else being equal, the clipped coin that retains its date is of substantially greater than one that is dateless.

Q. *How can I tell a mint-made clip from one made in someone's garage?*

A. The homemade clip, produced by punching out a bit of the metal with a round punch die, will show a flattened or buckled effect on the side of the coin opposite to that upon which the punch was applied. The rim of a genuine clip will taper off as it approaches the clipped area due to the free flow of metal in that direction during the striking process.

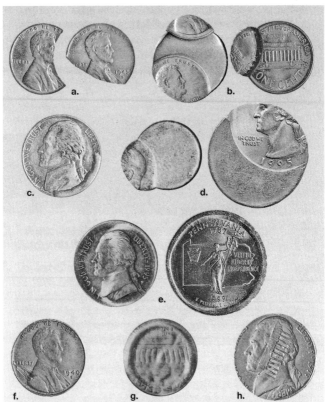

Mint errors. A variety of errors originating during the minting process have been identified and coveted by collectors. Among these errors are the ones pictured here: (a) clipped planchet, a coin missing 10–25 percent of its metal; (b) multiple strike, a coin with at least one additional image from being struck again off center; (c) defective die, a coin showing raised metal from a large die crack or small rim break; (d) off center, a coin struck out of collar or incorrectly centered so part of the design is missing; (e) broadstrike, a coin struck without a retaining collar; (f) lamination, a coin with a fragment of metal peeled off the coin surface; (g) brockage, a coin with a mirror image of the design impressed on the opposite side; (h) wrong planchet, a coin struck on a planchet intended for another denomination.

Q. *I have a nickel that has what appears to be a short length of wire firmly imbedded in Jefferson's cheek. Could this have happened at the mint?*

A. Error collectors will assure you that anything can happen at the mint. Your nickel is representative of the type of error known as an impressed error, and reflects the fact that a scrap of wire was between the coin planchet and the obverse die at the time the coin was struck. Such errors are uncommon and command significant premiums.

Q. *I have a naturally dark (not tarnished) Jefferson nickel. What caused the discoloration? Is it valuable?*

A. Off-color Jefferson nickels are not uncommon, and are known in hues ranging from smoky blue through deep purple, to black. The discoloration is caused by an incorrect alloy mix containing significantly too much copper. Some collectors are attracted to them, as some prefer toned Proof coins, and will pay a small premium for them.

The discoloration of poor alloy mix is more commonly encountered in the bronze cent, taking the form of coins with discernible yellow streaks on the surface or with a distinct yellowish cast. The coin is normally composed of 95 percent copper and 5 percent zinc. As the proportion of zinc to copper increases, the coins become progressively more yellow, until at a ratio of 30 to 70 percent the alloy becomes ordinary brass.

Q. *All of the U.S. coins I have ever seen have the reverse rotated 180 degrees in relation to the obverse. However, today I found a Lincoln cent which has the reverse rotated at about 90 degrees. How did this come about and what is such a coin worth?*

A. When the dies are attached to a coining press, they are locked in proper alignment with a key. Sometimes a key will be improperly set or will work loose, allowing a die to rotate away from its proper position and permit the striking or rotated die errors. The value of such oddities is determined by the degree of rotation involved, and by the type and denomination of the affected coin. The premium paid for coins of modest variance—under 15 degrees—and the type and denomination of the affected coin, with 90 and 180 degree rotations being the most sought after. The premiums paid for coins of modest variance and low denomination—high production quantities—is relatively low.

Q. *What is meant by a "first process" blank planchet and a "second process" blank?*

A. First process blanks are characterized by their sharp edges. Second process blanks have had their edges upset so that they are slightly higher than the surface of the blank, they being slightly smaller in diameter than the finished coin would be. These raised edges result from punched blanks being fed through upsetting mills prior to their being fed into the coining presses to improve metal flow to the raised coin edges in the striking process. Unmilled and milled would serve as more precise terminology for classification of these blanks.

Q. *What is a die trial as it relates to error coinage?*

A. The "die trial" error is a very weak strike caused by the dies being set too far apart during the adjustment process, or by the planchet being struck by a press slowing to a stop. The resulting raised design features appear weak. These imperfect coins are normally scrapped by the pressman, but examples occasionally escape into the receptacle for good finished coins. This error should not be confused with the die trial piece produced by the impression of an unfinished or completed die in soft metal to test the die.

Q. *Is there a book available that lists and provides valuations for minting varieties of U.S. coins?*

A. There is nothing available that comprehensively covers all of the wide variety of minting errors. There are a pair of volumes, however, that provide collectors with a wealth of detailed information on die varieties that have reasonably broad appeal to collectors—they are *The Cherrypickers' Guide* volumes authored by Bill Fivaz and J.T. Stanton, the first volume of which covers half cents through nickels, and the second embracing half dimes through gold and the classic commemoratives. These volumes, produced in new editions by Whitman Publishing, present the user with clearly detailed, enlarged illustrations of the struck design features that distinguish the listed varieties from regular strikes.

III.
AMERICAN
PAPER MONEY

About the images in this book: In general, coin denominations of 50 cents and higher are pictured at actual size; denominations below 50 cents and coins that are unusually small (e.g., gold dollars) are generally pictured at 150 percent of their actual size. Paper money is typically pictured at page width. Other items, such as medals, encased postage, and so on, may be enlarged for visibility. Appendix B lists the actual sizes of U.S. coins and currency.

CHAPTER TWENTY

Continental Currency and Broken Bank Notes

Q. *What is meant by the term "shinplaster?"*

A. The American War for Independence was a time of great ideals and small preparations. There was grand talk of inalienable rights and a dearth of supplies for the quartermaster. When a soldier bled, he stanched the flow with a plaster of papers. When his stockings wore out and his boots chafed his ankles, he wrapped his feet with a protective layer of paper. These papers acquired the name of "shinplasters" from the second use. Once used for either purpose, they were as worthless as a struck match. The term has since been applied to Continental Currency, U.S. Fractional Currency, and sometimes to state bank notes when their value was questionable and might have been used as "shinplasters," as was the destiny of some of the near-worthless Continental Currency.

Q. *You often hear the phrase "scarce as a $3 bill." Did such a piece of money ever exist?*

A. Yes, as did a $4 and $8 bill, along with a host of other odd denominations. They were all issued before the adoption of a federal currency in 1861. Between 1837 and 1857, states, banks, savings institutions, and various other organizations issued paper notes in such seemingly odd denominations as 6-1/4¢, 12-1/2¢, $1.25, $1.50, $1.75, $2.50, and $7.50. In reality, the denominations were logical and of benefit to everyday commerce at a time when U.S. and Spanish coins circulated concurrently, and people were accustomed to goods priced in terms of the Spanish bit (12-1/2¢) and its fractions and multiples. Such notes are no longer legal tender, but are prized by collectors, with many issues being excessively rare and very valuable.

Broken bank notes. Many odd denominations can be found among the broken bank notes, a name attached to them because most of the private banks did not redeem their issues.

Q. *What does the term "broken bank note" mean?*

A. The present system of United States paper money began with the Civil War. Prior to 1861, the chief form of paper currency was notes issued by banks operating under charters granted by individual states. These notes were generally backed only by a pledge of stock, a backing that merely reflected the anticipation that the institution would endure and prosper. Inevitably, many such banks were unable to withstand the effects of mismanagement, under-financing, or financial panic, went broke, and were unable to redeem their notes. Thus was born the term, "broken bank notes."

Q. *Why is it that some types of Colonial Currency once thought to be quite scarce are now encountered with greater frequency?*

A. Occasionally surplus notes or duplicates—or entire collections or old accumulations—of Colonial Currency are put on the market by museums and state archives. Some years ago many Connecticut issues, for example, once thought to be rare became available to collectors in this manner.

Q. *Is there any way of determining how many broken bank notes were issued?*

A. The gigantic task of cataloging broken bank notes, the largest series of U.S. paper money, has been undertaken by the Society of Paper Money Collectors, sponsoring an ongoing series of state books authored by specialists. That effort is far from complete. A comprehensive four-volume study authored by James A. Haxby in 1988 *(United States Obsolete Bank Notes, 1782–1866)* provides a detailed overview of the state chartered bank, its unchartered banking association predecessor, the state chartered savings bank, and fraudulent bank issues. It has been speculated that more than 30,000 varieties of notes were issued between 1782 and 1866 by some 1,600 banks operating in 35 states.

Q. *Recently at a state coin convention I saw an exhibit consisting of a number of $1.75 bank notes. How do you account for this unusual denomination?*

A. The notes were probably broken bank notes, which exist in such unusual denominations as $1.37-1/2, $1.75, $2.50, $3, $4, $6, $7, $8, $9, $12, $13, and even more exotic units of value. The $1.75 value was directly related to the eight reales coin, and its lesser units, which was legal tender in the United States until 1857. The piece-of-eight was divided into eight 12-1/2–cent "bits." Fourteen bits were exactly equal to $1.75.

Q. *When did the national identification "United States" first appear on a government issue of paper money?*

A. When first issued in May of 1775, Continental Currency bore the title "The United Colonies." That identification was continued following the signing of the Declaration of Independence until May 1777, when the title was changed to "The United States." The title was expanded to "The United States of North America" on the last issue of Continental Currency, dated January 14, 1779.

Three-dollar 1775 Continental Currency. Continental Currency such as this piece lost its value quickly, giving rise to the expression, "Not worth a Continental."

Q. *I've been told that the term "not worth a Continental" was derived from money. Is this correct?*

A. Yes. The first type of money issued by the Continental Congress, the first U.S. central government, was a form of paper money known as Continental Currency. In theory it was redeemable in Spanish milled dollars, but as the Continental Congress controlled no specie to back the note emissions it authorized, and no practical authority to implement and enforce its pronouncements, the paper rapidly inflated to the point that it had no meaningful value; in 1780, 27,733-1/2 Continental Dollars were required to purchase 10 head of cattle valued at 200 Spanish silver dollars. The Continental Currency was widely rejected by the public and never redeemed by the government; because of this, "not worth a Continental" came to denote the complete absence of value.

Chapter Twenty-one

U.S. Paper Money

Q. *I have a $5 bill issued on a hometown bank. It not only has the signatures of the "Register of the Treasury" and the "Treasurer of the United States," but is also signed by local bank officials, the "Cashier" and the "President." Is it any good?*

A. Take all you can get. You have a National Bank Note that is as sound as the day it was printed. In 1862, as part of a program to stabilize chaotic banking standards and revive a functioning banking system, the U.S. government began granting federal charters to banks with assets that could be deposited as security against the issue of "blue chip" government bonds. Concurrently the right of state banks to issue currency was revoked.

From 1862 to 1933, when the National Bank currency issuing privilege was terminated, 14,348 National Banks were authorized to issue National Bank Notes against their government deposits. These notes were exquisitely drafted, with historically attuned designs, which are as valid as monetary instruments today as they were when issued. Due to their rarity and artistic appeal they invariably command a collector premium that in most instances is many multiples in excess of their face value, unless they are in very poor condition and/or extremely common.

Q. *I have several Silver Certificate and Federal Reserve Note bills, along with a few that bear red seals, including some United States Note $2 bills that have red seals. All are of the same size and similar in design to those we were receiving from banks prior to the recent redesign and colorizing of our currency. The other day I found a note bearing a* *brown seal that had the name of a bank from a neighboring town on it. What can you tell me about these notes? Can they still be spent?*

A. Yes, they certainly can, but in most instances to do so would be to cheat yourself. All U.S. paper money issued since the first Demand Note obligations were released in 1861—to facilitate federal financing of the Civil War—remain legal tender for all debts pubic and private. While eleven different types of notes—Interest Bearing Note, Demand Note, Legal Tender or United States Note, Compound Interest Treasury Note, National Bank Note, National Gold Bank Note, Silver Certificate, Treasury or Coin Note, Federal Reserve Bank Note, Federal Reserve Note, and the Refunding Certificate (a $10 denominated issue of 1879 that was actually a bond, but is collected as a note)—were issued during the large-size currency era, 1861 through 1929, there have been only five types issued during the small-size currency era since that time, with Federal Reserve Note obligations being the only type still in production.

All U.S. note issues from 1862 through 1966 are overprinted with red Treasury seals; in the era of small size issues commencing in 1928, most notes were of $2 and $5 denominations, with $1 notes also being issued dated 1928 and $100 notes dated 1966. Silver Certificate notes were issued from 1886 through 1957, all overprinted with blue Treasury seals, with only $1, $5 and $10 notes being issued in the small size era, bearing series dates from 1928 to 1957. While the issue of Federal Reserve Note obligations commenced in 1914 as large size notes, they have been the backbone of our circulating currency since the first small size notes were issued in 1928 in denominations from $5 to $10,000, with the overprinted Treasury seals being green; no denomination above $100 has been printed since the 1940s. The series was expanded with the introduction of $1 issues commencing in 1963, and the $2 note being added with series dated 1976, 1995, and 2003.

Your brown seal note would be a National Bank Note issue, with all small-size currency issues carrying the date 1929; these notes were issued prior to 1933 under provisions of the National Bank Act. Gold Certificate paper money obligations were also issued as small size currency in $10, $20, $50, and $100 denominations; they bear gold Treasury seal overprints and appeared only in a 1928-dated series.

The "jackass" note. The Series 1869 Legal Tender note displays an eagle on the face that, turned upside down, resembles a jackass.

Q. *What is a "jackass note?"*

A. The note referred to is the Legal Tender Note of 1869 and subsequent series of 1875, 1878, and 1880. All feature a small vignette of an eagle with spread wings at bottom center on the face, which, when the note is inverted for viewing upside down, resembles the head of a donkey or "jackass."

Q. *What is the highest denomination note circulated by the U.S. government?*

A. Generally speaking, the $1,000 value is the highest face value that might have been encountered in circulation. Actually, no notes with face values higher than $100 have been printed since 1945, and since 1969 all higher value notes have been subject to permanent retirement as they circulate back into the Federal Reserve System. While a quantity (42,000) of $100,000 notes were printed in the 1934 Gold Certificate series, these were prepared for exclusive use within the nation's banking system at the federal level. Otherwise, the highest denominations printed and released for circulation between 1875 and 1934 were $5,000 and $10,000 notes.

During the large-size currency era, the $5,000 and $10,000 values were authorized for general issue only as Legal Tender or United States Note (1878 series), Gold Certificate (1882 and 1888 series) and Federal Reserve Note (1918 series) obligations, while there was also a $5,000 unit issued as one- and three-year Interest Bearing Note obligations in 1861 and 1863 dated series, of which no examples are known to have survived. In the small-size currency era, $5,000 and $10,000 notes were issued as Federal Reserve Note (1928 and 1934) and Gold Certificate (1928) obligations, with a $10,000 note issue existing as a 1934 Gold Certificate as well.

Security precautions. Hawaiian overprints with brown seals were issued just after Pearl Harbor to use in the islands. If the Japanese had invaded Hawaii, the distinctive notes could have been devalued with a minimum of confusion.

Q. *I have a $5 bill that has the word HAWAII printed on both the front and back. Can you tell me what I have and its value?*

A. You have one of the special "Hawaiian" precautionary notes introduced in the islands following the Japanese attack on Pearl Harbor on December 7, 1941. The Hawaiian series was printed in $1 Silver Certificate and $5, $10, and $20 San Francisco Federal Reserve Note obligations. The notes carried brown Treasury seals, rather than blue or green, and were overprinted with HAWAII in small letters on both sides of the front, and in large, open-face letters on the back. The purpose of the overprints were to distinguish the paper money in use in Hawaii and by troops stationed elsewhere in the Pacific theater, to facilitate invalidation of the circulation should it fall into enemy hands.

The series 1934 $20 is the scarcest note in the series by far. The 1935-A $1, 1934 $5, and 1934A $5, $10, and $20 all command values in the high three-figure range. Star notes exist of all four series, with the 1934-A $5 star note being truly rare, while star notes of the other series command high four-figure premiums or more. These notes remain legal tender today, but any note in fine or better condition commands a significant premium.

Q. *I have two $1 bills signed by Granahan and Dillon which look alike. The only difference is one series is designated as 1935-H and the other as 1957-B. Why are these two series designations used on notes bearing the same signatures?*

A. The difference between the 1935 and 1957 series notes is visually negligible, involving a technical consideration. Series 1935 notes are printed on paper that was mill-wet and contains 50-percent cotton and 50-percent linen. The subsequent drying process imparted a slight wrinkling to the notes. Series 1957 notes were dry-printed using paper that is 75-percent cotton and 25-percent linen. This process produced flat, wrinkle-free notes.

Q. *I have a pair of notes carrying the signatures of Ivy Baker Priest as Treasurer of the United States and Robert B. Anderson as Secretary of the Treasury, but one carries the series designation 1935-F and the other 1957. Why is this?*

A. The most discernible difference between your pair of notes concerns inclusion of the motto IN GOD WE TRUST above the word ONE on the back of the 1957 note, while it is not present on the back of the 1935-F note. The series 1957 $1 note was the first U.S. paper money obligation to incorporate the motto, as stipulated by the Act of July 11, 1955, which had been championed by Matt B. Rothert, who subsequently served as president of the American Numismatic Association. The first notes were placed in circulation on October 1, 1957. Subsequently, series 1935-G notes, bearing the signatures of Elizabeth Rudel Smith and C. Douglas Dillon, were produced both with and without the motto parallel with series 1957-A notes with the motto, while 1935-H notes, bearing the signatures of Kathryn O'Hay Granahan and C. Douglas Dillon, were produced only with the motto and parallel with series 1957-B notes. These parallel productions were required to meet circulation demands as the Bureau of Engraving and Printing was in the process of converting its press room from the wet to dry printing processes.

Q. *A friend of mine who used to run a retail shop had dutifully checked the receipts at the end of each day looking for and preserving "rare Barr notes." How rare are they? What are they worth?*

A. Joseph W. Barr served as Secretary of the Treasury for only one month, from December 20, 1968, to January 20, 1969. Despite his short tenure, more than 470 million of the Barr-Granahan $1 bills were printed, or more than two for every man, woman, and child in the United States. These were Federal Reserve Notes of the 1963-B series, they being printed for only the New York, Richmond, Chicago, Kansas City, and San Francisco banks. Even strictly uncirculated notes of this series are of only modest value, with the exception of the star notes of the San Francisco and Chicago banks, which do command a decent premium, well above those commanded by star notes of the New York and Richmond banks. Kansas City star notes were not produced.

Q. *Why are the signatures of Granahan and Dillon on notes dated 1935, 1957, and 1963, when their term of office was 1961 through 1963?*

A. Unlike coins, paper money is not generally dated in the year of its issue. The year dates refer to the year the basic design or issue of a currency was first produced. The alphabetic suffix appearing in combination with a date indicated the sequential introduction of a minor change, usually a signature change for the Treasurer of the United States or Secretary of the Treasury, or both. In the case of the 1935-H Granahan-Dillon signature combination, it represents the ninth minor change in the $1 Silver Certificate series of 1935, the third basic type of the small size currency era, of which eight were signature combinations. The 1957-B Granahan-Dillon signature combination was the third signature combination for the IN GOD WE TRUST design change under the dry printing process introduced that year. The 1963 Granahan-Dillon signature combination is the first issue in the Federal Reserve Note series. All three of these note issues were in overlapping production during their joint service tenure which extended from January 3, 1963, through March 31, 1965.

Q. *What do all those little numbers in the upper left portion of the field on the front of series 1957 one-dollar bills mean; i.e., A1, C3, D4, B2, etc.?*

A. This particular note was printed in a 32 subject sheet configuration. Each quarter has a numerical designation: 1, 2, 3, 4. Each numerical designation has an alphabetic designation to locate a particular note in relation to all the others within a given quarter of the sheet. The designations reveal the exact location on a 32 subject sheet from which the individual note came.

Q. *I have always understood that whenever there was any change in the design of a U.S. currency note the suffix letters of the series designation was changed. However, I have two series 1935-G $1 Silver Certificates which differ from each other. One includes the motto IN GOD WE TRUST, while the other does not. Can you explain why the suffix letter is the same on both notes?*

A. No, but we are not alone. Normally, the second variety of the series 1935-G note, the one with the motto, would have carried a new designation (H), but for some unexplained reason the change was not made. The second variety is generally considered to be the scarcer of the two by a factor of roughly three.

Q. *I am confused about the appearance of the national motto, IN GOD WE TRUST, on our paper currency. Can you tell me the why and the where of it?*

A. The Act requiring that the national motto to appear on U.S. paper currency was signed by President Eisenhower on July 11, 1955. It first appeared on $1 Silver Certificates dated 1957. It was not initially intended that the motto be added to the series 1935 Silver Certificates, but they, too, were converted in 1962, without the traditional change in suffix letter. It was not until March of 1964 that the motto was added to other denominations, in this case the twos and fives. It was added at that time in accordance with a conversion schedule announced early in 1964, calling for a complete conversion through the $100 denomination by January of 1965, which objective was not technically achieved. The $10 and $20 Federal Reserve Notes incorporated the motto effective with the 1963 series (Granahan-Dillon, tenure terminated March 31, 1965), while the change was effected for the $50 and $100 notes with the 1963-A series (Granahan-Fowler, tenure commenced April 1, 1965).

Q. *Is it illegal to hold Gold Certificates?*

A. Gold Certificates were called in the same as gold coin by the order of the Secretary of the Treasury on December 28, 1933; at that time, it was illegal to hold them. However, the Secret Service did not come looking for them because they could not be exchanged for gold and were technically no longer legal tender, although they were exchangeable for lawful money at any bank. Somewhat over 30 years later, in April 1964, the Treasury Department revised its ruling, and it has since been legal to own and display Gold Certificates for numismatic purposes.

Q. *I understand that if one were to take Silver Certificates to the Treasury in Washington seeking to redeem them for silver dollars, or "one dollar in silver" as the obligation printed on the notes pledges, that they would not be honored. I am told that the Treasury is no longer obligated to redeem the notes with either silver dollars or silver bullion. Why can't the government be held to its obligation?*

A. Prior to 1935 the government was obligated to redeem Silver Certificates with silver dollars, and thereafter with one dollar in silver bullion, which at the pegged silver price of $1.2929 per ounce amounted to .77 ounce of silver bullion per dollar. The traditional tie between silver and our circulating currency came to an end on June 24, 1968. Congress, by the Act of June 24, 1967, provided one year for the redemption of Silver Certificates in silver bullion. During that period notes to the amount of $150 million were redeemed, leaving approximately $245 million of Silver Certificates which the government is no longer obligated to redeem in silver, although they remain valid legal tender. The retired Silver Certificates have been replaced by Federal Reserve Notes.

Q. *I have a $20 bill that was partly destroyed by burning. Can I exchange it for a new one?*

A. Three-fifths or more of a mutilated note will be redeemed by the Treasurer of the United States at full face value. Less than three-fifths, but more than two-fifths will be redeemed at one-half face value. Fragments not more than two-fifths will not be redeemed unless accompanied by proof, in the form of affidavits, that the missing portions have been

Educational series. Popular with paper money collectors are the three silver certificates known as the "educational" series. On the $1 note, History instructs Youth, with the Constitution at right, the Capitol and Washington Monument in the background; Science presents the twin gifts of steam and electricity to Commerce and Manufacture on the $2 note, and the $5 denomination depicts Electricity as the dominant force in the world.

destroyed. Your local bank should be able to initiate the redemption process for you.

Q. *Is it legal to photograph coins or paper money?*

A. Coins may be reproduced on flat surfaces; that is, they must not have raised relief surfaces.

Prior to the liberalization of currency reproduction statutes on September 2, 1958, photographic or printed reproductions of currency were prohibited. "Printed illustrations of paper money, checks, bonds and other obligations and securities of the United States and foreign governments are permissible for numismatic, educational, historical and newsworthy purposes," read the new regulation. "The illustrations must be of a size less than three-fourths or more than one-and-a-half times the size of the genuine. No illustrations may be in color."

These restrictions were subsequently challenged in court. In 1984 their validity was upheld by the U.S. Supreme Court insofar as the size and color restrictions were concerned. More recently they have been revised to permit illustrative reproductions in color, provided the over and under size restrictions are observed.

Q. *What is the rarest $2 note that has been issued?*

A. There are two possible answers to this question. Authorities generally concede that the series 1878 Legal Tender deuce signed by Glenni W. Scofield as Register of the Treasury and James Gilfillan as Treasurer of the United States is the rarest in terms of availability. The original issue National Bank Note series, however, features the popular "Lazy 2" note, which in the Noah L. Jeffries / F.E. Spinner signature combination sometimes commands the higher premium when sold.

Q. *How many notes are there in a complete type set of $2 bills?*

A. Introduction of the new series 1976 Federal Reserve Note deuce—this type has been continued through 1995, 2003, and 2003-A signature combination series'—brought to 17 the number of basic type notes in this denomination which have been issued under the authority of the federal government since the first modern circulating paper money issues were authorized in 1861. Of this total, 13 were issued during the period of large size note issues (1861–1923): five in the Legal Tender or United States Note series, four Silver Certificates, two Treasury of Coin Note series, and one each in the National Bank Note and Federal Reserve Bank Note series. Three small size United States Note issues—series 1928, 1953, and 1963—preceded the new 1976 Bicentennial–oriented issue.

Undoubtedly the second most popular type note, and the best known aside from the distinctive "Lazy 2" is the series 1896 Silver Certificate, one of a trio of notes constituting the "educational" series. This note portrays science presenting steam and electricity to commerce and industry on the face side, while the back presents vignette portraits of inventors Robert Fulton and Samuel Morse.

1776 $2 note. Reproduction of Trumbull's painting shows delegates to the Constitutional Congress and Thomas Jefferson presenting the Declaration of Independence for signatures. In adapting the scene to the back of the $2 note, the Treasury cropped six delegates from the original, an omission that triggered protests from some historians.

Q. *Why are U.S. $2 notes no longer being actively printed and circulated? It seems that, with the $1 bill steadily declining in purchasing power, a $2 note would be a practical alternative?*

A. The U.S. Treasury came to the same conclusion a few years back, scheduling a new $2 note to enter commercial channels on April 13, 1976.

Except for the series designation (1976), signatures, and its designation as a Federal Reserve Note—all prior small-size $2 notes were Legal Tender or United States Note obligations—the front of the new paper $2 was similar to its predecessor. However, the back presented a large vignette representing John Trumbull's painting of the Signing of the Declaration of Independence, rather than the picture of Jefferson's home, Monticello.

The old $2 note, last printed in 1965, had been discontinued for a variety of reasons, both practical and frivolous. Merchants and customers complained because the denomination could be confused with the $1 note, and tradesmen objected because standard cash registers did not have a pocked for receiving the odd value. Superstition and myth also entered the picture—some despised the two-spot because of its reputation as a convenient monetary instrument at race tracks and in brothels. Conversely, some habitués of the tracks wouldn't place a bet with the deuce because to do so might bring "bad luck." Probably the biggest disadvantage was the small number printed. In 1965 less than four million were printed including star notes, and only a bit over 22 million over the prior two years.

The latter disadvantage can certainly not be attributed to the 1976 Bicentennial offering, as by June 30 of that year the Bureau of Engraving and Printing had produced roughly 400 million for distribution. Subsequent printings, by reducing the need for the $1 denomination, would have saved more than $5 million annually in costs to the government, officials estimated. However, the issue was almost totally shunned by the public. The subsequent 1995 series was available only in 12-bank sets, of which 9,999 were produced as "Millennium" sets, plus some 153 million bearing the Atlanta FRB imprint, while the 2003 series was limited to just 16,000 sets, plus some 121 million bearing the Minneapolis FRB imprint. The 2003-A production totaled in excess of 294 million, with individual bank quantities varying from a low of 6.4 million for St. Louis and Minneapolis to a high of 64 million for San Francisco. Star notes in the 2003-A series, of which only 320,000 were produced bearing the Atlanta FRB imprint, command a hefty premium.

Q. *A friend of mine has a one-dollar note with a beautiful blue reverse. How?*

A. The green pigment in the ink historically used to print the backs of U.S. paper money has blue and yellow components. If a printed note is exposed to certain acids, or even acid fumes, the yellow component may be destroyed, thus turning the color of the residual ink to blue. If the green-colored note is exposed to an alkali, the blue component may be destroyed, turning the color of the residual ink to yellow. These color changes can be brought about either accidentally or intentionally, but there is no known case of the color change having taken place during the production process at the Bureau of Engraving and Printing.

Peroxide will turn a note yellow within a very few minutes. A note left in clothing being laundered can be turned yellow by the alkali present in the washing product. A note carried in the pocket of anyone working with acid, or in an environment of acid fumes, can be turned blue. Needless to say, the change of color can also be obtained by deliberately exposing a note to acid or alkali. Your friend's "blueback" note has no premium value because the change was achieved after the note was placed in circulation, and it is therefore not a printing error.

Q. *Is it true that the United States issued a special Federal Reserve $1 note to mark the assassination of President Kennedy in Dallas, Texas, on November 22, 1963?*

A. The facts of the so-called "assassination note" are as follows: The note does bear the date 1963, the year of Kennedy's assassination. It does carry the figure "11" four times, that being the month of the assassination. It does carry the identification "Dallas, Texas," as an element of the Dallas FRB seal. It does carry a large letter "K" within the circular Dallas FRB seal, being the 11th letter of the alphabet and that assigned to Dallas as the 11th of 12 Federal Reserve districts, and in front of each serial number. None of these indications, however, have any connection whatsoever with Kennedy's death. They are standard features incorporated on all currency printed for the Dallas FRB.

1815 $10 Treasury note. This 1815 dated U.S. Treasury note, bearing the denominational value $10, was an interest bearing (7 percent) issue.

Q. *Why did the United States wait until 1861 before issuing paper money?*

A. It didn't. While it is true that paper money as we know it today began with the "greenbacks" of 1861, the government did issue interest bearing fiscal securities as Treasury Notes during times of excessive Treasury drain, such as the War of 1812, the Jacksonian Depression that lasted from 1837 through 1841, the Mexican War of 1846, the Panic of 1857, and during the unsettled years immediately prior to the Civil War. With the exception of the low denomination notes of 1815, which were not interest bearing and circulated briefly, however, these Treasury Notes generally did not circulate as money and were quickly retired. The "greenbacks" of 1861 were necessitated to meet Union military expenses, which were running at a level of about $3.5 million a day at a time when tax revenues amounted to only about a third of that requirement.

Q. *I have a Federal Reserve Note that has a star (*) in place of the last letter of the serial number. What does the star denote?*

A. The star (*) indicated that the original note was destroyed in the printing process or was deleted by inspection and was replaced by a star (*) series note to maintain an uninterrupted sequence of numbering within a stack of finished notes. The symbol was also utilized when the numbering machines reached 100,000,000, as the numbering counters carried only eight digits. Instead of the usual prefix letter, a star (*) also appears with the serial number on Gold Certificates, United States Notes and Silver Certificates; it appears in place of the suffix letter when used on Federal Reserve Notes and Federal Reserve Bank Notes. No star (*) notes were used in conjunction with National Bank Notes prior to 1908. The star (*) on the face of Treasury Notes is a decorative embellishment, and does not denote a replacement note.

Q. *Is it true that the song "Dixie" had its origin in a $10 bill?*

A. Dixie as a collective noun indicating the Southern states is thought to have originated from the practice of the Citizens Bank of Louisiana printing "Dix" (10 in French) on $10 bills as a convenience to that state's large French speaking population. Thus, the South was the land of the "Dixies."

Q. *My father left me a $1,000 bill issued by the Bank of the United States. It is printed on authentic parchment and bears the serial number 8894. A dealer told me it's a fake. Is he right?*

A. "Replica" would be a better word. Several years ago a chemist discovered a chemical solution that gives vegetable membrane paper the appearance of old parchment. He formed a company to manufacture replicas of famous U.S. documents, and also produced replicas of paper money used during the Colonial, Revolutionary, and Civil War periods. The most notorious of his numismatic replicas is a $1,000 note of the Bank of the United States numbered 8894.

Q. *I have a note classified as obsolete that has a pattern of rather large holes punched in it. Does this lessen the value of the note?*

A. The punch holes are almost certainly cancellation marks indicating that the note was redeemed for face value by the issuer. Such notes generally bring less than unmarked specimens.

Q. *What is the origin of the dollar sign ($) and why doesn't it appear on United States paper money?*

A. At least three theories have been advanced to explain the origin of the dollar sign. 1) It was derived from the ribbon-entwined "Pillars of Hercules" on the Spanish dollar. 2) It is a monogram combination of the letters "U" and "S" of United States. 3) It is a modification of the old Mexican symbol "Ps" for pesos. The third theory is the one that is most generally assumed to be correct. The dollar sign is not an official requirement of United States currency, the official practice being to indicate the value in word form. The sign frequently appears on federal postage, revenue, and fee stamps, and can be found on the $1,000, $5,000, and $10,000 denomination notes of Series 1918 Federal Reserve Notes, but it has never appeared on any piece of paper money of the denominations issued for general circulation.

Q. *What is the significance of the large eye in a triangle appearing above an unfinished pyramid on the back of the dollar bill?*

A. The complete device to which you refer is the reverse of the Great Seal of the United States. The eye in a triangle surrounded by a glory proper represents the Eye of Providence.

Q. *I understand that the small-size Legal Tender $1 note has a red seal, but I have never seen a dollar bill with a red seal in circulation. What happened to them?*

A. The $1 Legal Tender note of Series 1928 is the only small-size note of that denomination to bear a red seal. The notes were released mainly in Puerto Rico, years after they were printed, and are no longer in circulation. These notes bear the signatures of Woods and Woodin, a Treasurer of the U.S. and Secretary of the Treasury tenure which extended only from March 4, 1933, to May 31, 1933, with somewhat less than 1.9 million notes being printed.

Q. *Many collectors of small size currency notes of the United States try to obtain a specimen of each of the Treasurer of the United States–Secretary of the Treasury signature combinations. Has the signature of these two officials always appeared on small size notes?*

A. A distinctive feature of the Series 1929 National Bank Note issues is the use of a Register of the Treasury / Treasurer of the United States signature combination.

Q. *National Currency notes and Federal Reserve Bank notes both carry the designation NATIONAL CURRENCY at top of the face of the note. Is there any way to quickly distinguish between the two types of notes?*

A. Federal Reserve Bank notes are easily distinguished from National Currency notes by the presence of the bank's district letter in four positions on the face of the notes, and by the addition of the wording "Or By Like Deposit of Other Securities" to the bonding statement at the top, in addition to the name of the bank being spelled out.

Q. *Small-size Federal Reserve Notes were first issued in 1929. Why is it that the $1 bill so essential to everyday commerce wasn't issued until 1963?*

A. One dollar Federal Reserve Notes weren't required until the issuance of $1 Silver Certificates was discontinued in 1963.

Q. *I know how to tell a Federal Reserve Note from a Federal Reserve Bank Note, but there must be an underlying fundamental difference related to the economic system. What is it?*

A. Federal Reserve Note issues were released as obligations of the Federal Reserve System. Federal Reserve Bank Note issues were released as obligations of the individual banks within the system.

Q. *I have heard paper money collectors speak of "Experimental Issue" notes. What are they?*

A. In 1944, the Treasury Department released an experimental issue of 1935-A series $1 Silver Certificates bearing the overprinting of a "R" (regular) or "S" (special) appearing to the lower right of the Treasury Seal. The purpose of the issue was to test the wearing qualities of regular and a special experimental currency paper. Results of the test were inconclusive, and the regular paper was continued in use. The total printing of each version was 1.2 million examples, with the "R" version commanding a slightly higher collector value than does the "S" version.

Q. *Why do some of the $1, $5, and $10 small-size Silver Certificates have yellow Treasury Seals and blue serial numbers instead of the usual blue seals and serial numbers?*

A. A special issue of Silver Certificates was printed in 1942 for use during the North African campaign of World War II. These notes retained the customary blue serial numbers of Silver Certificates, but the Treasury Seal was printed a distinctive yellow to permit ready identification and demonetization of the notes in the event of military reverses. These specially identified notes were also used briefly during the 1943 assault on Sicily. Nearly 27 million $1 1934-A series notes were printed, while the production of the $5 note was somewhat less than 17 million. The $10 note was printed as both a 1934 and 1934-A series, with a combined production of nearly 22 million notes, with specimens of the 1934 series being extremely rare.

1862 $2 Legal Tender note.

Q. *I know that Continental Currency and broken bank notes were issued in a variety of odd denominations, but is it true that the United States once issued a $3 Legal Tender note?*

A. It is true that a Legal Tender specimen note of $3 denomination does exist, but notes of that denomination were never produced for circulation. Legal Tender notes of the second issue, dated August 1, 1862, were issued in denominations of $1 and $2 only. Interestingly, however, the face design of those notes includes the numerals 1, 2, and 3 in vertical linear arrangement with the denomination of the note encircled with a lathe-work generated security feature. Inclusion of the numeral 3 in this configuration indicates that a $3 note was certainly being seriously contemplated, as this had been a popular denomination of issue with state banks, and it would have served as a good companion to the silver 3-cent piece and $3 gold which had been circulating since the early 1850s.

Q. *What is the "Technicolor Note" of 1905?*

A. The 1905 series $20 Gold Certificate has the center of the face gold tinted and the Treasury Seal and serial numbers printed in red, along with the paper being imparted with a light gold tint, resulting in a spectacular color combination of gold, red, black, and white.

The "watermelon" note. The art on the back of this $100 Series 1890 Treasury note resembles a watermelon.

Q. *What are collectors referring to when they say the U.S. issued a "watermelon" note?*

A. This is an 1890 series Treasury or Coin Note of the $100 denomination, which displays the value on the back in large numerals rendered in a fanciful style causing the two zeros to take a form reminiscent of watermelons. There is also a companion $1,000 note of the same series which similarly treats the three zeros, it being referred to as the "Grand Watermelon" note.

1886 $5 large silver certificate.

Q. *I have been told that there is a United States bank note on which coin illustrations are used to indicate the value and series date. Do you know which note this is?*

A. The back design of the $5 note of the second issue large-size Silver Certificate of the series of 1886 features five actual-size facsimile Morgan silver dollars. The coin at the center is dated 1886. There is another popular example of coins on bank notes. All of the National Gold Bank notes have on the back an representation of an collage of U.S. gold coins having a total face value of $211 in $1 through $20 denominations of various dates up to 1871, the most prominent being a double eagle of that date.

Q. *I have a friend with whom I've been discussing when the motto "In God We Trust" was first placed on U.S. currency. According to anything I've ever seen, it was in 1957, but he says it was much earlier. Who is right?*

A. In a way, you are both right. Legislation enacted in 1955 resulted in the motto being incorporated on our currency as a formal requirement in 1957, some 93 years after it was first featured on our coinage. Appearing first on the two-cent pieces of 1864, it was incorporated on nickels (1866–1883), quarters, half dollars, silver dollars, half eagles, eagles, and double eagles in 1866, although its presence was not legislatively proscribed until enactment of the Coinage Act of 1873. Interestingly, however, it was not incorporated on the quarter eagle until 1908, on the cent until 1909, and on the dime until 1916, and was also absent from the Liberty Head and Indian Head / Buffalo nickel (1883–1938) series.

As the backs of Series 1866 $5 Silver Certificate obligations represent portions of the reverses of four silver dollars—a fifth silver dollar is represented by the obverse of an 1886 Morgan—the motto appeared prominently on that offering during its active production life-span from 1886 to 1893. An early variation of the motto—In God Is Our Trust—also appeared on the March 3, 1863, $100 Interest Bearing Note series, an abstraction from a line in one of the later stanzas of the Star Spangled Banner.

Q. *Has the United States ever issued a commemorative currency note?*

A. None has ever been officially designated as such, although the Series 1976 $2 Federal Reserve Note with a portrait of Thomas Jefferson on the face and a representation of Trumbull's painting of the signing of the Declaration of Independence on the back that was issued on Jefferson's birthday, during the nation's Bicentennial celebration year, would be difficult to classify in any other manner. By the timing of their issuance, some collectors also consider three large-size Silver Certificates—the $2 note of Series 1886 bearing the portrait of General Winfield Scott Hancock, the $2 note of Series 1891 bearing the portrait of Secretary of the Treasury William Windom, and the $10 note of Series 1886 and 1908 bearing the portrait of Vice President Thomas A. Hendricks—and the $5 National Bank Note of Series 1882 bearing the portrait of assassinated President James A. Garfield as being commemorative in theme.

Q. *The color green is so historically traditional to the backs of our paper money that we refer to U.S. paper currency as "greenbacks." Has the United States ever printed paper money in any other color before the turn into the 21st century introduction of multi-hued treatments?*

A. More times than you might suppose. The 1878 to 1880 series of large-size Silver Certificates utilized black ink printing on the backs. Paper tinted yellow was used to print the 1870 to 1884 National Bold Bank Note issues. Gold Certificates were printed with brilliant golden-orange backs to symbolize the gold coins they represented. Series 1882 National Bank Notes include the popular "Brown Back" type, which do display the bank charter number in the center in green, but with the color brown dominating. Fractional Currency issues of the Civil War period were also printed in various colors.

Q. *I have heard—but find it difficult to believe—that the United States has issued paper money that was not only circulating legal tender but also bore interest. Is this true?*

A. A number of profit inducements were devised by the Treasury Department in the mid-19th century to overcome America's traditional distrust of paper money. First Issue 1862 Legal Tender Notes could be exchanged for U.S. 6 percent bonds. An act of 1863 authorized an issue of Interest Bearing Notes that bore interest at the rate of 5 percent for one or two years, or 7.3 percent for three years. Three year notes had coupons attached that could be used for collecting the interest semiannually. The same act also authorized Compound Interest Treasury Notes that bore interest at 6 percent compounded semiannually but payable only at maturity. An Act of 1879 authorized $10 Refunding Certificates that bore interest indefinitely at the rate of 4 percent annually. Interest payments on these notes weren't terminated until 1907, when the interest on them amounted to $11.30, giving the $10 Refunding Certificates a redemption value of $21.30. All of these interest-bearing notes could also be used as circulating legal tender.

August 10, 1861, $10 demand note.

Q. *I understand the public was so distrustful of the first issue of paper money, the Demand Notes of 1861, that they discounted them as much as 65 percent against gold. Yet within a decade they were routinely accepting paper money at face value. How do you account for the change of attitude?*

A. The foundation for confidence in paper money was established by the National Banking Act of February 25, 1863, which authorized the federal chartering of banks, requiring them to secure their bank note issues with U.S. government bonds deposited with the Treasurer of the United States.

Q. *I have noticed that all National Bank Notes bear a full date. Is this the date the note was issued?*

A. The exact significance of the date on a National Bank Note has not been determined. It is not the date the note was issued. Nor is it necessarily the date the issuing bank was chartered; the date is usually later, but occasionally earlier, than the charter date of the bank. Most of the dates appearing on National Bank Note issues are either the date the bank was organized, or a 20-year or 40-year anniversary thereof, or the date that marked a change of title for a bank. It appears that the dates were sometimes rather arbitrary in nature, however, as a few notes carry such special dates as January 1, February 14, February 29, March 17, and December 25.

$2 First Issue National Bank note.

Q. *Can you tell me what a "Lazy 2" bank note is?*

A. The term "Lazy 2" is an identity collectors have given to the $2 note of "First Issue" or "Original Series" National Bank Notes. The name refers to the large numeral 2, represented reclining on its face, on the front of the note. Similarly treated large numerals can also be found on obsolete notes.

Q. *I have observed the term "Forbidden Titles" being used when referring to National Bank Note issues. What does that expression mean?*

A. An Act of May 24, 1926, relating to National Bank Note issues forbade the inclusion of the words "United States," "Federal," or "Reserve" in a bank title. A grandfather clause in the legislation permitted, however, existing banks to continue using these words in their titles.

Q. *I recently viewed a display which included a National Bank Note of the Bank of North America, and I am wondering how that is possible, as I had always understood that the words "National Bank" had to be included in the title of any bank granted a national charter.*

A. There was one exception, it being the Bank of North America in Philadelphia. After the National Currency Act was signed into law on February 25, 1863, by President Abraham Lincoln, the naming convention established by Secretary of the Treasury Salmon P. Chase required that only numerical titles—First, Second, Third, etc.—could be used in naming national banks. Many established eastern banks resisted this requirement, as their bank names were well established, declining to apply for national bank charters. Their voiced displeasures to Comptroller of the Currency Hugh McCulloch was heeded and the requirements were changed when the Act of June 3, 1864, became law, which henceforth required that only the words "national" and "bank" be included in the title. One exception permitted by provisions of the legislation was provided for The Bank of North America.

Q. *When was paper with silk threads first used as a deterrent to counterfeiting?*

A. Paper with silk threads was first used in printing the Series of 1869 Legal Tender Note issues. A warning against counterfeiting was also printed on the back of these notes.

$100 1862 Legal Tender note.

Q. *The Mint Act of April 2, 1792, provided that the figure of an eagle appear upon the reverse of all gold and silver coins. When did the eagle make its first appearance on paper money of the United States?*

A. The American eagle first appeared on U.S. paper currency on the face of the series 1862 Legal Tender $100 note. Eagles were prominently featured on many subsequent 19th century note issues, but only infrequently in the 20th century, aside from its presence on the back of all $1 notes since 1935. Since the modern era currency redesign was inaugurated commencing with Series 1996 Federal Reserve Note issues, the eagle has reappeared on the face of the $5, $10, $20, $50, and $100 notes, where it is presented in the Federal Reserve System seal that is incorporated thereon.

Center medallion of 1886 $5 silver certificate.

Q. *Why did nearly 100 years pass between the time when the motto "In God We Trust" was incorporated into the nation's coin designs and its adoption on paper money commencing with the 1957 series?*

A. That's not a question that can be answered with certainty. Initially, the motto just "happened" onto our coins, first with its incorporation on the new two-cent piece introduced in 1864, at which time religious sentiment had been heightened as a result of the Civil War. It was also incorporated into the similar design executed for the obverse of the nickel five-cents piece introduced in 1866. From 1883 to 1938, when the Liberty Head and Indian Head / Buffalo nickels were in current production, the motto was missing from the nickel, at which time it was also adapted to the existing silver coinages in the quarter through dollar denominations, along with the gold half eagles through double eagles.

When President Theodore Roosevelt in 1907 directed a redesign of the nation's gold coinage, the new eagle and double eagle designs by Augustus Saint-Gaudens were introduced without the motto. Saint-Gaudens had, with the support of the president (who personally objected to the use of the Deity's name on coins), eliminated this feature from his designs in the essence of artistic simplicity and expression. Congress acted in 1908 to override Roosevelt's objections, however, requiring that all future U.S. coin issues carry the motto. It was to first appear on the new Lincoln cent in 1909, but did not make its first appearance on the dime until Weinman's new winged Liberty Head design was introduced in 1916, and not on the nickel until the new Jefferson nickel was executed by Felix Schlag for 1938.

Another 47 years passed before Congress acted, and President Eisenhower on July 11, 1955, signed into law regulations requiring that the motto be featured on the nation's paper money as well, and in the interim it was never incorporated as a basic design element. It did appear as an incidental element of currency design on one occasion, however—that being on the 1886 series $5 Silver Certificate issue. The reverse of that design featured representations of five Morgan silver dollars, four of the pieces being reverses that flank an 1886 obverse, displaying the motto, with the word "Trust" as it appears on the second reverse from the right on some examples appearing to be spelled "Trast" due to an imperfection in the printing plate.

CHAPTER TWENTY-TWO

❧

Fractional
Currency — Really!

Q. *What can you tell me about a funny little 50-cents bill I have?*

A. Your "funny little 50-cents bill" is a piece of Fractional Currency that
replaced the short-lived Postage Currency in 1863, introduced in 1862
as a substitute for coinage, which had disappeared from circulation due
to hoarding as a consequence of the fiscal vagaries of the Civil War.
Postage Currency was initially issued in 5-, 10-, 25-, and 50-cents
denominations, while Fractional Currency was also offered in the additional denominations of 3- and 15-cents in 1864 and 1869 respectively.
Fractional Currency continued to be issued into early 1876, with its
redemption and retirement commencing in the summer of 1876, with
the circulation of fractional coins having been reestablished, but they
remain legal tender to this day. It has been estimated that of the total
issue of Postage and Fractional Currency, amounting to about $369 mil-
lion, approximately $1.8 million in value remained outstanding when
redemption dissipated.

5¢ Fractional currency note. Five cents fractional currency note featuring the portrait of Spencer Clark still is worth a nickel in redemption, but no collector would be foolish enough to sell it for such a pittance.

Q. *I have a 5-cents Fractional Currency note that looks like it has a picture of one of the Smith Brothers on it. I don't recognize him. Who is he?*

A. His name is Spencer M. Clark, and he is remembered by collectors as the man responsible for our coins and paper notes not bearing portraits of the living. The 5-cents note of the type you possess—authorized by the Act of June 30, 1864, this Third Issue note was issued December 5, 1864—bears the portrait of Spencer Clark, a civil servant in the Treasury Department, who at the time held the post of superintendent of the "National Currency Bureau," being the first person to hold that post. Most people at the time thought it to be the portrait of William Clark, the 1804–1806 Lewis and Clark Expedition explorer. Congress subsequently passed the Act of April 7, 1866, prohibiting the placing of the likeness of any living person upon any "bonds, securities, notes, Fractional or Postage Currency of the United States." Clark's portrait continued in production, however, until passage of the Act of May 17, 1866, was enacted authorizing the nickel five-cent piece and stipulating that no future Fractional Currency notes be produced in denominations under ten cents.

Postage currency. Earlier postage currency was issued in sheets, perforated like stamps, for easy tearing.

Q. *Is it true that the first issue of government stamp money, the only one of the five Fractional Currency issues to be called Postage Currency, was actually illegal?*

A. That is probably true. Rather than being strictly "postage and other stamps of the United States," and despite being "receivable for postage stamps at any U.S. post office," Postage Currency took the form of reproductions of postage stamps on paper carrying the promise of the government that it would be exchanged for United States Notes, thereby acquiring the attributes of a promissory note, which was not the intent of Congress.

Q. *There are error coins and error bank notes. Are there also error specimens of Fractional Currency?*

A. Through an engraver's oversight, the word CENTS does not appear on the 10-cent denomination of the third issue of Fractional Currency.

Q. *I have a specimen of Fractional Currency printed on paper watermarked "C.S." What does this indicate?*

A. Some specimen notes of the second and third issues of Fractional Currency were printed on paper made in Europe for the printing of Confederate currency. This paper was seized as contraband in 1862 from the

S.S. *Bermuda*, a captured blockade-runner. This paper was watermarked "C.S.A." (Confederate States of America) in block letters. Fractional Currency notes printed on this paper bear either the letters "C.S." or "S.A."

Q. *Why are the ends of Fractional Currency notes of the fourth and fifth issues tinted blue and violet?*

A. For the same reason that a surcharge was overprinted on the face and back of notes of the second and third issues, to make the work of counterfeiters more difficult.

3¢ Fractional currency note.

Q. *The third issue of Fractional Currency is the only one of the five issues to include a 3-cent note. Why was it necessary?*

A. The 3-cent note was required to facilitate purchases of the 3-cent first-class postage stamp, a role the silver 3-cent piece was no longer able to perform due to the hoarding of specie, which commenced in earnest in early 1862, after which time only token amounts of 3-cent silver pieces were minted annually until the issue was discontinued in 1873. With the introduction of the nickel 3-cent piece in 1865 the demand for continuance of the unit was no longer required when the fourth issue of Fractional Currency was placed in production in 1869.

IV.
MONEY OF THE
WAR BETWEEN
THE STATES

About the images in this book: In general, coin denominations of 50 cents and higher are pictured at actual size; denominations below 50 cents and coins that are unusually small (e.g., gold dollars) are generally pictured at 150 percent of their actual size. Paper money is typically pictured at page width. Other items, such as medals, encased postage, and so on, may be enlarged for visibility. Appendix B lists the actual sizes of U.S. coins and currency.

CHAPTER TWENTY-THREE

～

Confederate Coins and Currency

Q. *What is the difference between "Confederate money" and "Southern States currency"?*

A. "Confederate money" is considered to be that issued under the specific authorization of the Confederate States of America, with the first notes being issued in Montgomery and Richmond in early 1861, an authorized circulation limit of $1 million authorized by an Act of March 9, 1861, passed by the Confederate Congress. The seventh issue dated February 17, 1864, was the last, the authorization being for unlimited quantities, which likely amounted to about a billion dollars. It has been estimated that perhaps as much as $2.5 billion in currency was circulated in support of the Confederacy, including Confederate currency, along with state and local bank issues. "Southern States currency" is generally considered to be those notes issued under state authorization as early as 1815 in North Carolina, but largely during the Civil War conflict and the reconstruction period that followed, the latest being war claim certificates of Missouri dated May 19, 1871, very rare interest-bearing notes of Arkansas variously hand dated from 1871 to 1875, and Bank of Tennessee obligation "substitution notes" dated 1883 and 1885, some ten years following the end of the Reconstruction in 1874.

Q. *Is the Confederate half dollar a genuine coin?*

A. The Confederacy planned to issue a coinage using the facilities of the New Orleans Mint. Only one die was ever prepared, a half dollar reverse depicting Confederate shield displaying seven stars for the original seven states of the Confederacy, surmounted with a Liberty cap. This was muled with an obverse die for the U.S. 1861-O half dollar to produce four pattern strikes, which comprise the extent of official Confederate coinage.

In 1879, J. W. Scott purchased the original reverse die and made an associated purchase of five hundred 1861-O half dollars. He shaved the reverse from each of the coins purchased and in its place impressed the Confederate Seal with the original die. These "restrikes" are the Confederate half dollars that reside in collector holdings today, aside from a single "original" in private hands that traded for $632,500 in an October 2003, auction. Scott also struck 500 specimens in white metal, using the Confederate die to fashion the obverse and his own store card for the reverse. Also, at the time the centennial of the Civil War was being celebrated, a "replica" of the Confederate half dollar, combining a representation of the 1861 reverse with the Confederate Seal, was created and struck in six different metals including silver.

Incidentally, in 1861 the seceded state of Louisiana and the Confederacy also caused to be struck 2,202,633 half dollars which are "genuine" to the extent that they owe their origin to the auspices of the Confederacy. However, they were struck with the confiscated equipment and dies of the U.S. branch mint at New Orleans, and for the most part cannot be distinguished from the 1861-O half dollars struck by the U.S. prior to the seizure.

1861 CSA 1 cent.

Q. *Did the Confederate States ever issue their own one-cent piece?*

A. No, but an effort was made to do so. In 1861, Bailey & Co., Philadelphia jewelers, agreed to supply a minor coinage for the Confederacy and engaged well-known engraver Robert Lovett Jr. to prepare the dies. Lovett executed dies for a one-cent coin, employing for the obverse the same turbaned Liberty Head he had created for a Northern store card, and on the reverse a wreath of cotton, sugar cane and tobacco leaves enclosing the words 1 CENT. He placed the small initial "L" on a bale of cotton placed in the area of the wreath tie. After striking a dozen specimens in copper-nickel, he had second thoughts about the possible consequences of giving aid to the enemy and had hid the dies for the duration of the war.

These dies were eventually purchased by John Haseltine who, in 1874, caused the striking of seven cents in gold, 12 in silver, and 55 in copper before the dies broke. In 1962, Robert Bashlow, creating a transfer die, struck 30,000 specimens in platinum, silver, goldine, and bronze, which can be easily distinguished from the "original" restrikes by the presence of heavy die cracks on both the obverse and reverse. He then presented the original and transfer dies to the Smithsonian Institution.

Q. *I have seen advertisements offering Confederate dimes, half dimes, etc., yet they are not listed in coin catalogs. Why?*

A. These are fantasy pieces of post-Civil War vintage created by an imaginative coin dealer. They have no authentic connection with the Confederacy, and are not genuine coins. They exist in a variety of metals and denominations, with the denominations generally stated fractionally, as 1/10, etc.

February 17, 1864, CSA one dollar note.

Q. *I have a Confederate $5 note. Is it rare?*

A. Probably not. All genuine Confederate notes have a collector value, but this value is frequently a relatively nominal one. Strangely, Confederate currency has not enjoyed the prestige arbitrarily bestowed upon Colonial or Continental currency and broken bank notes, although the trend seems to have started changing in recent years. The most highly prized types of Confederate currency are the 1861 Montgomery notes issued at the first Confederate capital—February 7 to May 24, 1861—although there are rare individual notes of subsequent issues as well. A complete Confederate note numbers 72 distinctive pieces, produced in ten issues, generally consisting of 1-, 2-, 5-, 10-, 20-, 50-, and 100-dollar denominations, although 500- and 1,000-dollar denominations were included in the first issue of 1861, and 50-cents denomination shinplasters in the last two of 1863 and 1864.

The notes commonly encountered were issued at Richmond, the permanent capital. They are distinguished by their pink obverses and blue reverses. The last Richmond issue of 1864 was printed in astronomical quantities necessitated by the extreme depreciation of the purchasing power of the Confederate dollar. When the first Confederate notes were circulated in 1861 the dollar was worth 95 cents in gold; by 1863 the value had dropped to 33 cents and by Appomattox (April 9, 1865) it was 1.6 cents, with the last recorded trading on May 1, 1865, being 1,200 to one. Comparatively, the low point for the greenback dollar of the North was about 35 cents in gold in July of 1864, with recovery to 69 cents in April of 1865. These notes were secured by a pledge to redeem in Confederate stocks and bonds two years after ratification of a treaty of peace between the Confederacy and the United States. In short, they were secured by a fading hope, for by late 1864 the most dedicated adherents to the Southern cause regarded the prospect of a Southern victory to be as remote as the arrival of a voyager from Andromeda.

Large quantities of the 1864 issue survived the war to be distributed across the country as curios and premiums, which largely accounts for their prevalence today. Slightly less than 600,000 $1 notes from the issue of February 17, 1864, were printed, as contrasted to the more than nine million examples of the $10 note of that issue that were printed, making it the second smallest printing in the series, after the $500 note, of which only about 150,000 were printed. The $1 note commands a value in the $100 range, the $5, $10, and $20 notes in the $50 range, and the $500 approaches $1,000 in nice condition. The Richmond $500 and $1,000 notes of 1861, on the other hand, command premiums in the mid-five figure range.

Q. *Why didn't the Confederate States of America issue coins?*

A. On March 9, 1861, the Confederate Congress enacted legislation providing for continued operations of the New Orleans Mint, seized by Southern forces on January 31, 1861, and the Charlotte and Dahlonega mints seized thereafter, instructing that dies be prepared "for the coin of the Confederate States." However, it was quickly determined that the South did not have sufficient bullion to implement the law in a meaningful manner. Thereupon it was decided to reserve existing bullion to the government for its necessities, and by Act of May 14, 1861, Congress declared "that from & after June 1st operations of the several mints in the Confederate States shall be suspended."

Q. *Is it true that Northern note companies engraved plates for Confederate and Southern States currency during the Civil War?*

A. Notes are known bearing the name of the American Bank Note Co. and the National Bank Note Co., both of New York. American Bank Note had a branch at New Orleans. It is possible that it printed notes at New Orleans during the early part of the war under the name of the Southern Bank Note Co. (a name that appears on many note issues, although the company was not listed in the New Orleans directory) to conceal the fact that the notes were engraved by Northern engravers of a firm with a branch doing business in the South.

Q. *Is it true that Confederate paper money was not printed on watermarked paper?*

A. No. Confederate notes were printed on paper both with and without watermarks. The most frequently encountered watermark consists of the initials "C.S.A." (Confederate States of America) appearing in block or script letters. The watermarks "FIVE" and "TEN" frequently appear on notes of like denominations. Among the rarely found watermarks are "N.Y." in block letters, extending nearly the width of the note, and "Hodgkinson & Co. Wookey Hole Mills," the mark of an English paper mill. Watermarks can also be found on notes issued by the individual states of the Confederacy.

CSA $10 "Sweet Potato" note.

Q. *What can you tell me about the popular Confederate note known as the "Sweet Potato" note?*

A. Your reference is to the $10 Richmond note dated Sept. 2, 1861, the central vignette of which represents "General Marion's Sweet Potato Dinner." The design of this note, engraved by B. Duncan of Columbia, South Carolina, was taken from a famous painting by John R. White of Charleston, South Carolina, which depicts an authentic incident in the military career of Francis Marion, the "Swamp Fox," who was one of the originators of guerrilla warfare and a hero of the Southern campaigns of the American Revolution. After futilely trying to trap Marion's guerrilla army in the swamps of South Carolina, British Colonel Banastre "Bloody" Tarleton asked him for a truce. Marion responded by inviting his enemy to dinner at his swamp camp. Instead of the lavish display of Southern hospitality he expected, Tarleton found only a dinner of sweet potatoes served on a bare table in a swamp. He later reported to General Cornwallis that if the colonists were willing to fight without pay, proper clothes, or food, "they could not be conquered."

This design is not unique to Confederate currency. It was previously issued by the Bank of the State of South Carolina on $5 notes issued in 1853 and 1861. Nice examples of the Richmond $10 note trade in the mid-double figures range, while the $5 South Carolina bank notes command values in the low-triple figures range.

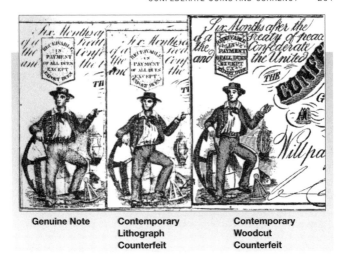

Genuine Note   **Contemporary Lithograph Counterfeit**   **Contemporary Woodcut Counterfeit**

Q. *I have heard that the shortage of skilled note engravers in the South was so critical that engravers had to be "imported," or the plates engraved in the North and abroad. Wasn't the lack of engravers in the South insurance against counterfeiting of the notes?*

A. Because of the lack of skilled craftsmen, equipment, and materials, few, if any, illicit notes were made in the South. Confederate currency was, however, extensively counterfeited in Louisville, New York City, Philadelphia, and even Havana, Cuba. Efforts to prevent counterfeiting by the use of watermarked bank note paper, or by using pink paper or printing the notes in multiple colors were ineffective. By the last year of the war, the supply of currency, swollen by counterfeits, was so over-abundant in the South that steps had to be taken to retire part of it from circulation. In reviewing a dealer price list of Confederate note offerings recently, I noted that the listing of contemporary counterfeit listings were about half as numerous as those of genuine issues.

Q. *I have heard the name of Samuel C. Upham of Philadelphia mentioned in discussions of Confederate paper money. What did a presumably loyal Northerner have to do with Confederate currency?*

A. Although Upham, a Philadelphia stationer, never represented himself as a counterfeiter, he was the most famous of the many printers of spurious Confederate currency notes. He called his excellent replicas "fac-similes" and "mementos of the rebellion," furnishing them to the trade, ostensibly as curiosities, at a cost of 50 cents per 100 notes, regardless of denomination. The dealers in turn sold them to interested parties for one cent each. Upham printed 28 different facsimiles of Rebel notes and shinplasters, and 15 different postage stamps during the period from March 12, 1862, to August 1, 1863. By his account, he produced a total of 1,564,050 facsimile Confederate era notes in denominations from 5-cent shinplasters of local bank, city, and county issue to 100 dollars.

Although Upham's notes were clearly marked "Fac-simile Confederate notes sold wholesale or retail, by S. C. Upham, 403 Chestnut Street, Phila. Pa.," in the margins, in the words of Confederate Senator Foote they "injured the Confederate cause more than General McClellan and his army." Large quantities of his notes with the "fac-simile" notice clipped off were smuggled into the South and placed in circulation, generally through the purchase of cotton from Rebel planters.

Q. *How much money did the Confederacy issue during the Civil War?*

A. The exact amount cannot be determined. Little effort was made to keep an accurate record of the amount issued after July 1864. The amount authorized by the various acts approximates $1.5 billion. To this must be added the amount of the issues of the individual states, as well as the amount issued by railroads, insurance companies, merchants, counties, and towns. The grand total was probably close to $2.5 billion. In the beginning notes issued were strictly limited to the authorizing laws. For the first issue of 1861 the total value of notes issued was $2,021,100, but the outstanding circulation never exceeding a $1 million authorization. The official retirement and replacement of the notes of this issue with notes of subsequent issues explains their great rarity. The second issue of July 25, 1861, authorized a circulation of $20 million.

Q. *Can money issued by the Confederate States of America be redeemed for current money?*

A. Redemption is specifically forbidden by Section 4 of the 14th Amendment to the Constitution, proposed in 1866 and ratified in 1868, which provides: "Neither the United States nor any State shall assume or pay any debt or obligation incurred in aid of insurrection or rebellion against the United States, or any claim for the loss or emancipation of any slave; but all such debts, obligations and claims shall be held illegal and void."

CHAPTER TWENTY-FOUR

Patriotics, Store Cards, and Sutlers' Tokens

Q. *I have a brass coin which on one side has, EL-RUS, BAR, IOLA, WISC., and on the other, 10c IN TRADE. It looks really old. What was it used for and what is it worth?*

A. You have what is known as a "Store Card" or "Merchant Token." They have been issued by merchants, tavern owners, clubs, restaurants, gaming houses, "company stores" in coal towns, etc., from the post-Colonial era to the present for advertising or trade purposes, and are redeemable to the stated amount in trade at the issuing establishment. The category includes such historic issues as Hard Times Tokens, Civil War Tokens, and the more modern 1930s Depression Era issues. Collectors particularly value the elaborately designed store cards issued from the mid-19th century through the 1990s, and the later issues of the early 20th century that feature geometric patterns, some of which command significant premiums. The piece you describe would appear to belong to the mid-1900s, and these are not especially valuable in most instances.

1863 Patriotic Civil War tokens.

Q. *I have a coin which is dated 1863, has an Indian head on the obverse, and is the same size as our current one-cent piece, but on the reverse it states NOT ONE CENT. Can you tell me what kind of a coin this is?*

A. Your "coin" quite possibly served as such, but is actually a privately issued patriotic Civil War token. These were issued by merchants during a severe coin shortage of Civil War days to provide a small coin for everyday transactions. Many were imitations of the Indian Head cent which had at the time only recently been introduced (1859) into circulation; others bore representations of such traditional devices as the Liberty Head; U.S. shield, flag, and eagle; and portraits of the founding fathers. Most were made of copper; other compositions were brass, zinc, nickel, copper-nickel, and lead. They were finally outlawed by congressional action in 1864.

These tokens generally bore a device symbolic of patriotism or a patriotic slogan, such as THE UNION MUST AND SHALL BE PRESERVED. The most familiar of this type is the famous "Dix Cent." On January 29, 1861, Secretary of the Treasury John Adams Dix ended a letter of instruction to a Lieutenant Caldwell with an unequivocal charge: "If anyone attempts to haul down the American flag, shoot him on the spot." Inevitably, the slogan ended up on Civil War tokens, but due to an engraver's error some examples read ". . . shoot him on the SPOOT."

Merchant Civil War tokens.

Q. *I have a round copper disc which has an Indian Head with 13 stars and the date 1863 on one side, and on the other some lettering which reads: PEKIN TEA STORE, N. 50 ST. CLAIR ST., PITTSBURGH. What is this item?*

A. The item you have is a one-cent trade token known as a Civil War store card, or merchant token. These pieces differ from patriotic Civil War tokens in bearing an advertisement of the issuing merchant. They were issued by merchants in almost 300 towns spread across 23 states, mostly in the North, with a few issues originating from the border states. It is estimated that the combined minting of store cards and patriotic tokens comprised more than 50 million pieces in about 10,000 varieties. The particular token you have is one of nearly 200 different Civil War store cards issued by some 30 firms in western Pennsylvania, mostly Pittsburgh and old Allegheny.

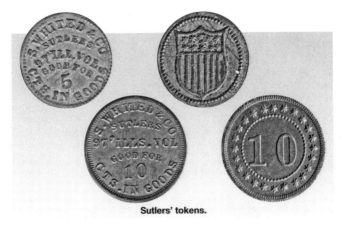

Sutlers' tokens.

Q. *I've seen small coins with Civil War regimental names on them and values indicated "in goods." Can you tell me their history?*

A. These coins are Civil War sutler tokens, issued by civilian traders (sutlers) who followed the troops of both armies. Sutlers set up shop wherever the troops camped, supplying the soldiers's needs from wagons full of a variety of items, including books, writing paper, patent medicines, and socks. However, the prices were often steep, and troops did not like to patronize them. When the armies turned their attention west after the war, private post traders took over the military trade and sutlers faded away. The tokens left behind are a highly prized.

CHAPTER TWENTY-FIVE

Encased Postage

Q. *Both coins and stamps are issued by the U.S. government and have face value. Why can't we use stamps as currency?*

A. Coins are legal tender, and as such are universally accepted as payment for goods or services. Stamps are affixed to mail as proof that postal services have been purchased. If you can find someone willing to barter for stamps, no one is stopping you. However, no one is required to accept stamps as a medium of exchange.

Encased postage. Introduced in 1862 as an emergency circulation medium, encased postage stamps soon were replaced by fractional currency. The brass holders were always embossed with advertising messages.

Q. *My scoutmaster says that people used postage stamps for money during the Civil War. Was this legal, and how did they carry the fragile bits of gummed paper?*

A. Stamps were declared a legal medium of exchange in amounts up to $5 after July 17, 1862. Until they were replaced by Postage and Fractional Currency—some issues of which bore reproductions of U.S. postage stamps—stamps were prepared for use as currency by pasting them on one half of a folded sheet of paper, by putting them in small envelopes, and by displaying them in small round brass holders with mica fronts through which the stamps could be viewed.

Encased postage reverses. A variety of companies and products were advertised on the back of encased postage.

Q. *I've noticed that the backs of encased postage stamps carry advertisements for various firms. How did this happen?*

A. Once Congress declared that stamps could be used as a legal medium of exchange, people began using them. However, bare stamps did not hold up well under constant handling. A Boston businessman, John Gault, came up with the idea to encase the stamps in a metal frame with a clear mica window on its face. He marketed them to 31 merchants in the Northeast and Midwest, and charged 2¢ per holder for the advertisements on the back. By the time the encasements came into use, the United States issued its first Postage Currency notes. Concurrent with its second run of Postage Currency in 1863, the government ordered all other types of postage being used as money to be turned in.

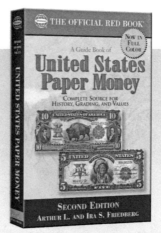

For more information: Encased postage stamps are discussed in the *Guide Book of United States Paper Money* (Friedberg).

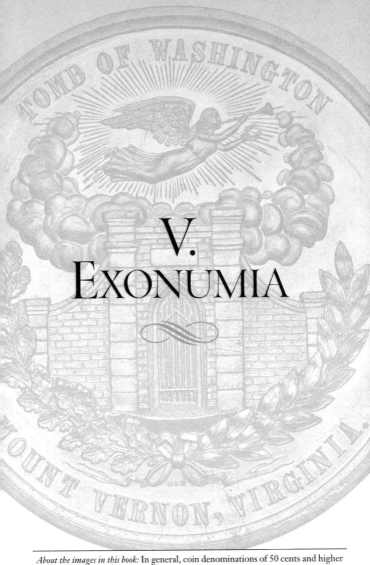

V.
EXONUMIA

CHAPTER TWENTY-SIX

Beautiful Medals

Q. *I have an eight-sided silver piece on the obverse of which is a mining complex identified as "Pikes Peak Silver Mine," and the legend, IN THE PEOPLE WE TRUST. A COMMODITY WILL GIVE IN EXCHANGE MERCHANDISE AT . . . The reverse carries the legend, JOS. LESHERS REFERENDUM SOUVENIR 1 OZ COIN SILVER PRICE $1.00, and a serial number. For what purpose was this item intended?*

A. The piece is a token known as the "Lesher Referendum Dollar" because they were to be referred to the people for acceptance or rejection. They were coined by Joseph Lesher in 1900 and 1901 at Victor, Colorado, in four basic varieties dated 1900 and one type dated 1901, each of which contained an ounce of .950 fine silver. It is believed the issue was intended to help open idle silver mines. They were distributed by interested merchants who redeemed them in merchandise at the indicated $1 value. One of the 1900 varieties carries the merchant name A.B. Bumstead die-stamped at the bottom on the obverse, while specimens of the 1901 type exist bearing the counterstamped identities of eight merchants, along with a variety without the name of any merchant counterstamped. All are impressed with serial numbers as well. Few specimens survived government seizure, with all specimens being considered rare and quite valuable.

Q. *I have a silver coin the same size as a U.S. silver dollar, and it has a portrait on the obverse along with the name HENDRIK HUDSON and the date 1609. The reverse shows a ship under full sail, with the lettering NIEUW AMSTERDAM MCMIX and 1 DAALER. From what country did this coin originate?*

A. What you have is neither a coin nor foreign. It is a private medal produced and distributed by Thomas L. Elder, a New York City coin dealer and prolific medal marketer, struck and issued in the United States in 1909 (MCMIX) to commemorate the exploration of the Hudson River by Henry Hudson in 1609. In addition to being struck in silver, this dollar-size medal was also struck in aluminum and bronze, the latter being a rare variety; a variety the size of the U.S. gold dollar was also struck in gold, as well as silver, bronze, and aluminum. It is believed that fewer than 100 examples each were struck of the large and small silver pieces and the small bronze piece, while the aluminum versions of both sizes are the common pieces with probably more than 200 struck.

The portrait on the obverse is that of the English captain Henry Hudson, who was commissioned by the Dutch to find a passage to the Indies by way of the North Pole. The ship represented on the reverse is the *Halve Maen* (Half Moon). This particular medal falls within a quaint class of numismatic items known as "so-called dollars." This category includes U.S. medals commemorating historical events of national and regional significance, along with some issues of a monetary nature issued from 1826 through 1948. In order to qualify, a piece must generally fall within the size range of 1-1/4 to 1-3/4 inches. The category was comprehensively cataloged in the book *So-Called Dollars* by Harold E. Hibler and Charles V. Kappen in 1963, and a second edition in 2008.

1896 Free Silver Sixteen to One Bryan dollar.

Q. *I have seen a number of large silver medals, the size of a silver dollar or larger, dated 1896. They all seem to have one of two phrases inscribed on them, 16 TO 1 NIT or FREE SILVER. What are these pieces?*

A. These medals are known as "Bryan Dollars." They were political campaign pieces associated with the 1896 and 1900 presidential bids of

William Jennings Bryan as nominee of the Democratic party and chief spokesman for the advocates of bimetallism at a ratio of 16-to-1 with free and unlimited coinage of silver. Holding sway as a leading political force of the Democratic Party for roughly 25 years commencing in 1893, Bryan gave prominent voice to the mining interests of the West throughout that time. Bryan Dollars are generally quite scarce today, and because of their size, silver content, nostalgic appeal, and historical significance command substantial premiums.

Many Bryan issue were satirical in nature, deprecating a gold standard, tight money, and the debased silver dollar. They bore such mottos as, IN GOD WE TRUST FOR THE OTHER 53 CENTS, a pointed reference to the United States silver dollar's 47-cent silver content. The 16 TO 1 NIT symbolism references the desired ratio of value between silver and gold, with NIT ("Not In Trust") indicating that the supporters of Bryan did not put their trust in a dollar valued in excess of its bullion worth. This was further emphasized by the huge size of some of the pieces which strikingly illustrated what a dollar's worth of silver really looked like.

Q. *Are the designs on the so-called "Olympic" medals struck for public sale the same as on those awarded to the victorious athletes? Is the large "gold" medal awarded to those who place first in their competitions really gold?*

A. The designs utilized on the official Olympic award medals are not made available to the general public. The gold medal is actually .925 fine (sterling) silver gilded with "at least 6 grams of the purest gold." The second place medal is .925 fine silver, and the third place medal is bronze. These standards were set in 1928, when it was also established that the medals should be no smaller than 50mm in diameter and 3mm thick. The winter and summer Olympic medals are of different design.

Q. *Are the medals that pour from the presses of private mints in seemingly endless streams good investment items?*

A. They haven't generally proven to be, but they are seldom purchased for that purpose. The appeal of medals derives from artistic, historical, or nostalgic considerations. Many of the silver issues and series promoted from the mid-1960s through the late 1970s were melted down for their bullion value when the silver price ballooned in the early 1980s, however, providing their purchasers with substantial profits. That phenomenon was repeated to a lesser degree about 25 years later when silver jumped from about $5 to the $20 level. The quantities of some issues and series that survive are probably quite limited, but they generally have not caught on with collectors of historic medals.

Q. *What is the difference between a medallion, a medal, and a medalet?*

A. All three can be issued to commemorate a person or event, or awarded for excellence or achievement. The difference is a matter of size, and that distinction isn't very finely drawn. Generally, a medallion is considered to be a medal greater than three inches in diameter. A medalet, on the other hand, is generally considered to be a medal roughly the size of a half dollar (1-3/16 inches) or smaller.

Q. *I am, of course, familiar with Proof coins. Are medals also produced in Proof?*

A. The majority of the medals produced and marketed by the better private mints since the 1960s are struck in Proof quality. Their manufacture requires highly polished dies and planchets and two or more strikings to produce sharpness of detail and height of relief. As an experiment in collector reception, the United States Mint struck a miniature Jimmy Carter presidential medal in Proof for sale at the 1977 ANA convention in Atlanta, Georgia.

Q. *During World War II, I was awarded the Distinguished Service Medal by the Army, but actual presentation of the medal never took place. Is it possible for me to obtain my medal at this late date?*

A. You can apply for your medal to the Army Records Center, 9700 Page Blvd., St. Louis, MO 63132. The Air Force Records Center and the Naval Records Center can also be contacted at the same address. The Marine Corps can be contacted at Arlington Annex, Washington, DC 20308, and the Coast Guard Commandant at Washington, DC 20591. Proof of service and your old military number must accompany your application. The delayed awards service applies only to service medals or decorations. Rifle, pistol, or combat infantry badges are not included.

1801 Jefferson Indian peace medal.

Q. *I have been told that it is possible to purchase commemorative medals from the U.S. Mint. Can you furnish details?*

A. More than 200 different historically attuned medals dating from Revolutionary War days to the present are stocked for sale by the U.S. Mint. They are bronze, from 11/16ths of an inch to three inches in diameter. Detailed availability information can be obtained by visiting the Mint's Web site at http://www.usmint.gov.

Q. *Is the striking of commemorative medals as active an enterprise as it was 40 years ago?*

A. It has been estimated that from the mid-1960s to the late 1970s, more medals were struck to commemorate a greater variety of events than were struck during the previous century. While the pace has slowed somewhat since that time, the past 30 years have witnessed the introduction of issue numbers and quantities greatly in excess of the rates that prevailed from the mid-19th to the mid-20th century.

Q. *I understand that the United States government issues national medals. When did the practice begin?*

A. As early as the Revolutionary War, the U.S. government began authorizing the striking of medals for presentation to outstanding military heroes. The first of these medals were made at the French Mint, principally under the direction of Thomas Jefferson, then the United States Ambassador to the Court of France. With the exception of the medal awarded to Major Henry ("Light Horse Harry") Lee for the Battle of

Paulus Hook, all of the Revolutionary medals were executed in Paris. Although positive proof is lacking, and is likely to remain so, it is believed that the Lee medal, for which Joseph Wright engraved the dies, was struck at the Philadelphia Mint between 1792 and 1796. Bronze copies of the Revolutionary period medals were made available to the public, starting in the 1860s.

Q. *I have heard that the U.S. Mint used "pure" gold and silver when striking national medals. Is this true?*

A. It is, with a few exceptions. As many as 80 blows were required to bring up the relief when medals were struck utilizing the old screw press process. Pure gold and silver, being softer than alloys, could be struck with fewer blows and extended the working life of dies. On a few occasions, .900 fine gold or silver was used. In at least one instance, the Mecklenburg Centennial (1875), the silver medal was apparently struck on regular-issue half dollar planchets.

Q. *Collectors of the copper or bronze medals of the U.S. Mint refer to them as "copper-bronzed," "mahogany," "dark chocolate," or "late bronze." Can you sort these terms out for me?*

A. Until about 1901, the mint struck medals of copper and then "bronzed" them by head and/or chemical treatment. "Copper bronzed" medals made from about 1825 to about 1891 are distinguished by a proof surface and a color ranging from light red to dark brown. Collectors call them "mahogany finish" medals. From about 1891 to about 1901, "copper-bronzed" medals have a dull surface and a dark brown color. They are called "dark chocolate" medals. From about 1901, the mint has employed a true bronze alloy (.950 copper, .050 tin and zinc). After being struck, the bronze medals are sandblasted. Medals made by this process are known to collectors as "late bronze" or "yellow bronze" specimens.

Q. *Has the U.S. Mint ever struck medals in any metal other than gold, silver, copper, and bronze?*

A. A very few were struck in nickel, aluminum, white metal, copper-nickel, goloid, brass, and lead over the years. Those in lead are almost certainly die trials.

Q. *I have seen relatively modern commemorative medals that carry the words BY ACT OF CONGRESS or something similar. What can you tell me about these pieces?*

A. These commemorative medals are part of a series of issues, referred to categorically as "national commemorative medals," that were produced under the authorization of Congress, subsequent to passage of the Act of February 12, 1873. The earliest of these issues was an 1875 offering marking the "Centennial Celebration of the Battle of Lexington," while the latest was a 1993 offering tied to enactment of a "Fire Service Bill of Rights" and Benjamin Franklin's 1736 organization of the first fire service. Of the 86 programs captured under this category, 54 of them were produced from 1954 to 1978, during the era of the suspension of U.S. Mint commemorative coin issues (1954 to 1982), with a substantial body of the resulting issues being sized from slightly larger than half dollars to roughly silver dollar–size. A comprehensive study and catalog of these issues was published in 2008 under the authorship of William Swoger (*National Commemorative Medals of the United States of America Since 1873*).

Q. *I once read somewhere that the U.S. Mint struck a series of medals that were strictly commemorative in nature. When was this, and are the medals still available?*

A. The Mint struck a most interesting series of commemorative medals prior to 1892, when the minting of commemorative coins began, several of which fall into the "so-called dollar" and "national commemorative medal" categories. The quality of workmanship revealed by many of them can be inferred from the names of some of the engravers: John Reich, Charles and William Barber, Augustin Dupre, George Morgan, Anthony Paquet, and James Longacre. These medals were struck in a variety of metals (copper, bronze, silver, gold, white metal, aluminum, and goloid) and range in size from a demure 19 mm to a generous 76 mm. While some were issued simply to cash in on the hour's enthusiasm for a particular person or event, along with the active collector interest in medals that surfaced during the last half of the 19th century, many are of lasting national significance.

A few of the commemorated events plucked at random from the list reveal a bemusing diversity of themes: U.S. Centennial, Emancipation Proclamation, Lexington Centennial, Valley Forge Centennial, Schuylkill Navy, National Convention of Cattlemen, the Chicago Fire, and the

Mighty Dollar. Several of these mint commemorative medals remain available for sale to the public today in current production versions. Most of the pre-20th century commemorative medal strikings are relatively scarce and provide the collector with a demanding acquisition challenge.

Q. *Is it true that the U.S. Mint once struck museum tokens and awards for dog shows?*

A. Yes, and also for kennel clubs, bicycle clubs, horse shows, athletic associations, fire companies, music societies, and many other clubs and organizations. These pieces were struck in copper, silver, and/or gold during the latter half of the 19th century, to the order of private individuals and club officials. The mintage of most pieces was quite small, in some instances less than a dozen examples were delivered. The "museum tokens" you refer to were made for the Charles Wilson Peale Philadelphia Museum piece produced late in the first half of the 19th century, one version of which is an admission token, with the words "Admit The Bearer" placed within the wreath on the reverse. They have been popular with collectors for more than a century, possibly because of the belief that they were engraved by Christian Gobrecht.

Q. *My grandfather had a school medal he always claimed was made by the U.S. Mint. Is this possible?*

A. From about 1831 until well into the 20th century, the U.S. Mint struck medals for various educational institutions which purchased them for use as scholastic achievement awards and, in at least one instance, for "punctuality and deportment." Many were still being struck after 1900. The practice was discontinued about 1947, when the last of the Franklin medals were struck for the Boston schools.

Q. *When did the U.S. Mint initiate the practice of striking copies of national medals specifically for sale to the general public?*

A. In January 1861, sixteen prominent numismatists, including inventor Samuel F. B. Morse, signed a letter addressed to Treasury Secretary John A. Dix in which they suggested that copies of national medals be struck for public sale. The secretary provided his assent on February 14 of that year.

Q. *How many so-called "official" Bicentennial medals were issued during 1975–1976?*

A. Official Bicentennial medals received their authority through Congress by the participation of their issuers in the medal program of the American Revolution Bicentennial Administration (ARBA). Forty-eight states issued a Bicentennial bearing the ARBA label, as did many cities. Mississippi and West Virginia did not participate in the "official" state medal program. It is generally acknowledged that "official" Bicentennial Commission issues numbered 106 distinctive medal issues.

Q. *Is it true that when the U.S. Mint first offered copies of national medals to the public, the large copper-bronzed pieces cost a mere $1.50?*

A. Yes, but it is equally true that in 1861 the average daily wage was less than two dollars.

Space medals.

Q. *What medals were most popular with collectors before those of the Bicentennial years?*

A. Space medals, particularly those relevant to the lunar voyages, and medals honoring the memory of former President John F. Kennedy were, and still are, enthusiastically collected.

Q. *What are Masonic "mark pennies," and are they still being made?*

A. Originally, Masonic or "mark" pennies were copper or bronze medal-like pieces of roughly large-cent size bearing the identity and location of the issuing lodge, the Masonic symbols and the private "mark" of a new member to whom the penny was given. The piece served to identify the member when presented at the issuing or other Masonic lodges. Today, mark pennies are produced principally as anniversary commemoratives for exchange between lodges and sale to members and non-members alike. During the last half of the 19th century, a number of Masonic lodges, including the New York Masonic Temple and St. John's Commandery in Philadelphia, had their mark pennies struck by the U.S. Mint.

Q. *How are elongated coins classified? Are they medals or still coins?*

A. I have never heard them referred to as other than elongated coins. If a choice has to be made between coins and medals, they can only be regarded as commemorative medals inasmuch as when the coins are squeezed through a pair of roller dies—one of which bears an engraved die for raising the devices and lettering which commemorate an event or person— the raised surface on the other side of the subject coin is flattened and all but obliterated by the process, which means the piece ceases to be a coin in the customary context.

Q. *Is it possible to obtain bronze copies of any medal the U.S. Mint has ever struck?*

A. No, only of a select few hundred considered to be of national interest. The mint began striking medals about 1800 and for many years actively sought private orders. The customer would either have the dies for his medals engraved by a private artist or would hire a mint engraver to prepare them, sometimes on his own time. In either case, the dies belonged to the customer, and were not deposited in the mint die collection. Consequently, the dies for literally thousands of private medals struck by the U.S. Mint likely no longer exist.

Q. *Are the copies of Indian Peace Medal issues available from the U. S. Mint today exact copies of those formerly presented to Indian chiefs?*

A. They differ in size and metal, but with a few exceptions the designs are authentic. The Indian Peace Medal issued under Washington's administration consisted of two hand-engraved silver plates bound together with a silver band. Its design bore no resemblance to the Washington peace or presidential medals available today, which were first struck after 1900. No medals for Indians were made during the administrations of John Adams and William Henry Harrison. They were designed and struck later to complete the presidential series.

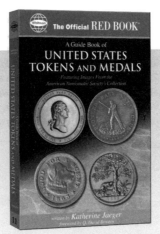

For more information: Consult the *Guide Book of United States Tokens and Medals* (Jaeger).

CHAPTER TWENTY-SEVEN

Utilitarian Tokens

Q. *I have a coin which has a head similar to the one on the old large United States cents, along with the date 1837. On the reverse is some lettering which reads, MILLIONS FOR DEFENSE, NOT ONE CENT FOR TRIBUTE. What do I have?*

A. You have an example of the privately issued necessity money of 1833 to 1844 known as "Hard Times Tokens." They are generally struck in copper, of the size of the large cent, and can be classified in one of two general groupings: political tokens and tradesmen's cards. Although they circulated as cents during a time of severe financial panic characterized by a lack of circulating coin caused by the hoarding of hard money, many bore a monetary disclaimer cleverly incorporated in patriotic slogans, such as "Millions for Defense, NOT ONE CENT for Tribute." The theme of the political tokens centers upon President Andrew Jackson's refusal to renew the charter of the Bank of the United States; many of the designs are strongly satirical, ridiculing Jackson's sketchy formal education, mule-like stubbornness and pretensions in office.

Q. *I recently came across a coin about the size of a current one-cent piece which I cannot identify. The obverse depicts a perched eagle and the date 1837, while on the reverse are the words FEUCHTWANGER'S COMPOSITION, in addition to "ONE CENT." What is this?*

A. The piece you have is commonly called a Feuchtwanger Cent. Dr. Lewis Feuchtwanger, a German-born chemist, perfected a metal which was really a variety of German silver, being an alloy of nickel, copper and some zinc. In 1837 he petitioned the U.S. government to consider using his metal as a substitute for copper in coinage, and struck a number of one-cent and three-cent trial pieces in the design you describe. Many tokens of the Hard Times period, including a number of his own store cards, were struck in Feuchtwanger's metal. Dr. Feuchtwanger was the first to suggest a small cent and a three-cent piece, coins the government later adopted.

Hard Times token.

Q. *I have a coin which depicts on the obverse a bird rising from flames, and lettering which reads: SUBSTITUTE FOR SHIN PLAS-TERS, NOVR., 1837. On the reverse is some wording which reads: SPECIE PAYMENTS SUSPENDED, MAY TENTH, 1837. What is this item?*

A. This is another of the political-motif Hard Times tokens. The symbol-ism of a phoenix rising from the flames is intended to suggest that the paper money of the time had become fit only to be burned; with its destruction, hard money would pump new life into the moribund econ-omy. The inspiration for the theme was derived from a convention of leading bankers who met in New York City in 1837. They determined to take the action of suspending specie payments as of May 10, 1837. Meeting again in early 1838, the bankers resolved that specie payments should be resumed, with most banks doing so during the course of the months that followed, temporarily abating the Hard Times, which were to return in October 1839, when the Bank of the United States of Philadelphia, the nation's largest, again suspended specie payments.

American Game Counter.

Q. *In my collection is a small coin which looks like gold and is about the size of a U.S. $2.50 gold piece. It has an odd-looking Liberty head on the obverse, along with the legend REPUBLICA ARGENTINA LIBERTAD. On the reverse is an eagle and the legend UNITED STATES OF AMERICA 2-1/2 D. Is this possibly a pattern for a proposed international coinage?*

A. It is not a pattern, but rather a relatively common numismatic item known as an "American game counter" or "spiel mark." These were produced for use as stakes or markers in games of chance during the mid-1800s, much as poker chips are employed today. Many were made in imitation of U.S. coins; others utilized Latin American designs in conjunction with U.S. designs. The majority of such pieces were manufactured in the private mints of Germany and in Birmingham, England. The scarcer varieties are highly valued, but most issues are relatively common. Their metallic composition is generally gilded bronze or brass, certainly not gold!

Q. *I have seen a token which has on both sides the elephant depicted on the famous American Colonial elephant tokens. On one side is the legend: ONLY 10 STRUCK. Is this a modern fantasy piece?*

A. Your token is one of the prestigious Colonial coin copies struck in the 1860s by J.A. Bolen. Ten were struck with the legend, and two without. The original tokens are great rarities bearing Carolina and New England imprints. The elephant obverse die of these two issues is shared with a rare series of London elephant tokens struck in the late 17th century. Copies were made of a great variety of Colonial coins from the middle of the 19th century into the opening years of the 20th century to provide facsimiles of rare issues that would otherwise be unobtainable. Time has given them a status denied current copies, which are not generally recognized as meaningful collector items.

Tokens. From left: Transportation token, sales tax token, and merchant's token, or store card.

Q. *I have what is identified as a "Colorado Retail Sales Tax Token." It also carries the figure "2" and has a cross shaped area removed from the center. It is about the size of a nickel and struck in aluminum. When and how was it used?*

A. Sales Tax Tokens were issued by various states in the mid-1930s to facilitate fractional payments of sales tax before the amount due was calculated in even cents. The piece you mention was valued at two mills. They were round, square, or rectangular in shape; with or without center holes; were made of metal, fiber, or plastic; and were frequently distinguished by a color code, such as black, white, green, and red.

Q. *I have a piece of paper which somewhat resembles a dollar bill. It is prominently labeled ONE DOLLAR SCRIP NOTE and was issued on the 6th day of March, 1933, by the Industrial Loan and Investment Co. of Fort Wayne, Indiana. What is the nature of this note?*

A. This note is one of an extensive array of "Depression Scrip" issued in the 1930s. It was issued during the bank holiday proclaimed by President

Roosevelt in March of 1933, when no other medium of exchange was available for everyday commerce. The use of various forms of Depression Scrip was widespread during the decade of hardship and tight money; scrip has been documented to exist from over 500 communities, representing 48 states, the District of Columbia, and the Territory of Hawaii. It was issued by employers for payroll purposes, by cities in the form of Tax Anticipation Notes, and by banks, clearing houses, chambers of commerce, prominent individuals, and so forth. Most scrip notes were printed on paper, but some unusual issues were printed on wood, aluminum, rubber, leather, shells, sheepskin, buckskin, and fish skin. As anticipated, small quantities of most of these issues were retained as souvenirs rather than being presented for redemption. Most of the paper scrip was redeemed and destroyed, however, and consequently many of those issues are very rare today.

Q. *I have often heard that old expression, "Don't take any wooden nickels," and I have seen many of them, and even saved a few. Does anyone collect them?*

A. There are many who collect nothing else. The dictionary defines a wooden nickel as "a small wooden disc, souvenir, token, or the like, having a value five cents, or no value." Numismatically, it is much more. A wooden nickel can be round or rectangular, and if round, of any size from a nickel or smaller up to a dollar or larger. While the devices and wording on a wooden nickel are usually printed, sometimes they are cut into the surface. It can be of any thickness from paper-thin to half an inch. It can be a valid trade token, frequently of commemorative design, usually redeemable as payment on merchandise; a souvenir of a meeting or celebration; or simply a personal calling or advertising card.

The history of wooden money can actually be traced back to the Byzantine Empire (AD 395–1435) when an attempt was made to circulate wooden money with little success. Since then, various forms of wooden money have served as a medium of exchange in England, Tibet, China, Africa, Oceania, the South Sea Islands, and Canada. Many of these issues were introduced during times of emergency, due to military operations or other political considerations. The first "official" issue of wooden money in the United States was circulated in 1931 in Tenino, Washington, to provide a medium of exchange during a bank failure which resulted in an acute shortage of circulating money.

OPA tokens.

Q. *I have read that during World War II "colored OPA tokens" were required to purchase canned goods and meats. What did the colors indicate, and are these war-related items collected as "tokens?"*

A. The OPA (Office of Price Administration) "tokens" to which you refer are of a sandwich-type fiber construction, consisting of red or blue outer layers bonded to an uncolored (gray) core. They are round, 16.4 mm in diameter, 1.4 mm thick, and weigh about 4 grains. Strictly speaking, they are not "tokens." They are "points" that were used in conjunction with, rather than in place of money, when purchasing designated food items. A specified number of blue "points" were required to purchase specified amounts of crop foods, such as canned fruits and vegetables, fruit juices, soups, baby foods, dried peas, beans, and preserves. Red "points" were require to purchase animal foods, such as meats, butter, oleo, edible fats and oils, cheese, canned milk, and canned fish.

They are collected, usually with emphasis upon the distinguishing two letter alphabet codes they bear. There are 54 documented alphabetical combinations—30 blue and 24 red—involving the letters C, H. T, U, V, X, Y, and occasionally W and M. The "rare" tokens in the set are the red bearing "MM" and "MV" letter combinations. Ration stamps, which were of similar purpose, were required for the purchase of gasoline, shoes, clothes, sugar, coffee, and other scarce items are also collected.

Q. *The fact that copper tokens of private origin circulated freely during the first 80 years of our nation's existence would seem to indicate that they possessed at least an implied legality. On what was it based?*

A. The legal status of private copper tokens prior to the Law of June 8, 1864, which provided for fines of up to $5,000 and 10 years at hard labor for the issuing of a private coinage of any kind, has never been clarified.

A law enacted in 1792 made it a misdemeanor punishable by a $10 fine to pay or receive in payment in any copper coins other than those of the United States. However, a subsequent law empowered the Secretary of the Treasury to annul by proclamation all private and foreign coppers six months after the U.S. Mint had issued $50,000 worth of half-cents and cents. There is no documented evidence that the required proclamation was ever issued and the issue of private tokens on an issue and circulation basis continued concurrently with U.S. coppers until 1857.

Q. *My brother told me that a token struck in 1796 for use in the United States is still being minted. Can he be right?*

A. In 1792 many French families of wealth and rank fled the French Revolution and established French settlements at Castorville and what is now Carthage, New York. In 1796, French designer Duvivier (designer of some of the early medals subsequently struck at the U.S. Mint) prepared a silver piece sometimes referenced as the "Castorland half dollar" or "jeton," either as an honorarium for the Paris Commissioners of Castorland or as a pattern for a coinage to serve the settlement. A reeded edge and the similarity of size and weight to the U.S. half dollar suggest a monetary purpose. This attractive piece can still be ordered from the Paris Mint in gold, silver, bronze, or copper, in matte or brilliant finishes. These restrikes carry incuse lettering—ARGENT (silver), CUIVER (copper) or OR (gold)—indicating their metallic content.

Q. *My mother had a coin or something which she wore as a pendant for many years. She said her grandfather, a sailor, gave it to her. On one side there are crossed sprays, the initials W.P. and the date 1880. There isn't anything on the other side but HALF REAL. What is it?*

A. Your great-grandfather had evidently been to Hawaii. The piece you describe is a plantation token used as small change on the Islands during the latter half of the 19th century. The initials W.P. are those of the Wailuku Plantation on the island of Maui. There is a companion one-real piece. There is also another pair of issues, attributed to the year 1871, with values of 6 cents and 12-1/2 cents. All of these tokens were hand-struck in the plantation's blacksmith shop.

Q. *I have heard that the United States government (not a private agency) once issued a $10 trade token. If true, when did it happen?*

A. It's true, and it happened in 1935. The brass $10 token was part of a series that also included aluminum 1¢, 5¢, 10¢, 25¢, 50¢, $1, and $5 (brass) tokens. The "Bingles," as they were called, were issued for the use of the colonists of the Matanuska Valley Colonization Project in Alaska Territory to provide them with needed federal aid. They were redeemable only at the stores of the Alaska Rural Rehabilitation Corporation (ARRC), and were in use for about six months in 1935 and 1936, after which they were redeemed for regular U.S. money and destroyed. With the exception of the octagonal one-cent piece, the tokens are round and of the same size as the corresponding U.S. coin.

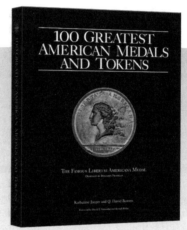

For more information: Learn about U.S. Exonumia in *100 Greatest American Medals and Tokens* (Jaeger/Bowers).

VI.
MONEY FROM OTHER COUNTRIES

CHAPTER TWENTY-EIGHT

Canadian Coins and Currency

Q. *How many mints are there in Canada, and do they have mintmarks?*

A. The Royal Canadian Mint at Ottawa, established in 1908, was the sole Canadian minting facility until mid-summer of 1975, when a large, modern facility at Winnipeg, Manitoba, began production. Eventually, the Manitoba plant assumed all production of coins for circulation, and the execution of circulating coinage under contracts with foreign governments, freeing up the Ottawa facility for production of special collector items. The Canadian "C" mintmark has appeared only on gold sovereigns minted for the British Empire and on certain Newfoundland coins struck before Newfoundland became a province of Canada.

Canadian tokens. Tokens played a prominent role in the commerce of early Canada. Two of the most common were the penny and halfpenny tokens issued in the 1850s by the Bank of Upper Canada.

Q. *I have a large Canadian coin or token that bears the denomination ONE PENNY. Also, the legend on this coin states that it is a bank token of Upper Canada. Just what is Upper Canada and what does this token represent?*

A. Ontario was largely founded by the immigration of English Loyalists into Canada following the Declaration of Independence by the United States and attendant activities in the colonies. The Constitutional Acts adopted by England in 1792 divided the Canadian territory that England had won from France as a consequence of the Seven Years' War into two separate provinces called Upper Canada, chiefly English-speaking and Lower Canada, the French stronghold. Upper Canada consisted of the southern part of present Ontario, that territory south of the Ottawa River and along the upper reaches of the St. Lawrence River, and Lower Canada can be identified with Quebec, that territory north of the Ottawa River and the lower reaches of the St. Lawrence River. In the instance of the token you describe, it is from an issue known as the St. George tokens, which were an authorized issue of the Bank of Upper Canada in Ottawa. They were issued in denominations of penny and halfpenny in the years 1850, 1852, 1854, and 1857.

Q. *Does the obverse of Canadian coins always bear the portrait of the ruling monarch of the British Empire?*

A. It isn't mandatory, but coins of the British colonies and associated Commonwealth nations typically bear the portrait of the ruling British monarch. The king or queen of England is by Canadian law designated as head of state.

Q. *I have a Canadian large cent that has an "H" on its reverse. Of what significance is this letter?*

A. The "H" stands for Heaton, it being the mintmark of a private mint located in Birmingham, England, to which the Royal Mint subcontracted some productions for coins serving its colonial possessions. Most of the early coins of Canada (before 1908) were struck at the Tower Mint in London and do not bear mintmarks.

Q. *Has the Royal Canadian Mint at Ottawa ever placed any type of mintmark on any of the coins it has produced for Canada?*

A. The Ottawa Mint has at no time placed any type of mintmark on any of the coins struck specifically for domestic use in Canada. However, the

Royal Canadian did mint gold sovereigns for the British Empire from 1908 to 1919 which do carry a distinguishing "C" mintmark on the reverse to indicate they were struck in Canada at the Ottawa Mint.

1947 Newfoundland one cent.

Q. *I have a coin dated 1941 that bears the word "Newfoundland." I always thought that Newfoundland was part of Canada. Can you explain this dilemma?*

A. Newfoundland became a British colony in 1713 under the provisions of the Treaty of Utrecht, along with its Labrador dependency, and did not become a province of the Dominion of Canada until April 1, 1949. Prior to that time, Newfoundland had its own monetary system. Newfoundland's distinctive coinage—minted from 1865 to 1947—was struck in London, Birmingham, and Ottawa. The Tower Mint coins (London) have no mintmark, the Birmingham coins have the characteristic Heaton "H," and those produced in Ottawa bear the Canadian "C" mintmark.

Q. *I have noticed that Canada, the United States, and Newfoundland have all issued 20-cent coins at one time or another. Can you shed any light on why this coin ever came into being and why it was never accepted?*

A. A 20-cent piece is a logical unit of a decimal coinage system; a 25-cent piece is an anomaly. However, the pre-national currency experience of both the United States and Canada was predominantly influenced by the Spanish dollar and its eight subdivisions, of which the two reales (two bits) had a value of 25 cents. It should be remembered that the Spanish dollar and its minor coins were legal tender in the United States until

1857, and that U.S. coins circulated freely in Canada before that country established its monetary system. Familiarity with the 25-cent denomination, and the desirability of maximum equivalence in the minor coins of concurrent currencies, established a use precedent for the quarter which a 20-cent piece was unable to replace in Canada, although the 20-cents denomination was readily accepted in more remote Newfoundland from 1865 to 1917, when the switch was made to the 25-cent denomination, likely due to the interchange of coins between Newfoundland and Canada, since Canada had produced the 20-cent pieces only with its initial coinage of 1858 and switched to a 25-cent denomination in 1870.

1945 Canadian "Victory Nickel."

Q. *I have a 1944 Canadian nickel that has a large "V" on the reverse and a border of dots and dashes resembling the Morse Code. Can you explain this?*

A. This is the famous Canadian "Victory Nickel" minted from 1943 through 1945. The torch and "V" are symbols of the victory of Liberty. The border of dots and dashes are an inscription in Morse Code: "We Win When We Work Willingly."

Q. *What is meant by the 1947 Maple Leaf cent? All of the cents of Canada that I have in my collection have a maple leaf on the reverse.*

A. Two issues of the Canadian cent bearing the date 1947 were released; the regular issue of 1947 and another with a small maple leaf placed immediately to the right of the date. The latter production took place in early 1948, when the Ottawa Mint was forced to utilize old 1947 dated dies to meet circulation demands. The granting of independence to India necessitated removal of a portion of the regnal legend—ET IND:

IMP:—on the obverse of all coinage, that had been traditional on all Colonial coinages of the English Empire, in 1948. The 1948 dies incorporating this change being prepared by the Royal Mint in London were delayed, necessitating improvisation of the part of the Ottawa Mint staff. The tiny maple leaf present on 1947 cents indicates that the coins so identified were actually struck in 1948.

Q. *What is meant by the term "Arnprior" that is sometimes referenced when talking about Canadian silver dollars? I have never seen that word on any of the dollars I've examined.*

A. In December of 1955, after the production of silver dollars had been officially completed for that year, the Royal Canadian Mint was called upon to produce a supplemental quantity of 2,000 additional dollars for a firm located in Arnprior, Ontario. These dollars differed from the previously struck ones in evidencing only one and one-half water lines in front of the canoe on the reverse of the coin, rather than the more typical three or four water lines. Collectors refer to them as "Arnpriors." A small quantity of similar dollars in Proof-like condition were included in 1955 mint sets released in late 1955 as well. A 1950 dollar of like characteristics belatedly acquired the same identification; subsequently similar deficient water line treatments have been discovered and actively collected of all years from 1950 to 1957 with the exceptions of 1954 and 1956.

Q. *I have noticed that a lot more attention is devoted to minor die varieties in collecting mid-20th century Canadian coins as opposed to U.S. coins of the same period. Can you explain this?*

A. In one word: boredom. Canada was not producing mintmarked variety coins, and it was producing sufficient quantities of each denomination to enable the collector of Canadian coins to easily acquire the year specimens for his collection. To sustain his interest, the Canadian collector began looking for die varieties and the repetitious imperfections inherent to any mass-produced item. Branch mints with their distinctive mintmarks and occasional small mintages of a particular denomination greatly increased the challenge confronting the collector of U.S. coinage. Active collecting of the Canadian varieties and their inclusion in the catalogs and price lists of the day resulted in them becoming a long-term pursuit of hobbyists.

1911 1¢ George V "Godless" coin.

Q. *What is meant by the "Godless" coins of Canada?*

A. In one year only, 1911—the year George V assumed the reign following the death of Edward VII—the words "Dei Gratia," meaning "By the Grace of God," were omitted from the obverse legend of all Canadian coins. Because of that absence, they are frequently referred to as the "Graceless" or "Godless" coins. The gold sovereigns of that year bore the abbreviated reverence "D.G."

Q. *What is meant by a 1926 "near 6" or "far 6" nickel?*

A. The description refers to the location of the date numeral 6 in relation to the right-hand maple leaf on the reverse of the coin. On the "near 6" variety, the stem of the 6 almost touches the leaf; on the "far 6" there is a narrow but quite obvious gap. The "far 6" is considered the scarcer of the two varieties by far.

Q. *To what do the expressions "blunt 7" and "pointed 7" refer?*

A. The terms refer to the manner in which the bottom tip of the stem of the date numeral 7 of the 1947 silver dollar is pointed. The point of the "blunt 7" variety is formed by a single downward diagonal achieving a point where it intersects the left lineament of the stem. The point of the "pointed 7" variety is formed by downward diagonals from each side intersecting at a point in line with the center of the stem.

Q. *Did Canada issue any gold coins prior to the introduction of the $100 issue in the Montreal Olympics commemorative coinage series in 1976?*

A. In 1912, 1913, and 1914, Canada minted a limited quantity of $5 and $10 gold coins, of which the coins of 1914 are considered to be the rarest, the 1914 $5 decidedly so. In 1967, Canada minted a commemorative $20 gold piece for inclusion in the specimen sets of commemorative coins marking the 100th anniversary of the Confederation of Canada. These gold coins bear no mintmark, and their reverse design portrays the armorial bearings of Canada. These Canadian gold coins should not be confused with the gold sovereigns minted at the Ottawa Mint from 1908 to 1919 (with the exception of 1912 and 1915) for the British Empire. These sovereigns are the Edward VII and George V type of Great Britain, and can be distinguished from them only by the Canadian mintmark "C" placed immediately above the date on the reverse of the coin.

Q. *What are my chances of finding a 1936 dot cent of Canada?*

A. You probably have a better chance of being elected president. The three know specimens are both uncirculated and unauthenticated. Officially, 678,823 of these dot cents were minted. Two theories have been advanced to account for their virtual non-existence: none were ever released for general circulation, or the dot on the die filled up very early in the production run and the distinguishing mark was raised on only a very few of the coins minted. The dot coinage of 1936 also included the dime and quarter. The quarters, of which 153,322 examples were struck, were released to circulation and a limited quantity are available to collectors at modest prices in the lower grades. Only four specimens are known of the 191,237 dot dimes minted according to official records. The dot was placed at the bottom of the reverse dies to enable them to be used to strike the 1937 George V coinage, until new dies for the George VI coinage could be placed in production.

Q. *Did Newfoundland ever issue gold coins?*

A. Newfoundland issued $2 gold coins in eight different years from 1865 to 1888, in consecutive years only from 1880 through 1882. Curiously, Newfoundland never issued a $1 denomination coin.

1954 paper money issue. The portrait of Queen Elizabeth on this note issued by the Bank of Canada created controversy until the art was corrected. Details show Devil in Hair (left) and No Devil (right).

Q. *To what does the term "devil in the hair" refer, as applied to Canadian paper money?*

A. It has reference to the initial 1954 Bank of Canada currency issue featuring the portrait of Queen Elizabeth II, and a resemblance to a devil's face that was noticed in the arrangement of the curls behind the left ear of her portrait on all denominations of the issue. Due to protests, the engravings were reworked to remove this fascinating, but objectionable, feature.

Q. *I have a Canadian coin dated 1942 and another dated 1943 that resemble a regular Canadian nickel. But they are of a bronze-colored material and 12-sided. Is this a coin of regular mintage, or do I have something special?*

A. Because of a shortage of nickel caused by war requirements, the metallic content of the Canadian was changed during 1942 to a bronze-colored alloy of 88 percent copper and 12 percent zinc, called tombac. It was made 12-sided to distinguish it from the bronze cent. It wasn't a success. The coin turned black and it was confused with the cent. While a reported 8,000 tombac nickels were struck in 1944, only one example is know to exist, with the balance of that production having been destroyed. During 1944 and 1945 the nickel was made of chrome-plated steel.

Q. *Does Canada mint any Proof sets?*

A. While the Canadian Mint has regularly offered "Uncirculated" or "Proof-like" sets since 1953, it did not begin offering Proof sets for general sale until 1981. These sets have typically consisted of one example of each coin minted for general circulation during a given year, they being struck on selected and specially handled blanks and contained in various styles of packaging. While "Proof" or "specimen" sets were prepared in very limited numbers for many years fr om 1858 through 1965, the first Proof sets marketed to the general public were not issued until 1981. In 1971 the Royal Canadian Mint began offering Proof-quality "specimen" coin sets in presentation cases similar to those utilized in marketing the Canadian Confederation commemorative sets of 1967. The coins contained in these sets were double struck, but, technically speaking, not of "Proof" quality. Annual issuance of these sets continued parallel with the "Proof" sets commencing in 1981.

Q. *I have noted that the Canadian monetary system very closely resembles that of the United States. Was there any direct planning for this between the two countries?*

A. There was no formal agreement. None was necessary. The proximity of the two nations, the common origins and traditions of the majority of their citizens, a common history of monetary experience with the Spanish dollar, and the tendency of the people of both nations to use each other's money, would have made any other decision irrational. While the exchange rates between the two currencies do ebb and flow over time, they generally float in relatively close balance.

Q. *In view of the fact that the Canadian currency has long been designated by various colors, why did it take so long for the United States to add color to the various denominations, and why didn't we match our color treatments to theirs?*

A. The desirability of colored currency was discussed in the United States for decades. The chief argument for it being that distinctive color for each denomination would enable it to be more readily identified and reduce the chance of improper payment or change. Opponents, on the other hand, argued that familiarity with the established designs was sufficient to enable quick identification without a color code. That, of course, was really untrue. Identification is made by the denomination numbers on the face of notes, not the design; not one person in five knows whose portrait is on the five-dollar or ten-dollar bills. Whatever the reason, it remains that comparatively few mistakes are made. And now, over the past decade, color has been subtly added to U.S. notes as an anti-counterfeiting measure.

1870 Dominion of Canada 25¢ fractional currency.

Q. *For what were the paper 25-cent notes of Canada used?*

A. In 1870, when the 25-cent fractional notes first appeared, Canadian officials were worried about the large amount of U.S. silver coinage circulating in Canada in default of an adequate supply of regal coins of that denomination. They were worried because the U.S. dollar was worth but 80 cents in Canada, and the trusting people who accepted the U.S. coins at face value suffered a 20 percent loss when they presented them for conversion to Canadian funds. The decision was made to withdraw the U.S. coins from circulation and replace them with the 25-cent notes until sufficient Canadian 25-cent coins could be minted. In the first three years of production for the Canadian 25-cent coin, nearly 4.3 million were struck. While the 25-cent notes were intended to be of temporary issue, as the public liked them, particularly for sending small amounts of money through the mail, further issues were released in 1900 and 1923, and it wasn't until 1935 that the Bank of Canada decided to formally call for their retirement.

Q. *The 1951 Canadian nickel lacks the normal reverse of the beaver, and in its place there is some type of factory with the additional legend NICKEL, 1751–1951. What is the significance of this change of design?*

A. About 75 percent of the 1951 Canadian nickels, struck of pure nickel, bear this commemorative reverse celebrating the 200th anniversary of the isolation of the metal nickel by a Swedish chemist in 1751 and remind consumers that Canada has historically accounted for 86 percent of the world's nickel production. The factory on the coin was a stylized rendition of a contemporary nickel refinery, likely styled after structures in the Sudbury mining district. A shortage of nickel late in 1951 forced the mint to return to the regular beaver design in chromium and nickel-plated steel.

Q. *A friend told me that Canada once used playing cards for money. Was he putting me on?*

A. Playing card money was used in the French colonies of Canada for approximately 75 years. Full cards, half cards, quarter cards, and oddly dimensioned clips were utilized. The first issue, in 1685, as an emergency issue, occasioned when troop payments from France were delayed. To quell the talk of mutiny, the governor collected all the packs of paying cards in the garrison, wrote an assigned value on the face of the cards and signed them. Both the soldiers and the colonists accepted this do-it-yourself money, and it became so popular that the government was forced to invoke it in larger quantities. Playing card money was of convenient size, relatively durable, difficult to forge . . . and the first paper money issued on the North American continent.

Q. *I have a Canadian dollar bill on which an asterisk precedes the serial number. Can you explain this, and does the asterisk increase the value of the note as a collector's item?*

A. The asterisk indicates that the note is a replacement for a defective one removed and destroyed during the printing process. They are inserted in packs of notes to maintain the integrity of the serial numbering sequence. Notes so marked acquire additional value, the increment sometimes being substantial.

Early Canadian money. As was true in other parts of colonial North America, the void between wampum and real coins was bridged in Canada by a variety of tokens, notes, and other forms of exchange. The piece of playing card money, dated 1735, is French. The Hudson's Bay Co. token was good for 1/2 made beaver (abbreviated NB in error); 1815 Magdalen Island one penny token proclaims "Success to the Fisheries;" and the holed Spanish dollar passed for five shillings on Prince Edward Island.

1967 25¢, 50¢, and $1.00 Canadian commemorative circulating coins.

Q. *Is it true that every coin Canada issued in 1967 is a commemorative?*

A. Yes. Canada's philosophy of commemorative distribution for many years differed fundamentally from that employed by the United States. Canadian commemoratives in the trade coin denominations have typically replaced regular-issue coin releases for specified periods, usually one year; the coins are struck in quantity and released to circulation in the normal manner. In 1967, Canada replaced all of the regular-issue coins (1¢ through $1) with commemoratives to celebrate the 100th anniversary of Canadian Confederation as a nation.

Q. *I have a 1967 Canadian dollar bill that has the dates 1867–1967 where the serial numbers would normally appear. Is this dollar related to the 1967 Centennial Celebration?*

A. You dollar bill was issued by the Bank of Canada in Ottawa to commemorate one hundred years of Canadian Confederation as a nation. This particular issue could only be obtained directly from the bank itself, and bears the dates 1867–1967 in place of the regular bill serial numbers. It was produced at the request of and particularly for collectors. A similar commemorative dollar bill, but with normal serial numbers, was issued for general circulation. While the bill was sold at a premium, it was honored in trade when presented in payment as well.

1967 $20 gold coin.

Q. *What is the story behind the 1967 $20 gold coin of Canada?*

A. The $20 gold coin was a special issue struck only for inclusion in the Gold Presentation Sets of 1967 coinage commemorating the 100th anniversary of Canadian Confederation as a nation. The seven Proof-quality coins were encased in a black, morocco leather presentation case and sold for $40 a set. This is a coin of many "firsts": the first commemorative gold coin of Canada, the dominion's first gold coin since 1914, the first commemorative gold coin of North America since 1926, the first $20 coin Canada ever minted, and the dominion's largest denomination gold coin up to that time. It was struck in .900 fine gold, with a bullion value of $20 Canadian, or about $18.50 U.S.

American collectors were denied the opportunity to legally purchase the coin at the time of issue. Officials of the U.S. Treasury's Office of Domestic Gold and Silver Operations did not consider the coin to be of sufficient merit for exclusion from the ban then in force which severely limited the ownership of modern gold coins by U.S. citizens. This ban was rescinded at midnight, December 30, 1974. It is a fact, however, that many U.S. collectors had the coins in their possession prior to that time. In fact, many purchased them at the time of issue and initially placed them in bank safe deposit boxes in Canada, which action was also technically unlawful.

CHAPTER TWENTY-NINE

Mexican Coins and Currency

Q. *What did the natives use for exchange before the arrival of the Spanish?*

A. In a slave-owning culture such as the Aztec Empire, slaves constituted the wealth of the owner and provided the standard, if not the unit, of value. There may have been a need for small change in such communities, but it existed only as a convenient subdivision of the real wealth. Consequently, there was a scarcity of primitive money in Mexico.

  The highest Aztec monetary unit was a sack containing about 24,000 cocoa beans. Interestingly, the cocoa-bean money was debased by being hollowed out and repacked with dirt and counterfeited with imitation beans of varnished clay. Pieces of cotton cloth, stone beads, and colored shells were also employed as a low-level medium of exchange. Extremely expensive purchases were made with transparent duck quills packed with flakes of gold.

  Some authorities cite a small copper axe (sometimes called a hoe or hide scraper) as a form of token money. Others believe the axe money was introduced about a quarter century after the conquest to facilitate trade between the Spaniards and Indians in lieu of sufficient small Spanish coins.

Q. *Did the Spaniards bring their own coins to the New World, use the native exchange media, or did they begin making coins as soon as they arrived?*

A. Spain never made a serious attempt to supply New Spain (Mexico) with coinage from the Old World. At the beginning there was no need for it;

the conquistadores came as looters, not traders. When developing trade created a need for coinage, it was considered more convenient, cheaper, and safer (in view of the action of privateers) to coin the silver at its source. The first mint in the New World was established at Mexico City in 1535, and coined one-quarter, one-half, one, two, and four real pieces. Two and four copper maravedies were also coined, but were not accepted by the natives, who also refused the fractional silver reales because of their smallness. The consequent shortage of coins of sufficiently low denomination for trading with the impoverished natives forced the Spaniards to utilize native currencies, principally the copper hoe and cocoa bean. According to a Spanish document from 1548, four new hoes were equal to five Spanish reales; by 1551, another document pegged the official value of the cocoa bean at 140 to the real.

First coins. Cobs, crude pieces minted by the Spanish, were the first coins in the Western Hemisphere. They were sliced from silver bars, then struck with hand dies.

Q. *What does the term "Cob" mean used in relation to early real pieces?*

A. The term refers to a crude type of Spanish dollar coined at Mexico City from the reign of Philip II until the middle of the reign of Philip V (1556–1728), and until 1751 during the reign of Ferdinand VI at the Potosi Mint in Peru. The cob was hastily coined by hand-stamping slices of crude, irregularly rolled silver bars with crudely prepared dies, but with no sacrifice of weight and fineness. The word "Cob" is a corruption of the Spanish "cabo de barra," meaning quite literally "end of the bar."

Piece of eight. Storied piece of eight, or Spanish milled dollar, had a decorative edge to prevent clipping. Fractional parts, or "bits," gave birth to the term still in use.

Q. *What is a "Piece of Eight?"*

A. The term "piece of eight" is an unofficial name given to the Spanish eight reales coin by the Brotherhood of Buccaneers. The coin was not itself a monetary unit, but a multiple of the Spanish monetary unit, the real. The real was the equivalent of 12-1/2 U.S. cents.

Q. *What is a "Doubloon?"*

A. The doubloon was a gold coin of Spain and Spanish America, first struck during the 14th century. Originally it was equal in value to eight gold escudos or 16 silver reales (pesos). When Spain adopted the metric system in 1849, the doubloon was made equal to ten escudos or 100 reales, about the equivalent of five dollars.

Q. *What is a "Pillar Dollar" and what is a "Milled Dollar?"*

A. The pillar dollar and the milled dollar were created simultaneously in the same coin in 1732 when the standard of the Spanish dollar was lowered slightly, the old design replaced with the imaginative Dos Mundos (Two

Worlds) design, and the edge protected for the first time against clipping and shaving by a milling of floral design. The pillar dollar is the most famous crown of the Western Hemisphere. An example belongs in the cabinet of every collector of America's coinage.

The design of two conjoined hemispheres resting upon the sea between two pillars and capped with the crown of Spain is symbolic of the Age of Exploration and the Spain's expansionist ambitions. The conjoined worlds beneath the Spanish crown symbolize the unity of hemispheres under the rule of Spain. The waves and the Pillars of Hercules symbolize that the western sea, rather than being the end of the world, is the gateway to new worlds. The amended motto—Plus Ultra—on the pillars attests that, contrary to the warning of Hercules, there is "more beyond" the Straits of Gibraltar.

Q. *Was the Spanish-American piece-of-eight ever used in the United States?*

A. The coins of Spain, minted in Mexico, served as the principal medium of exchange in the American colonies prior to and immediately following the American Revolution. They continued to circulate concurrently with U.S. coinage well after the establishment of the U.S. Mint, being officially recognized as a legal tender medium until 1857.

Q. *What is a "bit" piece?*

A. "Bit" was a popular expression for the Spanish and Mexican silver 1-real coin and 1/8 portions "cut" from piece-of-eight coins for circulation at a 1-real value. The value of a real or bit, 12-1/2 cents U.S., was derived from the real being one eighth the value of a piece-of-eight reales, which was officially decreed as being equal in value to the U.S. dollar. Logically, two reales or two bits were equal to a U.S. quarter dollar and four bits to a half dollar. The practice of calling a quarter "two bits" has survived to our time. A persistent shortage of small change had given rise to the practice of cutting a piece-of-eight reales into appropriate half-moon and pie-shaped bit units which passed freely as minor coinage.

1974 20 centavos.

Q. *Can Mexico's history be traced through its coinage?*

A. The thread of history is woven through the coinage of most nations, with Mexico certainly being no exception. Mexican coins relate the tales of feeble-minded monarchs, rabid revolutionaries, fighting priests, forceful reactionaries, an Austrian pretender, bandit presidents, and the birth and evolution of a republic. They also tell of a city founded on two marshy islands where an eagle devoured a snake; of a Great Temple erected atop a pyramid and sanctified with the blood of 20,000 captives; of a warrior-priest society sufficiently advanced to devise calendars, irrigate crops, and build walled cities, and still primitive enough to cut the beating hearts from children to forestall calamities foretold by the entrails of goats.

Mexican coins also recount the coming of the Great White God from across the seas, and of how he preached salvation through faith while he looted the enslaved; of a cruel and sanguinary struggle against the tyranny of foreign despot and native adventurer; of the triumph of humanism over reaction; and the emergence of democracy's light from the dark night of suppression and indignity. But in all the capture, they but again relate to the theme of all men in all ages: the ceaseless struggle between superstition and intelligence, and between aspiration and the intransigence of power.

1975 un peso.

Q. *I thought Mexico's peso was a silver coin, but I have one dated 1972 which appears to be struck of a nickel alloy. What's the story?*

A. Mexico's peso is one of history's more storied silver coins. Its origins are tied to the right heritage of the Spanish colonial eight reales coin which achieved such widespread international respect and was produced in great numbers at the mints of colonial Mexico. The coin's fine silver content was .9027 fine until 1918, when the fineness was debased to .800 and the total weight of the coin reduced by more than 30 percent. The fineness declined again in 1920, this time to .720, at which time the weight was again reduced, this time from 18.125 grams to 16.86 grams. The peso remained a stable coin for the next 25 years, but in 1947 the standard was again reduced, this time to a .500 fineness and 14 grams weight. That lasted until 1950 when the standards became .300 fine and 13.333 grams for a single year coin issue. Coinage of the peso was resumed in 1957 with the weight raised to 16 grams, but the fineness debased to .100, at which it remained until the last silver (billon) pesos were struck in 1967. The peso was reintroduced as a nine gram copper-nickel coin in 1970, followed by a stainless steel piece with a weight of 6.07 grams in 1984. Following a monetary reform, in 1992 a new peso was introduced as a bimetallic coin, the issue of which continues to this day.

Q. *How many mints have there been in Mexico?*

A. The exact number is still debated. Including Crown and Revolutionary mints, there were probably no less than 23. The first and principal mint was at Mexico City. Other well-known mints were located at Chihuahua, Guadalajara, Sombrerete, Zacatecas, Durango, Oaxaca, Valladolid, and San Luis Potosi.

1822 dos pesos note.

Q. *When did Mexico first use paper money?*

A. Mexico issued paper money for the first time in 1822, during the First Empire of Augustin I (Iturbide). This issue took the form of 1-, 2-, and 10-peso promissory notes, printed with blank backs, and redeemable a year from issuance. General disapproval of the notes discredited the government and contributed to the downfall of Iturbide. The notes were demonetized on April 11, 1823, and their use authorized for part payment of taxes. Curiously, on May 12, 1823, a series of one-peso notes was authorized to redeem the unwanted first issue notes. They were printed on the blank backs of Papal Bulls of Indulgence, for which reason they are widely referenced as "Bull Notes."

Q. *Under how many monarchs did Mexico mint coins?*

A. Coins were struck at mints located in Mexico during the reigns of eleven Spanish monarchs: Charles I (and Johanna), Philip II, Philip III, Philip IV, Charles II, Philip V, Louis I, Ferdinand VI, Charles III, and Ferdinand VII, a time span stretching from 1535 to 1821. To these may be added the usurpers, Iturbide (Augustin) I (1821–1823) and Maximilian (1864–1867).

Q. *What is the monetary unit used in Mexico today?*

A. It is still the peso, divided into 100 centavos. This reformed or "new peso" was introduced in 1992; the current exchange rate is around 11 U.S. cents to the peso. "Peso" is Spanish for "weight," of "unit of weight."

Q. *Was the piece-of-eight known by any other names?*

A. Many of them. They include Spanish dollar, milled dollar, pillar dollar, peso, piaster, 'dobe dollar, and cob.

Q. *I have a number of different Mexican pesos featuring the patriot-priest Morelos. In each instance he is presented with his head wrapped in a cloth. Why is he depicted in this unusual manner?*

A. The coins you mention are an unusual example of realistic, rather than idealistic, coin portraiture. Morelos is said to have suffered continuously from severe headaches, the pain of which he sought to relieve by tightly binding his head with a kerchief. Morelos was depicted on all peso coins minted from 1947 through 1987, with the exception of the 1957 Constitution Centennial commemorative depicting Benito Juarez, the Minister of Justice at the time of its adoption, five types in all.

Q. *What do the terms "Maximiliano," "Balanza," and "Caballito" mean?*

A. They are names given by Mexicans to various types of their peso. "Maximiliano" refers to the peso issued from 1866 through 1867 under Emperor Maximilian; "Balanza" to the peso issued from 1869 through 1873 featuring a balance scales design; "Caballito" to the peso minted from 1910 through 1914 featuring Liberty astride a horse.

Q. *I am confused by the identity of the king who ruled Spain (and Mexico) from 1516 to 1556. Some call him Charles I, and other Charles V. Which is correct?*

A. Both. Johanna, the third child of Ferdinand and Isabella, succeeded to the Spanish throne upon the death of Ferdinand in 1516, but because she was mentally incompetent, her son Charles was appointed to rule in her name. Charles ruled as both Charles I, King of Spain, and as Charles V, Holy Roman Emperor.

Q. *How many different mintmarks were used by the mint at Mexico City?*

A. The mark most frequently utilized by the mint at Mexico City consists of the small letter "o" placed in tight proximity over the capital letter "M," but instances are known where it appears as M, Mo, *M.X*, and the letters Mxo in a vertical arrangement of small "o" above medium "x" above large "M." The Mxo mintmark appears exclusively on gold coins issued from approximately 1681 to 1713. The mark *M.X* was used on all denominations of silver in 1733.

Q. *When did Mexico issue a coin in the unusual denomination of "1 onza?"*

A. It didn't. The 1 onza is a silver bullion piece containing 1 troy ounce (480 grains) of .925 fine silver. It was produced and sold initially in 1949 to help dispose of a large amount of silver bullion held in government storage, and to demonstrate the exceptional quality of the work of the Mexico City Mint in hopes of enticing orders for the minting of foreign coinage. Substantial additional quantities were struck dating from 1978 to 1980. Collectors include the 1 onza in collections of Mexican coinage or world crowns because it is crown size, and because its design depicts the coinage themes of a screw press and balance scales.

About the images in this book: In general, coin denominations of 50 cents and higher are pictured at actual size; denominations below 50 cents and coins that are unusually small (e.g., gold dollars) are generally pictured at 150 percent of their actual size. Paper money is typically pictured at page width. Other items, such as medals, encased postage, and so on, may be enlarged for visibility. Appendix B lists the actual sizes of U.S. coins and currency.

1914 Pancho Villa "Muera Huerta" silver peso.

Q. *I recently saw a Mexican peso which bore the unusual motto "Muera Huerta," which in loose translation wills or wishes the death of Huerta, one of the prominent figures of the Mexican Revolution of 1910–1917. Can you tell me the origin of this coin?*

A. The 1910–1917 Revolution was a time of unparalleled violence and confusion in Mexico. The various guerrilla leaders—Villa, Zapata, Carranza, Obregon—fought each other even as they struggled to unseat Huerta, who had seized control of the Mexican government, and install his successor. Pancho Villa in particular hated Huerta intensely for causing the death of Madero, the mild intellectual who started the modern revolution, and for his own close brush with death at the hands of Huerta's firing squad. To publicize his hatred, he caused a silver peso to be struck in 1914 at Cuencame, Durango, on which was inscribed the motto MUERA HUERTA, or "Death to Huerta." Huerta was so incensed by the existence of Villa's "Death Wish" peso that he ordered the immediate execution of anyone found with the coin in his possession.

CHAPTER THIRTY

Coins From Around the World

Q. *I have a silver-dollar-sized coin that portrays a queen on the obverse and a double-headed eagle with shield on the reverse. It is dated 1780, but it looks brand new. Is this a real coin?*

A. You have the Queen of Current Coins, the Fat Lady of Numismatics, the dollar that is not a dollar. You have an example of the renowned Maria Theresa thaler of Austria, which is not a thaler (dollar), but a bullion disc of 26.0668 grams of .833 fine silver, which does not bear a mark of value and is not legal tender in its homeland. You have an unofficial trade dollar that was maintained in production for more than 200 years. First minted in 1780, it was restruck on an ongoing basis utilizing original tools and without changing dates until 1984, sometimes as a product of mints other than the Austrian Mint in Vienna, with untold millions being produced. This coin was a favorite trade dollar of traders and tribesmen in the coastal areas of the Red Sea and Persian Gulf because of its constant standard, unchanging design, and its intricate engraving and edge, which made it difficult to counterfeit and impossible to shave. You do not have a valuable coin, but you do have a very historic one, it being one of the most romantic issues in the lore of Coindom.

Q. *What is a "cartwheel," as the term is applied to foreign coins?*

A. During the 18th century, the obsolete equipment of the Royal Mint in London proved to be incapable of supplying the expanded coinage requirement of England. The coinage of copper was neglected to produce gold and silver coins. By the late 1700s, the only copper coins in circulation were regal coins of earlier monarchs that had worn smooth from years of use, underweight counterfeits, and a hodgepodge of private tokens issued by exasperated merchants to facilitate business transactions. Finally, in 1797, England issued pence and two-pence coins of sufficient weight to discourage counterfeiting. The penny contained an ounce of copper, and the two-penny, which was as large as a U.S. silver dollar and twice as thick, contained two ounces. They were promptly dubbed "cartwheels" because of their tremendous size and because they were made with a broad, flat rim on which the legend was incused. These were the first English regal coins to be manufactured with steam power.

The term "cartwheel" has also been fairly widely applied to U.S. silver dollars issued in the late 1800s and early 1900s, primarily the Morgan type, and similar sized silver coins of other countries are sometimes similarly referenced.

Q. *I have a United States silver dollar dated 1875 which on the back says TRADE DOLLAR. There are a couple marks counterstamped into the surface of the coin which resemble Chinese characters. Could you explain this?*

A. The U.S. trade dollar was introduced in 1873 to compete with the Mexican silver peso, which had gained recognition and popularity as a "trade dollar" with merchants in the Orient. The Chinese merchant was a suspicious fellow who examined each coin closely to determine its genuineness. Certain merchants who commanded the respect of their fellows stamped their "chop mark" on authenticated coins to inform others of their acceptance as being genuine. Some such dollars are so covered with chop marks as to be bent and nearly unrecognizable. Others with just a few—perhaps as many as four or five—neatly executed and spaced marks are prized by some collectors.

1935 Filipino five centavos.

Q. *Did the United States ever issue colonial coins of its own?*

A. The United States coinage for the Philippines might be so considered. After liberating the Philippine Islands from Spanish domination, the United States issued a regular coinage for the island commencing in 1903 and continuing through 1945, which remained in active circulation following the 1946 proclamation of the republic until new national issues of similar design were introduced in 1958. The reverse of the issues under U.S. administration bore the legend UNITED STATES OF AMERICA and on the obverse the figure of a male seated by an anvil with a volcano in the background (on the base metal 1/2, 1, and 5 centavos) or a female standing at an anvil with a volcano again in the background (on silver 10, 20, and 50 centavos, and one peso). The republic coinage of from 1958 through 1966 retained the obverse treatments on the various denominations for the reverse, with a treatment of the arms of the republic being rendered on the obverse.

Q. *Can I exchange foreign coins for U.S. money?*

A. The capability for so doing is available in the foreign exchange departments of some commercial banks in the larger cities. However, in view of the fluctuating rate of exchange, the low value of most foreign coins, the commission charged for exchange—due to handling considerations, they are greater than for paper currency—and the fact that many issues of older foreign coinage have been devalued, the transaction is of dubious worth unless you have a great deal of higher denomination foreign coins to exchange.

1883 Hawaiian Akahi Dali.

Q. *Did Hawaii ever issue its own coins?*

A. Prior to becoming a territory of the United States, the independent Kingdom of Hawaii issued a modest number and variety of coins. The first official coins were copper cents of 1847 bearing a facing portrait of King Kamehameha III on the obverse and with the denomination stated as "Hapa Haneri," meaning "one hundredth part," on the reverse. Apart from some pattern 5-cent coins prepared in 1881, presumably struck at the Paris Mint, the second and last coinage of Hawaii was struck in 1883 as silver dimes, quarters, halves, and dollars for circulation, to the standards of U.S. coinage, with a 1/8 dollar pattern of like style being prepared as well. This coinage rendered a right facing profile portrait of King Kalakaua I on the obverse, with the arms of the republic rendered on the reverses of the quarter, half, and dollar coins, and was struck at the San Francisco Mint. With the exception of the 1883 quarter, all Hawaiian coins are considered relatively rare.

1906 British Honduras one cent.

Q. *I have seen a number of coins which carry a portrait of a King of England on the obverse along with legends which attest to his being King of England. However, on the reverse is carried the name of several other countries, such as South Africa, West Africa, East Africa, etc. What is the reason for this?*

A. At the height of colonialism prior to World War I, the British Empire embraced a fourth of the habitable land area of the globe and influenced the happiness of a fifth of its people. The colonies, which were permitted their own coinage, acknowledged British sovereignty by depicting the British monarch on the obverse of their coins. At this time it was said that 80 percent of the coins in the pocket of an American sailor home from the sea had been minted under British auspices. The surge of nationalism born between World Wars I and II resulted in the Union Jack being lowered upon dune and headland, bringing independence to most of the larger British colonies. A second surge of nationalism in the 1960s led to most of the rest becoming independent. Those which chose independence within the British Commonwealth have, in most instances, continued the tradition of monarchic coinage.

1936 Edward VIII coin from East Africa.

Q. *Does the portrait of Edward VIII, the king who gave up a throne for love, appear on coins of England or the colonies?*

A. No English or colonial coins bearing a portrait of Edward VIII were produced for circulation, although preparations for 1937-dated coinage were completed. The Royal Mint struck a few complete sets of Edward VIII coinage, farthing through silver crown and gold sovereign, for English institutions. Possibly a dozen of the 12-side, brass threepence pieces were released to vending machine companies for testing purposes. Most were returned, but a few are in private collections. The Royal Mint classifies them as patterns. Colonial coins bearing the name of Edward VIII, but not his portrait, were released by East Africa, West Africa, New Guinea, Fiji, and the Indian states of Kutch and Jodhpur.

Q. *I have what appears to be an English copper halfpenny, dated 1793, which bears the portrait of Sir Isaac Newton. However, I can't find it listed among English coins of that period. What do I have?*

A. You have an 18th century English trade token of the type issued by merchants in England, Scotland, Ireland, and Wales from 1787 to 1804. They are generally called Conder tokens, in recognition of James Conder, who compiled the first comprehensive catalog of the series in 1798. These tokens were issued by private sources to alleviate an annoying shortage of regal copper coins. It is estimated that the series contains approximately 10,000 historically attuned tokens, including counterfeits, mules, and varieties of date, die treatment, and edges.

Q. *What is the largest official silver coin that was circulated in the 20th century?*

A. It's a giant 1975-dated 20-pa'anga coin from the Pacific Kingdom of Tonga. The piece measures 62 millimeters (almost 2-1/2 inches) in diameter and weighs 140 grams (4.4971 ounces) of .999 fine silver. The previous titleholder was Panama's 1971 silver 20 Balboas, measuring 61 millimeters, with 2,000 grains of .925 fine silver. Both coins were issued for circulation, but the extent of commercial use is questionable. In 1985 a limited issue £25 coin commemorative of the Falkland Islands' "self-sufficiency," with a diameter of 65 millimeters and silver weight of 4.82 ounces sterling (2,313.6 grains), technically supplanted the Tonga coin as the world's heaviest silver coin. This offering was subsequently supplanted by Communist China's 1986 dated 50 Yuan coin commemorating the 120th anniversary of the birth of Dr. Sun Yat-Sen, it being a 70mm diameter issue struck of .999 fine silver and weighing five ounces (155.52 grams).

Q. *In recent years I have seen more and more advertised coins designated as "NCLT's." What are they?*

A. Coins designated non-circulating legal tender (NCLT) are those created and marketed under the agencies of sovereign governments expressly for sale to into the collector marketplace. They are primarily individual coins of a commemorative nature which invariably are sold at prices substantially in excess of their face values, and which often do not have a counterpart in the same or a base metal which were released to circulation. Officially declared legal tender by the governing authority, and technically subject to being honored as such, they are not intended to serve as a medium of exchange.

Q. *Is it really a fact that English pennies were once made of gold?*

A. The deeper one delves into the numismatic discipline, the more one comes to realize that money isn't what is used to be. The now lowly English penny was the principal coin of the Middle Ages, being made of silver in England until a change to copper was made in 1797. In the 12th century, a silver English penny would pay the rent of a cottage for a year. In 1257, Henry III caused gold pennies to be struck to represent the value of 20 silver pennies.

1797 two-pence.

Q. *I have been told that when Matthew Boulton produced the massive 1797 "Cartwheel" coinage for England, he intended that in addition to their utility as coins, they be used for gauging weights and measures. Can you explain if this is true and how it worked?*

A. Matthew Boulton can explain it better; "I intend there shall be a coincidence between our Money, Weight and Measures, by making 8 two-penny pieces 1 lb, and to measure 1 foot; 16 penny pieces 1 lb, and 17 to measure 2 feet; 32 half-pence 1 lb, and 10 to measure 1 foot."

Q. *I recently picked up a brass piece dated 1837 that appears to be English. It has a young Victoria head on the obverse and a horseman and multi-headed dragon on the reverse. The legend reads, TO HANOVER. Is this a 19th century British token?*

A. Although the TO HANOVER pieces may have seen limited service as tokens, they are generally considered to be game counters inspired by an incident in British history. Hanover, a small independent kingdom in Germany, was from 1714 to 1837 ruled by the same sovereign as Great Britain. Victoria became Queen of Great Britain in 1837 upon the death of William IV. She did not, however, become Queen of Hanover. By the law of Hanover, a woman could not ascend the throne. Accordingly,

Ernest Augustus, Duke of Cumberland, fifth son of George III, was appointed sovereign and took up residence in Hanover. Hence the legend, TO HANOVER.

Q. *Were the British "Model Coins" that resemble the 1792 U.S. silver-center cents of Henry Voight intended to be patterns for a copper coinage of convenient size but good intrinsic value?*

A. Joseph Moore may have had something like that in mind when he privately produced the so-called "Model Coins," although the center plug, made in imitation of a genuine British coin, is white-metal, not silver. Moore issued the "Model Coins" (the name refers to the word MODEL that appears on them) in great quantities, in denominations of 1/2, 1/4, 1/8, 1/16, and 1/32 of a farthing. Whatever the pieces were intended to be, they proved to be so popular with the people that the Royal Mint had to publicly disown them as official coin issues.

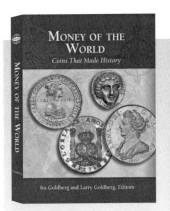 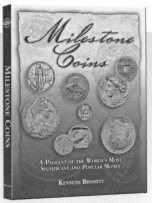

For more information: Learn about money from other countries in *Money of the World: Coins That Made History* (Goldberg) and *Milestone Coins: A Pageant of the Word's Most Significant and Popular Money* (Bressett).

Appendix A

Numismatic Investment

Q. *I have often been told that when buying a given coin, one should always buy an example of the best quality available, but I am wondering if there is valid justification for paying a multiple of ten times more for an MS-65 (Select) than for an MS-63 (uncirculated with attractive eye appeal), or a like multiple for an MS-67 (Gem) over an MS-65.*

A. The practice of buying the best quality available is certainly an appropriate and applicable rule . . . up to a point. Let's assess, for example, an 1892 or 1893 World's Columbian Exposition commemorative half dollar. In "Select" quality, these coins today carry a value of approximately $800, but twenty years ago they traded for about $1,000. Stepping up to "Gem" quality, today the price is in excess of $10,000. While the best reported grade for specimens of either date is MS-67, hundreds of examples of each exist at or above the MS-65 grade level. Referred to in the trade as "ultra-high" grades, with only the most miniscule difference between specimens, it is questionable that they would be worth that amount from the collector perspective. Rather, this is a speculator market, where the demand support is very thin. The market is much more broadly supported at the MS-63 level, where either coin carries $100 level price tags, at which one could acquire perhaps eight to ten, or perhaps even more examples that would be more readily marketable. The Columbian issue is, however, a very common issue within the classic commemoratives series (1892–1954). Assessing where one might direct their monies when price appreciation is an objective, you should buy coins that are basically scarce and numismatically desirable, that are possessed of a broad base of collector interest, always buying high quality specimens, but avoiding the ultra-high grades.

1957 Proof set.

Q. *Is it true that you can buy Proof sets each year and be assured of a profit?*

A. You can buy Proof sets each year—from the Mint if your order is placed on a timely basis and from dealers thereafter—and in most years when Proof sets have been issued (from 1936 to 1942, again from 1950 to 1964 and from 1968 to the present) the sets have appreciated in value by the year's end. However, generally speaking, annual Proof sets have been produced in excess of the demand that exists in the secondary market-place. At this point they become simple commodities, or articles of commerce, and as such are subject to the same laws of supply and demand that govern economic performance of pork bellies or peanuts. Over the

Modern Silver Proof set.

years, the values of Proof sets have risen and fallen in response to the supply and demand factors.

The 1957 Proof sets, with roughly 1.25 million sets produced, in contrast to about 670,000 in 1956 and 875,000 in 1958, depreciated to the point where they could only be sold into the secondary marketplace at less than their $2.10 initial cost before they recovered to a satisfactory level. The 1964 Kennedy Proof set rode a wave of nostalgia to an initial high of $16, then tumbled to a value of about $5 in 1977, recovering to the present mid-teens level. In recent years, the profit performance of Proof sets has lagged behind that of commemoratives, type coins, and gold, with most sets from the mid-1970s to the mid-1990s regularly trading below their issue prices. It is unrealistic, however, to suppose than any of the regular high mintage sets of the past 60 years will ever parallel the performance of the 1936 set, which is presently valued in the high four-figure range.

Q. *What makes rolls of coins worth more than their face value?*

A. Hope, where most issues of the past 50 years are concerned. Investing in Uncirculated rolls is taking a calculated gamble based on the experience of prior times. If you check a price list of Uncirculated Lincoln cents (to cite but one example), you will notice that the pre-1934 coins are considerably higher priced than those that follow. The short supply of pre-1934 Uncirculated cents—revealed by their higher prices—was created when the rolls that collectors had squirreled away from the teens and twenties were taken from cigar box and trunk during the hardship of the Great Depression years and given to the butcher, who fed them into circulation.

The erosion of supply wasn't fully appreciated until the hobby entered an expansionary phase following World War II. Then collectors, sadly realizing the extent of the profit that had gone awry, began squirreling away rolls of late 1940s and 1950s coinages and turning a handsome profit on them within an acceptable time. Their success attracted the speculators, and in the early 1960s the roll market boomed with an artificial prosperity created by speculators selling their rolls to each other. Inevitably, the bubble burst, with a lot of them "taking a bath." Today, most uncirculated rolls of cents and nickels after 1958 and dimes after 1969 are moderately priced, as are quarters from 1970 through 1981 and halves after 1993. While intelligent roll collecting is essential to the future growth of the hobby, it should be remembered that the rolls must ultimately be broken up and sold to collectors as individual coins in a marketplace where the laws of supply and demand remain operative. Any quantity release at one time can only depress the value of the coins.

Q. *Is collecting any type of coin a good investment?*

A. No! The hobby collector—be it of coins, back-scratchers, or Bavarian beer mugs—is occasionally persuaded to purchase by impulse or sentiment. Indulging frequent lapses into irrationality is part of the fun of maintaining a hobby. But the strictly investment collector cannot afford to indulge impulse or sentiment. His purchases must be informed and selective. He must avoid historically rewarding but neglected types, slow movers, common dates, and low grades. He must regard his collection not as an end, but as the means to an end outside the hobby.

Q. *Is it really true that I can put my children through college with the profit from investing in coins?*

A. It has happened. Likewise, not a few collectors have made down payments on vacation homes from sales out of their collections. Judicious coin investment can result in such substantial profit gains, even as the cost of college educations and the value of the most desirable coins have mushroomed in recent years. Realistically, however, there is a risk inherent in any investment and there can be no real assurance that your coin investments will create the necessary income to provide a college education for each of your children or a down payment on that vacation home of your dreams.

Q. *Are coins a good investment? Can they go down in price?*

A. Coins can be a good investment. And they can go down in price as well. A phenomenon of coin investment is that casual collectors, who wouldn't think of buying a stock without consulting with a broker, will plunge into coin investment with the random restraint of a bull in a china shop. Coin investment should be approached with the same research and intelligent concern you would bring to investment in real estate, stocks and bonds, or commodity futures.

Q. *Could I buy any new coin, hold it for a few years and make money on it?*

A. Not necessarily. Time is an essential ingredient in increasing coin value, and "a few years" might not be enough of it. It is true that collectors prefer Uncirculated specimens that are within their price range, and that even collectors of modest means are not reluctant to pay a small premium to upgrade the appearance of their collection and its long-run potential for appreciation. It is also true that in most instances uncirculated coins properly stored to prevent tarnish and discoloration, and kept a sufficient number of years, appreciate in value—sometimes spectacularly. Still, the indiscriminate buying of new coins for investment should not be recommended. It should be remembered that even a profit can mean losing money if the capital could have been more profitably employed in more selective coin investment.

Q. *Are freak "mint errors" a good investment?*

A. A number of specific major mint errors—1922 plain or filled die cent, 1955 double die obverse cent, 1937-D 3-legged Buffalo nickel, a number of overdates—have long been established as highly desirable and valuable collector issues. Numerous examples of off-center strikes, multiple strikes, clipped planchet strikes, and coins struck on planchets of incorrect size or metal also command substantial premiums. Many mint errors of lesser significance—die breaks, blobs, multiple mintmarks, laminations, rotated dies, etc.—have no widely accepted fixed price, and are generally worth premiums that are highly variable. However, the rapid growth in the number of mint error enthusiasts in recent years, along with a declining supply caused by quality control production enhancements at the mints introduced in the late 1990s, have tended to drive prices dramatically higher on a relative basis.

Q. *Can anybody make money on coins?*

A. Only in the sense that anyone can become president; the opportunity is available to all. Certainly money has been made on coins regularly by some individuals over extended time-frames. Almost invariably, the one who makes money buying and selling coins is also one who is well grounded in the fundamentals of the hobby. Compulsive gambling is not an investment.

Q. *Is there any course available which would teach me the "know-how" of the hobby of coin collecting?*

A. Not in the academic sense, but neither is there a school to train presidents. Desire is the motive and application is the means to acquiring a working knowledge of coin collecting. There are, of course, valuable aids to a thoughtful program of self-application. The better-run coin clubs include lectures and panel discussions of hobby community perspectives in their activities. Authoritative books, embracing virtually every phase and field of the hobby, are readily available from coin shops, mail-order dealers, and at coin shows and conventions, as well as being frequently available for purchase at bookstores and on a loan basis from libraries in even small communities. Subscribe to one or more of the national coin publications. They will keep you informed of the references currently available, and through the book reviews they publish, they will acquaint you with the theme of the latest offerings that become available. You should also build yourself a personal library as you build your collection. "Growth through knowledge" is more than a catch phrase.

Q. *It seems to me that this hobby of coin collecting is based entirely on dollars and cents. Is this correct?*

A. If your premise were correct, there would be little collector interest in Conder tokens, which have appreciated but slightly, relatively speaking, over the past 200 years, nor an expanding interest in transportation tokens, minor mint errors, wooden nickels, and literally dozens of other specialized categories within the numismatic realm. The hobby collector—one who is motivated to build a collection chiefly for the pleasure, relaxation, and increased knowledge that it affords him—is the kingpin of the hobby community. Without him, the dealers, coin press, and numismatic speculators would not exist for an hour. The collector came first; the others followed to serve his need. It is collector demand that underpins the market; absent that factor and the value ingredient would not exist.

Q. *What types of coins are best to buy for investment?*

A. Supply and demand are the dominant persuasions of the marketplace. In the world of coins, the demand is expressed in two ways. First, the demand of type; there is a greater demand for the relatively common Lincoln cent than for scarce Byzantine bronze. Within the desired type, the demand is greatest for the coins of lower mintage and higher grade. Supply is meaningless unless there is a demand for the type; an 800-plus-year-old denier of Richard the Lionheart can be purchased for a low two-figure expenditure. Over the years, the higher grades of the lowest mintage coins within a demand type have proven to be the soundest investment.

Q. *Can you offer a short-cut method of making a quick profit in coins?*

A. If we could, we wouldn't be writing books. An honest quick profit is more often the result of fortunate coincidence rather than focused judgment and timing.

1852 U.S. $20 Gold Double Eagle.

Q. *Are gold coins a good investment?*

A. Gold coins contain a dual investment potential, one derived from their value as collector items and the other from their intrinsic bullion value. Gold coins on the numismatic market have exhibited a modest but determined rate of value increase, tending to advance somewhat in tandem with the bullion marketplace, with the rarities and highest grades of given issues exhibiting exceptional performance. It has been calculated that if a collector had obtained one each of the double eagles ($20 gold pieces) by year and mintmark (exclusive of the 1927-D) from 1908 to 1932, and they had been held by the family until 2008, the collection would have cost $920 and would be worth in excess of $1,000,000 today. This is equal to an effective annual interest rate yield of more than 9.5 percent.

The double eagle contains slightly less than an ounce of gold. Based on the present official price of gold ($42.44 per ounce), each coin contains $40.85 worth of the metal. Now that the gold-reserve requirements for Federal Reserve Notes and deposits have been abolished, however, both the monetary role and official price of gold are symbolic. At the $900 value level for an ounce of gold, the bullion value of a double eagle is approximately $870. While one never knows what their value might be from the bullion perspective, the age-old lure of gold should ensure the continuing popularity of double eagles and other gold coins as collector items.

Q. *I have several old large-size paper notes with consecutive numbers. Are they a good investment that I should hold onto?*

A. Paper money in general has historically not been considered to have the investment potential of coins. Collector enthusiasm has been discouraged by the higher face values of paper money. However, there is a definite market for paper money, and the consequent potential for the emergence of "blue chips" has evidenced itself in recent years, particularly with respect to National Bank Note issues and high grade type notes. It must be kept in mind that the marketplace for paper money is much narrower than that for coins by a minimal factor of ten. In regard to the series numbers, each paper note is unique in that it has a serial number that is not duplicated elsewhere in the series. Consequently, the serial number in itself is generally inconsequential.

Q. *What affect did the withdrawing and melting of silver coins by the government, and by private citizens when bullion values ballooned, have on their individual value and investment potential?*

A. The Federal Reserve's three-year attempt to cull the nation's silver coinage and melt it for industrial use was less than 20 percent successful, leaving something in excess of $1,784,120,000 worth of silver coinage minted subsequent to 1940 in the hands of dealers, collectors, numismatic investors, and bullion speculators. A substantial portion of that outstanding volume was melted privately when the bullion market ballooned from time to time, with no record being available of the volumes involved. The ultimate effect of the hoarding and melting upon the value of individual silver coins can be determined only by the supply and demand factors that emerge. Certainly, the validity of mintage figures as determinants of rarity are somewhat suspect as a result. It's likely that some of the silver coins now considered to be relative rarities will, in years to come, prove to be more plentiful than some of the high-mintage issues that were liberally consigned to the melting pot.

Q. *At what point did the bullion value of U.S. silver coins surpass their face value? What is the value of the silver in these coins at today's bullion value levels?*

A. The monetary value of silver was $1.2929 per ounce. At the time the market value of silver bullion hit that level, the precious metal content in a regular issue dime, quarter, half dollar, or dollar minted from 1873 through 1964 matched the coin's face value. In the case of silver wartime nickels (1942–1945), the break point was a bullion market value of approximately 90¢. The following chart (next page) shows the relationship between the bullion value of U.S. silver coins and incremental bullion market levels, including .400 fine silver halves (1965–1970) and dollars (1971–1976). This chart also presents values for the bullion contents of Canadian silver coins minted from 1920 through 1968.

Silver Price Per Ounce		$12	$13	$14	$15	$16	$17	$18	$19	$20	$21
U.S. 5¢ .350 Fine (Wartime)	0.05626	$0.68	$0.73	$0.79	$0.84	$0.90	$0.96	$1.01	$1.07	$1.13	$1.18
U.S. 50¢ .400 Fine (1965–1970)	0.14792	1.78	1.92	2.07	2.22	2.37	2.51	2.66	2.81	2.96	3.11
U.S. $1.00 .400 Fine (1971–1976)	0.31610	3.79	4.11	4.43	4.74	5.06	5.37	5.69	6.01	6.32	6.64
U.S. 10¢ .900 Fine (Pre-1965)	0.07234	0.87	0.94	1.01	1.09	1.16	1.23	1.30	1.37	1.45	1.52
U.S. 25¢ .900 Fine (Pre-1965)	0.18084	2.17	2.35	2.53	2.71	2.89	3.07	3.26	3.44	3.62	3.80
U.S. 50¢ .900 Fine (Pre-1965)	0.36169	4.34	4.70	5.06	5.43	5.79	6.15	6.51	6.87	7.23	7.60
U.S. $1.00 .900 Fine (To 1935)	0.77344	9.28	10.05	10.83	11.60	12.38	13.15	13.92	14.70	15.47	16.24
Canada 10¢ .800 Fine (1920–1967)	0.06000	0.72	0.78	0.84	0.90	0.96	1.02	1.08	1.14	1.20	1.26
Canada 25¢ .800 Fine (1920–1967)	0.15000	1.80	1.95	2.10	2.25	2.40	2.55	2.70	2.85	3.00	3.15
Canada 50¢ .800 Fine (1920–1967)	0.30000	3.60	3.90	4.20	4.50	4.80	5.10	5.40	5.70	6.00	6.30
Canada $1.00 .800 Fine (1935–1967)	0.60000	7.20	7.80	8.40	9.00	9.60	10.20	10.80	11.40	12.00	12.60
Canada 10¢ .500 Fine (1967–1968)	0.03720	0.45	0.48	0.52	0.56	0.60	0.63	0.67	0.71	0.74	0.78
Canada 25¢ .500 (1967–1968)	0.09370	1.12	1.22	1.31	1.41	1.50	1.59	1.69	1.78	1.87	1.97

Silver Price Per Ounce		$22	$23	$24	$25	$26	$27	$28	$29	$30
U.S. 5¢ .350 Fine (Wartime)	0.05626	$1.24	$1.29	$1.35	$1.41	$1.46	$1.52	$1.58	$1.63	$1.69
U.S. 50¢ .400 Fine (1965–1970)	0.14792	3.25	3.40	3.55	3.70	3.85	3.99	4.14	4.29	4.44
U.S. $1.00 .400 Fine (1971–1976)	0.31610	6.95	7.27	7.59	7.90	8.22	8.53	8.85	9.17	9.48
U.S. 10¢ .900 Fine (Pre-1965)	0.07234	1.59	1.66	1.74	1.81	1.88	1.95	2.03	2.10	2.17
U.S. 25¢ .900 Fine (Pre-1965)	0.18084	3.98	4.16	4.34	4.52	4.70	4.88	5.06	5.24	5.43
U.S. 50¢ .900 Fine (Pre-1965)	0.36169	7.96	8.32	8.68	9.04	9.40	9.77	10.13	10.49	10.85
U.S. $1.00 .900 Fine (To 1935)	0.77344	17.02	17.79	18.56	19.34	20.11	20.88	21.66	22.43	23.20
Canada 10¢ .800 Fine (1920–1967)	0.06000	1.32	1.38	1.44	1.50	1.56	1.62	1.68	1.74	1.80
Canada 25¢ .800 Fine (1920–1967)	0.15000	3.30	3.45	3.60	3.75	3.90	4.05	4.20	4.35	4.50
Canada 50¢ .800 Fine (1920–1967)	0.30000	6.60	6.90	7.20	7.50	7.80	8.10	8.40	8.70	9.00
Canada $1.00 .800 Fine (1935–1967)	0.60000	13.20	13.80	14.40	15.00	15.60	16.20	16.80	17.40	18.00
Canada 10¢ .500 Fine (1967–1968)	0.03720	0.82	0.86	0.89	0.93	0.97	1.00	1.04	1.08	1.12
Canada 25¢ .500 Fine (1967–1968)	0.09370	2.06	2.16	2.25	2.34	2.44	2.53	2.62	2.72	2.81

Dimensions of U.S. Coins and Paper Money

COINS

Type	Years	Size
Half Cents		
Liberty Cap, Head Facing Left	1793	22 mm
Liberty Cap, Head Facing Right	1794–1797	23.5 mm
Draped Bust	1800–1808	23.5 mm
Classic Head	1809–1836	23.5 mm
Braided Hair	1840–1857	23 mm
Large Cents		
Flowing Hair, Chain Reverse	1793	26–27 mm
Flowing Hair, Wreath Reverse	1793	26–28 mm
Liberty Cap	1793–1796	29 mm
Draped Bust	1796–1807	29 mm
Classic Head	1808–1814	29 mm
Liberty Head, Matron Head	1816–1836	28–29 mm
Liberty Head, Matron Head Modified / Braided Hair	1837–1857	27.5 mm
Small Cents		
Flying Eagle	1857–1864	19 mm
Indian Head (Bronze)	1864–1909	19 mm
Lincoln Head	1909–Date	19 mm
Two Cents		
All	1864–1873	23 mm

Three Cents

Trimes	1851–1873	14 mm
Nickel Three Cents	1865–1889	17.9 mm

Nickels

Shield	1866–1883	20.5 mm
Liberty Head	1883–1912	21.2 mm
Indian Head / Buffalo	1913–1938	21.2 mm
Jefferson	1938–Date	21.2 mm

Half Dimes

Flowing Hair	1794–1795	16.5 mm
Draped Bust	1796–1805	16.5 mm
Capped Bust	1829–1837	15.5 mm
Liberty Seated	1837–1873	15.5 mm

Dimes

Draped Bust	1796–1807	19 mm
Capped Bust	1809–1837	18.5 mm
Liberty Seated	1837–1874	17.9 mm
Liberty Head (Barber)	1892–1916	17.9 mm
Winged Liberty	1916–1945	17.9 mm
Roosevelt	1946–Date	17.9 mm

Twenty Cents

All	1875–1878	22 mm

Quarters

Draped Bust	1796, 1804–1807	27.5 mm
Capped Bust Large	1815–1828	27 mm
Capped Bust Small	1831–1838	24.3 mm
Liberty Seated	1838–1891	24.3 mm
Liberty Head (Barber)	1892–1916	24.3 mm
Liberty Standing	1916–1930	24.3 mm
Washington	1932–Date	24.3 mm

Half Dollars

Flowing Hair	1794–1795	32.5 mm
Draped Bust	1796–1797, 1801–1807	32.5 mm
Liberty Cap (Lettered Edge)	1807–1836	32.5 mm
Capped Bust, Reeded Edge	1836–1839	30 mm
Liberty Seated	1839–1891	30.6 mm

Liberty Head (Barber)	1892–1915	30.6 mm
Liberty Walking	1916–1947	30.6 mm
Franklin Head	1948–1963	30.6 mm
Kennedy Head	1964–Date	30.6 mm

Silver Dollars

Flowing Hair	1794–1795	39–40 mm
Draped Bust	1795–1803	39–40 mm
Gobrecht	1836–1839	39–40 mm
Liberty Seated	1840–1873	38.1 mm
Trade Dollar	1873–1885	38.1 mm
Liberty Head (Morgan)	1878–1921	38.1 mm
Liberty Head (Peace)	1921–1935	38.1 mm
Eisenhower Head	1971–1974, 1976–1978	38.1 mm

Modern Dollars

Susan B. Anthony	1979–1999	26.5 mm
Sacagawea	2000–date	26.5 mm
Presidentials	2007–2016	26.5 mm

Gold Dollars

Liberty Head	1849–1854	13 mm
Indian Princess Small	1854–1856	15 mm
Indian Princess Large	1856–1889	15 mm

Quarter Eagles

Capped Bust to Right	1796–1807	20 mm
Capped Bust to Left Large	1808	20 mm
Capped Head to Left Large	1821–1827	18.5 mm
Capped Head to Left Small	1829–1834	18.2 mm
Classic Head	1834–1839	18.2 mm
Liberty Head	1840–1907	18 mm
Indian Head	1908–1929	18 mm

Three Dollars

| Indian Princess Head | 1854–1889 | 20.5 mm |

Four Dollars

| Stella | 1879–1880 | 22 mm |

Half Eagles

| Capped Bust to Right | 1795–1807 | 25 mm |
| Capped Bust to Left | 1807–1812 | 25 mm |

Capped Head to Left Large	1813–1829	25 mm
Capped Head to Left Small	1829–1834	23.8 mm
Classic Head	1834–1838	22.5 mm
Liberty Head	1839–1866	22.5 mm
Liberty Head, Variety 2	1866–1908	21.6 mm
Indian Head	1908–1929	21.6 mm

Eagles

Capped Bust to Right	1795–1804	33 mm
Liberty Head	1838–1907	27 mm
Indian Head	1907–1933	27 mm

Double Eagles

| Liberty Head | 1849–1907 | 34 mm |
| Saint-Gaudens | 1907–1933 | 34 mm |

PAPER MONEY

The size of most federal notes 1861 and later can be divided into two categories: large size and small size. Large-size notes, printed from 1861 to 1928, measure 7.5" × 3.25", although there are some variations. The width of the margins can vary considerably, especially among National Bank bills, which effects the size. Small-size notes, issued since 1929, measure 6.14" × 2.61".

APPENDIX C

Selling Your Coins

Is it time to sell your coins? Perhaps you don't consider yourself a collector, but you've inherited a cigar box full of Grandpa's old pocket change. Or maybe you've spent years in the hobby, and you feel like it's time to explore new paths. You might be drawn to a different collecting specialty within numismatics, or even to a completely new hobby. Perhaps your life circumstances have changed, and you need to cash in (however reluctantly) on your investment. Or maybe you want to take advantage of the current "hot" coin market by selling off some of your collection's duplicates.

Regardless of why you're selling, you now have some decisions to make. Will you sell your collection privately, to a local coin dealer? Shop it around to dealers nationwide? Consign it at a public auction? Or maybe auction it yourself, on the Internet? What are the benefits of each path, and which will bring the greatest profits?

To get started, the first question you should answer is, "What kind of collection do I have?"

What Am I Selling?
Rolls of Modern Coins, Proof Sets, Modern Commemoratives, Bullion, etc. This includes bulk investment coins, such as American Eagle bullion pieces, bags of common circulated silver coins, rolls of Uncirculated statehood quarters, and so on. It also includes modern commemoratives and Proof and Uncirculated sets from the U.S. Mint, not all of which have increased in value in the secondary market. Such coins and accumulations are best sold privately to a coin dealer or to another collector. Auctioning them yourself, on the Internet, is also a potential route. Consigning them to an auction house is not likely to be your best option, as this venue is typically reserved for scarcer coins.

Coins With Sentimental—but Not Necessarily High-Dollar—Value. You might have inherited or gathered an *accumulation* (as opposed to a studiously compiled *collection*) of coins—for example, a coffee can full of wheat cents, or a jar full of Buffalo nickels pulled years ago from pocket change. Your local coin dealer can make you an offer on such coins, either buying the entire lot or searching through them to "cherrypick" the better pieces. If you have the time and inclination, you might sell them yourself, through an Internet auction site. The same advice applies to individual lower-value coins, tokens, and medals. Additionally, you might consider donating such coins to a local Boy Scout troop or similar organization (this encourages coin collecting as a hobby, and may be tax-deductible).

Rare and/or Significant Coins. For rare, valuable, and historically significant coins, a public consigned auction is often the best way to sell, potentially bringing much higher prices than you could get selling to a dealer. Dedicated collectors subscribe to auction firm catalogs, knowing they are good sources for scarce and expensive coins. When you consign your collection to a well-established auction house with numismatic experience, your coins will be carefully studied, cataloged, publicized, and presented to an audience of serious collectors with money to spend. You save the time and effort of searching for potential buyers, perhaps traveling, worrying about security, etc. The auction firm makes money by collecting a commission on each sale.

Another option for selling your rare and significant coins is to approach a dealer nationally recognized as an expert in the field—for example, a specialist in 18th-century gold, or a dealer who focuses on colonial coins.

You can also receive tax benefits from donating your rare or significant coins to the American Numismatic Association, the American Numismatic Society, or a museum.

After you've considered the scope of your collection, you can decide the best venue for selling.

Selling to a Coin Shop

Your local coin shop has the advantage of the personal touch that might be lacking in, for example, mail-order sales or Internet auctions. Good coin-shop proprietors do more than just run a cash register: they are fonts of numismatic knowledge, and are happy to educate and advise their customers. An active coin dealer stays up to date on the hobby and the market, knows about tax and estate laws that might affect your sale, and has the resources and experience to study your collection and make educated decisions. Many dealers attend multiple coin conventions yearly, and maintain connections with other dealers and collectors. This gives them a wide arena for selling coins—which provides the leverage to offer you a good price.

A coin shop can be a venue for selling numismatic items of any value. Keep in mind, though, that very rare or specialized coins will likely fetch a higher price at public auction. An advantage of selling to a coin shop is that the owner can often make you an offer and write you a check on the spot.

As with any other commercial venue, you should feel comfortable with the integrity of the shop's proprietor and staff. If you haven't dealt with them before, talk to coin-collector friends, inquire at the local coin club, and check with the Better Business Bureau. Look at the shop's Web site, advertisements, and any in-house flyers or publications—do they project fairness and professionalism?

Coin shops can be found in your phone book's business directory. Before you take your coins to a shop, call ahead to make sure the owner or a qualified assistant will be there to examine your coins. A busy dealer might be away from the office at a coin show, and can schedule a convenient time to meet with you or to examine your coins at your home or bank. It is always a good policy to solicit at least two quotes before you decide to sell.

Selling Through the Mail

If you don't live within driving distance of a coin shop, you can ship your coins to a dealer for their offer. Again, trust is an important factor in such a sale. Does the dealer belong to national organizations such as the American Numismatic Association and the Professional Numismatists Guild? Does he advertise in hobby newspapers such as Coin World and Numismatic News? Search the dealer's name on the Internet: do you find numerous reports of fair transactions and satisfied customers, or a discomforting number of complaints and concerns?

You should inquire by mail, email, or phone before shipping any coins. The dealer might request a list beforehand, and should be able to give you some general advice and a ballpark idea of value without seeing the coins in person. Once you're comfortable and have decided to sell, ask the dealer for advice on shipping and insurance.

Keep in mind that the dealer will need to examine your coins before fine-tuning a firm offer.

Even if you live near a coin shop, you can broaden the playing field and get multiple offers if you're open to selling your coins through the mail to established, respected dealers. This is a good option if you have the time. The entire transaction (researching dealers, packaging and shipping your coins, and waiting for the check) will likely take longer than getting a local offer.

Selling to a Dealer at a Coin Show

The United States is home to hundreds of city and regional coin clubs, and many of them sponsor regularly scheduled coin shows. There are national (and even international) shows as well; some are always held in the same place, some are set up in different cities each time. No matter where you live, chances are a show is held somewhere nearby at least once per year.

At a coin show, with dozens or even hundreds of dealers gathered all at once, you can shop your coins around, getting multiple offers before deciding to sell. As with a coin-shop transaction, your payment will be immediate.

Remember that a coin show is a public venue—be alert and mindful of security, and use common sense. Outside the show (for example, in the parking lot), do not draw attention to yourself or publicize the fact that you're carrying valuable coins.

Most shows will have a program or flyer listing the dealers in attendance. If you've done your homework ahead of time, you'll know the ones you want to approach—for example, the silver-dollar specialists, if you have Morgan dollars to sell. Or you can simply stroll the aisles, looking for dealers who sell items similar to those in your collection. Introduce yourself, strike up a conversation, and ask if the dealer is interested in your coins. This is all part of the fun of a coin show.

Consigning at a Public Auction

Numismatic auction firms are often connected to larger retail operations that also sell through the mail, online, at coin shows or from a storefront, etc. As with any other venue, reputation is a prime consideration. Study a potential auctioneer's web site, examine the results of past sales, learn about their numismatic staff, read any coverage they might receive in the hobby's newspapers and magazines. Look at the firm's advertisements and catalogs. Are their catalogs professionally made, with attractive photographs and informative lot descriptions? The effort and experience an auction firm brings to its work will affect the bottom line—how much your coins sell for.

Selling Online

Selling your coins yourself, in online auctions, can be fun if you have the time and talent to do it. This typically requires some skill with scanning or photography (buyers like to examine potential purchases). Each auction site has its own rules and policies, commission rates, etc., that you should read carefully. When it comes to transactions, as always, be security-conscious— for example, you might want to rent a Post Office box instead of using your home address, and you should insist on full, guaranteed payment before you ship any coins.

You can also use the Internet to sell your coins at a fixed price, through a bulletin board posting or other announcement.

Any online sale to the public requires you to take on responsibilities similar to those of a retail coin shop or auction firm. There is work involved, but the experience can be enjoyable and profitable.

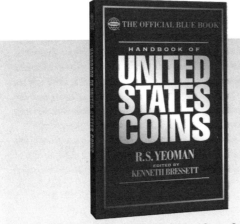

For more information: The *Handbook of United States Coins,* known to collectors as THE OFFICIAL BLUE BOOK®, gives average prices paid by coin dealers nationwide.

INDEX